The Pharisees

The Pharisees

*Their History, Character, and
New Testament Portrait*

Kent L. Yinger

FOREWORD BY
Craig A. Evans

CASCADE *Books* · Eugene, Oregon

THE PHARISEES
Their History, Character, and New Testament Portrait

Copyright © 2022 Kent L. Yinger. All rights reserved. Except for brief quotations in critical publications or reviews, no part of this book may be reproduced in any manner without prior written permission from the publisher. Write: Permissions, Wipf and Stock Publishers, 199 W. 8th Ave., Suite 3, Eugene, OR 97401.

Cascade Books
An Imprint of Wipf and Stock Publishers
199 W. 8th Ave., Suite 3
Eugene, OR 97401

www.wipfandstock.com

PAPERBACK ISBN: 978-1-6667-3136-1
HARDCOVER ISBN: 978-1-6667-2378-6
EBOOK ISBN: 978-1-6667-2379-3

Cataloguing-in-Publication data:

Names: Yinger, Kent L., author. | Evans, Craig A., foreword.

Title: The Pharisees : their history, character, and New Testament portrait / by Kent L. Yinger ; foreword by Craig A. Evans.

Description: Eugene, OR: Cascade Books, 2022 | Includes bibliographical references and index.

Identifiers: ISBN 978-1-6667-3136-1 (paperback) | ISBN 978-1-6667-2378-6 (hardcover) | ISBN 978-1-6667-2379-3 (ebook)

Subjects: LCSH: Pharisees. | Judaism—History. | Rabbinical literature—History and criticism. | Bible. Gospels—Criticism, interpretation, etc.

Classification: BM175.P4 Y56 2022 (print) | BM175.P4 (ebook)

05/17/22

New Revised Standard Version Bible, copyright © 1989 National Council of the Churches of Christ in the United States of America. Used by permission. All rights reserved worldwide.

Contents

Foreword by Craig A. Evans | vii
Preface | ix
Acknowledgments | xi
Abbreviations | xiii

Introduction | xv

Part 1: Origin and History of the Pharisees

1 Josephus and the Beginnings of the Pharisees | 3
2 Josephus and the Historical Development of the Pharisees | 16

Part 2: Character of the Pharisees

3 Distinctives in Josephus | 31
4 Echoes in the DSS and Rabbinic Literature | 50
5 Common Identity with Other Jews | 60

Part 3: New Testament Portrait: Disagreements with Pharisees

6 Jesus and the Pharisees: Introductory Matters | 75
7 Never on Saturday: Disagreements over Sabbath Rules | 90
8 Eating with Sinners: Dinner with Levi the Toll-Collector | 100
9 Don't Touch That! Eating with Unclean Hands and Other Disagreements over Purity Rules | 112

10 Who are You? Core Disagreements over Kingdom, Authority, and Identity | 124

11 Political Dynamite: Pharisees, Politics, and Power | 134

12 Why Do You Eat So Much? Jesus, Fasting, and the Pharisees | 142

Part 4: New Testament Portrait: Attitudes toward Pharisees

13 Were the Pharisees legalists? | 151

14 Woe to You Hypocrites | 159

15 A More Positive Spin on the Pharisees in Acts and Paul? | 177

Taking Stock of the Pharisees: Conclusions and Suggestions | 183

Appendix: Interview with a Pharisee | 189
Bibliography | 195
Author Index | 207
Subject Index | 209
Ancient Documents Index | 213

Foreword

THE GREAT STRENGTH OF Kent Yinger's *The Pharisees* is the way he puts this important topic into full context. He rightly avoids the old caricatures and the simplistic idea that the Pharisees were legalistic, corrupt hypocrites. In his Introduction Professor Yinger sorts out the epistemology and the hermeneutics. He explains to his readers how historians learn things and how they interpret them. He reviews our sources and rightly underscores the varying portraits of the Pharisees that we find in them. These sources, which are Jewish and Christian, are sometimes sympathetic to the Pharisees and sometimes not.

Getting the Pharisees right is very important, of course, because they play such a significant role in the public activities of Jesus. Sometimes these men are hardly more than a foil, providing Jesus with the opportunity to make known his position on a given topic. The questions and objections that the Pharisees and their allied scribes ask of Jesus are very helpful, for they give Jesus the opportunity to clarify his own position on the law of Moses and the way it should be applied.

Based on a careful assessment of the relevant materials, both the New Testament as well as the Jewish sources, Professor Yinger rightly describes the Pharisees as serious pursuers of God and holiness. To be sure, on occasion Jesus did criticize some Pharisees, but we should not assume that he criticized all Pharisees or that this criticism implied that there was no hope of their salvation. Jesus used invective and hyperbole to criticize some Pharisees, but he didn't apply it universally. The debates were in-house, but Jesus never condemned the whole of Judaism or the Jewish people. Christians shouldn't either.

Professor Yinger raises a very interesting question with respect to Saul of Tarsus, who in the story of the early Church becomes the Apostle Paul. Did Paul give up his Pharisaic identity after his conversion? It is usually assumed that he did, but did he? That Paul changed his mind with regard to Jesus and significantly altered his understanding of works with respect to righteousness is clear, but that he no longer considered himself a Pharisee is not clear.

Professor Yinger draws attention to a number of Pharisees, among them Nicodemus in the Gospel of John, who were drawn to Jesus and were willing to learn from him. In Acts 15 we learn that a number of Pharisees joined the Jesus movement. Why would they do that, if Jesus and his disciples viewed the Pharisees as beyond all hope? The narrative in Acts describes these men as both followers of the Way and as belonging to the party of Pharisees. There is no hint that to become a disciple of Jesus one could no longer be a Pharisee.

Jesus and the Pharisees apparently differed on a number of matters. What one could and couldn't do on the Sabbath, what did and did not constitute purity or impurity, what company one could keep, and so one. The question was not whether the Sabbath should be honored, but what honoring it entailed. The question was not whether purity was important, but what constituted true purity, and so forth. The Pharisees were committed to the observation of God's law and keeping the commandments. What was wrong with that? The issue was how that was to be done, how it was to be applied, and how all of it was to be balanced with the pressing needs of the poor and disadvantaged.

Professor Yinger's clearly written, tightly argued book addresses these important questions. The ancient texts that are discussed are well chosen, the exegeses are informed and persuasive, the engagement with scholars who hold to similar or very different views is always fair, and the conclusions that are reached invariably make good sense. Professor Yinger's book will benefit scholars and students alike and should result in better and more accurate descriptions of the Pharisees in exegesis papers, sermons, and Bible studies. The Pharisees will serve well academy, church, and synagogue.

Craig A. Evans
Houston Baptist University

Preface

THE IMPETUS FOR THIS book struck while sitting in a church pew. Not a single pew in one particular church, but in churches of all sorts, all around the United States and in countries outside the US. Sermon after sermon echoed the identical view of the Pharisees in the Gospel accounts . . . legalists trying to earn their way to heaven, loading burdens on others, hypocrites who taught others but didn't obey themselves . . . the perfect counterexample to what we in the pews should strive to be.

Preachers of differing backgrounds and denominations are not always known for agreeing on everything in the Bible, but on the nature of the Pharisees most are in lock-step. How could this be? And then it hit me, "Maybe I'm partly at fault." Or, more accurately, maybe it's partly *our* fault, the guild of Bible teachers and professors. We have trained future leaders in our Bible classes and seminaries to think about the Pharisees this way. And that shouldn't really be a surprise, since that's the picture of the Pharisees and of first-century Judaism on which we ourselves were nurtured as budding academics.

The problem now is, most of us in academia have moved on . . . to a more benign view of ancient Judaism and of the Pharisees. And rightly so. Reading more carefully what ancient Jewish authors said about their own beliefs and concerns has convinced us we had been wrongfully caricaturing the Pharisees for decades, for centuries, in fact. While most of us in the Bible teaching profession have been trying to turn this ship for a while, it takes more than a single seminary class to chart a new direction for the larger church.

It is my hope that this book will help serious modern students of Scripture to give another group of serious (ancient) Bible students a fair shake, and to paint a portrait of the Pharisees for which we will no longer need to apologize.

Acknowledgments

This book would have been impossible without the generous and professional assistance of the Murdock Library staff at George Fox University. Hats off from one of your "power users."

Abbreviations

ad loc.	*ad locum*, at the placed discussed
Ag. Ap.	Josephus, *Against Apion*
A.J.	Josephus, *Jewish Antiquities*
BCE	before the common era (= BC)
BDAG	Bauer's *Greek English Lexicon*, 3rd. ed.
ca.	circa (about, around)
CE	common era (= AD)
cf.	*confer*, compare
ch(s).	chapter(s)
DSS	Dead Sea Scrolls
e.g.	*exempli gratia*, for example
esp.	especially
FRLANT	Forschungen zur Religion und Literatur des Alten und Neuen Testaments
Gk.	Greek
J.W.	Josephus, *Jewish War*
LCL	Loeb Classical Library
Life	Josephus, *Life*
lit.	literally
LSJ	Liddell-Scott-Jones *Greek English Lexicon*
MS(S)	manuscript(s)

n./nn.	note(s)
NT	New Testament
OT	Old Testament
par.	parallel
StrB	Strack-Billerbeck, *Kommentar zum Neuen Testament aus Talmud und Midrasch*
s.v.	*sub verbo*, under the word; i.e., see the entry
TDNT	*Theological Dictionary of the New Testament*
v/vv	verse/s
vl./vll.	*varia lectio*, variant reading/s

For other abbreviations, see *The SBL Handbook of Style, Second Edition* (Atlanta: SBL, 2014).

Introduction

The Holy One, blessed be He, said to Moses:
"Go and say to Israel,

'My children, as I am a pharisee [*parush*],
so be you pharisees [*parushin*].'"

(paraphrase of Lev. Rab. on Lev 20:26)

Good guys or bad guys?

IT'S EASY TO READ the gospel story as a simple tale of good guys versus bad guys. Jesus and the disciples are the good guys; the Jerusalem chief priests, the Romans, and especially the Pharisees, are the bad guys. This way of reading the story has been reinforced in hundreds of sermons I've heard in many different churches over the years; probably you have, too. There would seem to be no question, the Pharisees are the bad guys, hypocrites, legalists who feel no compunction at loading burdens on widows and sick people.

So it came as a shock when I learned that Jewish tradition actually views the Pharisees as the good guys. They "stood for the interests and beliefs of the Jewish masses, and stressed the ethical and compassionate elements of Jewish law."[1] "Jewish tradition for most of the last two thousand years viewed the Pharisees as the rabbis of our heritage . . . the teachers of authentic Judaism."[2] According to many, this tradition saw the early rabbis, whose **Torah** debates are enshrined in the

> "Torah" is Hebrew for teaching, instruction or law. Although technically it refers only to the five books of Moses (Gen–Deut), it is used widely to refer to the entirety of the Jewish Scripture, what Jews call the Jewish Bible or Tanakh and Christians the OT.

---

1. Karesh and Hurvitz, "Pharisees."
2. Kendall and Rosen, *Christian and the Pharisee*, 7.

Mishnah and Talmud, as spiritual descendants of the Pharisees. "Pharisaism was a heroic effort to prepare the ground for the kingdom of God. The name belongs to the past; the meaning contained in it has remained ideal reality."[3] Many religiously engaged modern Jews see themselves proudly as the Pharisees' spiritual offspring, and lay the blame for the negative portrait on the "biased" portrayal in the Gospels.

If that's not jarring enough, scholars of Judaism and of the NT have been painstakingly correcting, even rehabilitating the image of the first century Pharisees.[4] A leading expert on the Pharisees calls them "good guys with bad press."[5] A prominent Jewish NT scholar pleads with us to "quit picking on the Pharisees."[6] A Christian OT scholar wants to "reclaim the reputation" of the Pharisees.[7] And a respected Jewish scholar urges us to see Jesus himself as a Pharisee.[8] Underlying much of this rethinking has been the growing recognition that first-century Judaism, including the Pharisees, was *not* characterized by harsh legalism and hypocrisy (see ch. 5).

So, as one recent book puts it, were they hypocrites or heroes?[9] If the latter, or something tending more in that direction, what are we to make of Jesus' attacks on them as hypocrites and white-washed tombs? If they were such good guys, why did they and Jesus get in each other's hair so often? Resolving these and many other related conundrums will occupy us in this book. Who were the real Pharisees? And, most importantly for Christian readers, how does this picture help us understand Jesus and the Gospels better?

Why Does This Matter?

Getting the Pharisees right is important for many reasons. I can think of at least four good ones. First, what about basic human decency and fairness? It angers us when someone unfairly accuses us or paints us as someone or something we are not. Moses commanded not to "bear false witness" and Jesus said "do unto others." Have we readers of the Gospels unwittingly been doing wrong by the Pharisees? Second, anti-Semitism has dogged the Christian movement from very early days and continues to raise its head.

---

3. Baeck, *Pharisees*, 50.
4. See now the essays in Sievers and Levine, *Pharisees*.
5. Deines, "Pharisees," 22, 57–58.
6. Levine, "Quit Picking on the Pharisees!" 26–29.
7. Pratheron, "Reclaiming the Reputation."
8. Maccoby, *Jesus the Pharisee*.
9. Amos, *Hypocrites or Heroes?*

The strongly negative perception of the Pharisees built upon the Gospels has played a significant role in this anti-Jewish sentiment. They were seen as typical of Judaism as a whole. We were warned to beware of "the hidden Pharisee" (= sinful, unbelieving hypocrite) in all of us. Third, if our picture of the Pharisees has been skewed, what was it that really separated them from Jesus? What have we been missing that was really going on with Jesus and the Pharisees in these Gospel stories? And last, what about the NT and truth? Some of what I've said might seem to raise doubts about the reliability of the Gospel accounts. In fact, as we'll see, not a few biblical scholars solve the question of the Pharisees by declaring the Gospel stories unhistorical. Either Jesus never said such harsh things to them or the Pharisees didn't act as portrayed. This is not the path I will follow in this book. Instead, I find the Gospel accounts reliable reports of what actually happened. But I will also argue that too many of us have missed the truth as to what was really going on between Jesus and the Pharisees, in part because we have misunderstood who they were. And that's what we're out to clear up.

Where to Find Information

We'd be way ahead in the game if some reliable ancient person had taken the time to talk about this group called Pharisees, to tell us where they came from and what sort of folks they were. Unfortunately, the closest we'll come to that is a first-century Jewish author named Josephus; and it turns out he has only limited comments on the Pharisees, and even in these he was probably not giving us unbiased reporting.

Didn't Pharisees themselves write anything, you may ask? Informed Bible students might chime in, "Paul claimed to be a Pharisee, and he certainly wrote quite a bit." True enough. But other than simply stating that he had been a Pharisee ("as to the law, a Pharisee," Phil 3:5), he said nothing further explicitly to describe them or to outline what he believed as a Pharisee. Some scholars used to think that a first-century BCE writing, The Psalms of Solomon, was a Pharisaic document, but that view has been abandoned.[10] Also, Josephus, whom we've mentioned, claimed to have followed the way of the Pharisees, but he hardly appears to have been a convinced supporter (ch. 2).

So, it looks like we have to rely on what others said about this group—on people who spoke about Pharisees as "them," not on people who spoke as convinced insiders of the movement. As always when evaluating what an outsider says about some other group, we will want to be cautious. None

---

10. Wright, "Psalms of Solomon," 2.642.

of our sources is wearing a t-shirt with "Pharisee—And Proud Of It!" They usually had other reasons for talking about this group (warn against them, castigate any who are like them, etc.).

That all sounds like bad news for reconstructing the ancient Pharisees.[11] But we do have literary sources that give us some information ... we just have to be discerning in how we digest this information. First, in the remainder of this chapter I'll give a brief overview of the whole landscape of literary sources and then we'll use them to reconstruct the Pharisees. Josephus is our richest source for their history, so in chapters 1 and 2 we will work our way through the relevant texts in Josephus gleaning whatever possible about their origins and history. Then chapters 3–5 will synthesize what we can conclude about their character, beliefs, and social status, and will draw in potential evidence from other sources such as 1 and 2 Maccabees and the Dead Sea Scrolls. Some of it may surprise you.

Quick Survey of Sources

Believe it or not, our earliest explicit literary witness to a group called Pharisees is the apostle Paul.[12] His letter to the Philippians contains his sole reference to being a Pharisee (Phil 3:5). He tells us only that

- he had been a Pharisee (and still considered himself to be?), and
- he understood Pharisaic identity to be tied particularly to Torah.

This is our first notice that a group called Pharisees even existed, and it doesn't come until mid-way through the first century, though it implies they probably existed several decades earlier.

Next to mention Pharisees are the NT Gospels and the book of Acts. They are typically dated somewhere between 64 (Mark) and 100 CE (John),[13] and they usually portray the Pharisees in opposition to Jesus,

---

11. Scholarly work on the Pharisees tends toward skepticism that our current state of sources and knowledge can produce a confident, composite picture of the historical Pharisees. See many of the essays in Neusner and Chilton, *In Quest of the Historical Pharisees*. While agreeing with the cautions, I am convinced a coherent and reliable picture can be drawn. For a similarly positive assessment, see Wilk, "Die synoptischen Evangelien des Neuen Testaments als Quellen."

12. Although Jesus preceded Paul as an historical figure, Paul's letter to the Philippians (c. 55–60 CE) is earlier than the earliest Gospel (Mark: c. 64 CE), earlier even than Josephus' *Jewish War* (75–82 CE). The DSS precede Paul as literary documents, but the term "Pharisee" does not occur in the DSS.

13. The dating of the Gospels and Acts is not an exact science. For this basic chronology of Pharisee-notices, I have taken an early date for Mark (usually placed

although occasionally they appear as friends or, at least, as undecided. Because the Gospels are our richest source of information about the first-century Pharisees, and because this book is largely about how to understand the Pharisees in the Gospel stories, we will spend a lot of time in later chapters (7–14) mining what they reveal.

Overlapping with the Gospels come the works of the Jewish historian, Josephus. He lived from 37–110/120 CE and penned four works we still possess. Three of these mention Pharisees explicitly:

- *The Jewish War*, dated 75–82 CE, contains several mentions of Pharisees

- *Jewish Antiquities*, dated 93/94 CE, compares Pharisees with Sadducees and Essenes (twice, similar to comparison in *J.W.*), and recounts further events involving Pharisees

- *Life*, dated 95–100 CE, brief description of Josephus' own involvement with Pharisees and others

In addition, he mentioned other groups and events (e.g., scribes, Sadducees) which may be related to Pharisees. Although he did not say a great deal about their points of view, Josephus' works are without doubt our richest source of information about the pre-Christian history of the Pharisees; yet, they leave plenty of gaps.

Last in our chronological list of sources is the voluminous rabbinic writings. The earliest, the Mishnah, was put into writing around 200 CE, and the remainder, the Tosefta, the Palestinian and Babylonian Talmuds, and various midrashim, are dated in the following centuries up to the fifth or sixth. Although they are all considerably later than the period of our main interest, they claim to contain traditions and teaching of rabbis, some of whom lived and taught in the first century and may have been Pharisees (see ch. 4).

Concise Roadmap to This Book

Our study will follow the three elements of the book's sub-title. Part 1 covers the history of the Pharisees, their origin and development, according to Josephus (chs. 1–2). Part 2 explores their character as revealed in Jewish sources (chs. 3–5). Part 3 builds on the Jewish foundation of Parts 1 and

---

somewhere shortly before or around the destruction of Jerusalem in 70 CE) and a later date for John (usually dated in the final decade of the first century, though some place it, as well as Acts, in the second century). Readers should consult any good introduction to the NT for details, for example, Hagner, *New Testament*.

2, and moves on to the profile of the Pharisees found in the NT Gospels, especially their points of disagreement with Jesus (chs. 6–12). Finally, Part 4 completes this New Testament profile by exploring the various attitudes toward Pharisees found in these documents, both negative and positive (chs. 13–15). A concluding chapter summarizes what we have discovered and suggests some differences this might make.

── Part 1 ──

Origin and History of the Pharisees

CHAPTER 1

Josephus and the Beginnings of the Pharisees

LISTENING CAREFULLY TO JOSEPHUS is key to understanding the Pharisees.[1] He was himself a Jew, claimed personal acquaintance with the Pharisaic movement, and spoke explicitly of Pharisees numerous times. Listening carefully is important because a number of earlier misunderstandings of the Pharisees were built on misreading these passages in Josephus.

Not long after the crucifixion of Jesus of Nazareth, Joseph ben Matthias was born in Jerusalem with both priestly (paternal) and royal (maternal) ancestry. During the Jewish revolt against Rome (66–70 CE), Joseph apparently had a leading military role for the Jewish troops in Galilee. However, after a 47-day siege in the town of Jotapata in 67 CE, he was captured, and allegedly prophesied that his captor, Vespasian, the Roman general, would become emperor. That is, Joseph switched sides. When Vespasian did, indeed, become emperor two years later, he rewarded Joseph with freedom and took him as an interpreter and mediator while he sought to finish off the Jewish revolt. In gratitude, Joseph latinized his name to Josephus and took Vespasian's family name, Flavius. He thus became Flavius Josephus as we know him today.

Shortly after the destruction of Jerusalem by the Romans in 70 CE, Josephus began to use his newfound position of influence to help the Romans better understand his ancient people, the Jews. He did this by writing a *History of the Jewish War against the Romans*, followed about twenty

---

1. While most older studies tended toward historical gullibility regarding what Josephus said about the Pharisees, others practically mute his voice with hyper-skepticism. On such methodological issues, see Mason, *Flavius Josephus on the Pharisees*, 1–17, whose approach, however, leaves Josephus with little to say about the historical Pharisees.

years later by his magnum opus, his *Antiquities of the Jews*, and near the end of his life a short autobiography (*Life*).[2]

The first thing we should note about the Pharisees in Josephus's writings is what minor roles they actually play in the whole narrative. In the *Jewish War*, for example, they appear in only four fairly brief narrative sections. For the original readers in the Roman Empire, the Pharisees would certainly have come across as little more than bit-players in the larger drama. Only during the reign of Salome Alexandra mid-first century BCE do they seem to exercise much significant influence (see on *J.W.* 1.110–114 below).[3] This should be kept in mind when seeking to evaluate how powerful in society and religion the Pharisees might have been.

Josephus, a Pharisee himself?

We begin with a passage from his *Life*, since here he details his personal acquaintance with the Pharisees. At age sixteen, claims Josephus, he decided to personally try out each of the leading schools of thought, Pharisees, Sadducees and Essenes (*Life* 10–12). He was, however, "not content with the experience," so he decided to spend three years as a disciple of Bannus "who dwelt in the wilderness, wearing only such clothing as trees provided, feeding on such things as grew of themselves, and using frequent ablutions of cold water, by day and night, for purity's sake." Following this three-year ascetic apprenticeship, during which he became a "devoted disciple" of Bannus, he "returned to the city. Being now in my nineteenth year I began to govern my life by the rules of the Pharisees, a sect having points of resemblance to that which the Greeks call the Stoic school."

The phrase "I began to govern my life by the rules of the Pharisees" has been understood traditionally to show that Josephus himself was a convinced Pharisee. This turns out on closer inspection not to have been the case. First, as we will see in numerous passages to come, Josephus does not sound like a convinced Pharisee. His praise nearly always has a critical edge. When speaking of their popularity or virtues he stops short of unqualified praise, willing to say only that they "are reputed to" have some good quality or "happened to" be the most popular; hardly the words of an

---

2. Around the time of *Life* he also produced *Against Apion*, a defense of Judaism against slander and misunderstanding in the Greek world. It does not mention Pharisees.

3. Unless otherwise noted translations and reference-numbering of Josephus are from the multi-volume Loeb edition (LCL), edited and translated by H. St J. Thackeray, Ralph Marcus, Allen Paul Wikgren, and Louis H. Feldman (Cambridge: Harvard, various dates).

ardent supporter. Further, in the passage quoted above, he says he was "not content . . . with the experiences thus gained" with the Pharisees and with the other two schools. Following on this dissatisfaction he then tried out the asceticism of Bannus. There are no indications that this Bannus represented Pharisaism, but rather a sort of eremitic lifestyle we also encounter with John the Baptist and others. In reference to this three-year experience with Bannus he then says he "accomplished my purpose," or better "fulfilled my desire" to find the best path of Jewish life. That is, Josephus's quest resulted not in the choice of one of the three Jewish schools of thought, but in preferring the way of rigorous Jewish asceticism. His "return to the city," however, meant that this ascetic choice would have mainly personal, private significance for his further path. The key phrase ("I began to govern my life [*politeuesthai*] by the rules of the Pharisees") refers to his return to the urban environment and meant he would have to choose *how to shape his public life* [*politeuesthai*: to engage in public life]. For this public purpose rather than for his personal spirituality, he chose the school of the Pharisees, which made the best social-political sense in light of their widespread popularity and influence. Thus, Josephus was not a convinced Pharisee, but chose to accommodate himself to their stance in his public dealings.[4]

A Hint of Pharisaic Origins

The Pharisees make their earliest appearance in *A.J.* 13.171-173.

> Now at this time there were three schools of thought among the Jews, which held different opinions concerning human affairs; the first being that of the Pharisees, the second that of the Sadducees, and the third that of the Essenes.

Josephus goes on to describe how they differed in regard to the concepts of fate (providence) and free will (see ch. 4 for details). This is a much-abbreviated version of material he had given two decades earlier in *J.W.* 2.119-166 and will repeat again in *A.J.* 18.11-25. These other two descriptions of the three Jewish schools of thought are inserted, however, at a much later point, namely, when commenting on the Fourth Philosophy, or Zealot movement during the reign of Caesar Augustus (27 BCE-14 CE). The insertion at that later point makes good sense in order to clarify

---

4. My reading follows a number of recent interpreters, esp. Mason, *Flavius Josephus*, 356; and Saldarini, *Pharisees, Scribes, and Sadducees*, 119. Grabbe, *Judaic Religion*, 191, is skeptical of this "public life" reading, but ultimately agrees "there is no evidence that he was himself ever a member of either movement."

the roles of the various Jewish groups in regard to uprisings against Rome. The insertion in *A.J.* 13 comes much earlier, namely, during the account of the Maccabean leader and high priest, Jonathan (160–143 BCE). But why this earlier insertion?

The text begins, "Now at this time there were three schools of thought among the Jews." The connecting phrase ("now at this time") would appear to signal the presence of these Jewish sects *at this point in Jewish history*.[5] The origin of the groups, including the Pharisees, has to reach at least back to the mid-second century BCE.[6]

This group called Pharisees shows up again in Josephus's account a few decades later during the reign of the Hasmonean ruler and high priest, John Hyrcanus (134–104 BCE). The story begins with harmony between them (*A.J.* 13.289). This is, however, quickly disrupted by a dinner-guest, Eleazar, who upbraided Hyrcanus for arrogating the high priesthood to himself. When challenged, Eleazar repeats a slander that Hyrcanus had no right to the priesthood since his mother was a captive under Antiochus Epiphanes, and thus stood under suspicion of having been violated sexually.[7] This incensed Hyrcanus as well as all the Pharisees. Now, however, a Sadducee whispers in Hyrcanus's ear that the Pharisees were actually in league with Eleazar in this slanderous action. To test their loyalty, Hyrcanus asks them to suggest a punishment for Eleazar. When the Pharisees suggest a mild punishment, Hyrcanus believes they are on Eleazar's side, and himself switches to the Saddducean side.

This story contains quite a few notes of potential value for our reconstruction of Pharisaic history. "And so great is their influence with the masses that even when they speak against a king or high priest, they immediately gain credence." As we will see in other texts, the Pharisees are not portrayed as members of the noble or ruling classes but are aligned more with the general populace. They do, however, have access to ruling circles and they exercise considerable political influence, at least in terms of swaying public opinion rather than through the exercise of official authority. As always, we need to be cautious in simply accepting Josephus's assertions

---

5. Debate over the rationale for the insertion of this material at this point in *A.J.* remains intense and unresolved. See, for example, Schwartz, "Josephus and Nicolaus on the Pharisees," 157–71. On the debate, with openness to the chronological reason, Mason, *Flavius Josephus on the Pharisees*, 197–202.

6. Pharisaic origins in the mid-second century BCE in connection with Maccabean developments has become a consensus opinion. For example, Rivkin, *Hidden Revolution*, ch. 4; Schaper, "Pharisees," 402–27. For an earlier attempt to stretch Pharisaic origins clear back to Ezra(!), see Herford, *Pharisees*, ch. 1.

7. Lev 21:14 says the high priest's lineage shall not include "a woman who has been defiled."

about their power. Here and elsewhere, he appears concerned to protect the reputation of these Hasmonean rulers and to explain why they were generally unpopular with their Jewish subjects.[8] As he notes in the opening of this story, "the envy of the Jews was aroused against him by his own successes." And as he will stress in a moment, "there is nothing more powerful than envy and calumny, nor anything that more easily disrupts friendship and the ties of nature than these influences" (*A.J.* 13.310). This particular story is all about how envy worked to the disadvantage of a good and effective leader (*A.J.* 13.299). Whether the Pharisees' influence over public opinion was quite so pervasive as this story asserts, it served the purpose of an easily understood picture: the Pharisees and the populace on one side, Hyrcanus and the nobles on the other.

This episode also reinforces what we will see in other Josephan narratives regarding Sadducees. They "hav[e] the confidence of the wealthy alone but no following among the populace" (*A.J.* 13.298). Alongside their higher socio-economic status, this text adds a religious dimension to their differentiation from Pharisees. The latter passed on unwritten laws and traditions, but these "are rejected by the Sadducaean group, who hold that only those regulations should be considered valid which were written down" (*A.J.* 13.297). In fact, the Pharisees are portrayed as having "established [regulations] for the people" (*A.J.* 13.296), thus having notable authority in Jewish praxis. Readers of the NT Gospels will immediately think of Jesus' disputes with Pharisees over the "traditions of the fathers" and sitting in the "seat of Moses."

This passage also portrays the Pharisees as fundamentally interested in righteousness, virtue, and pleasing God. "They knew [Hyrcanus] wished to be righteous and in everything he did tried to please God and them—for the Pharisees profess such beliefs" (*A.J.* 13.289). In fact, Hyrcanus refers to them as his religious guides. "He begged them, if they observed him doing anything wrong or straying from the right path, to lead him back to it and correct him" (*A.J.* 13.290).

Finally, the Pharisees in this story do not adopt the negative position of Eleazar regarding the legitimacy of Hyrcanus as high priest. On a stricter reading of Torah, one might have expected them to side with those questioning Hyrcanus's assumption of this priestly role.[9] Yet, they appear quite at peace with this, and, in fact, become indignant when Eleazar presses his

---

8. Josephus himself claims to be a Hasmonean descendant (*Life* 1-6).

9. See below (pp. 9-10) on the earlier opposition of the pious to unlawful high priestly appointments in the Maccabean period.

point of view. Thus, at least in this instance, the Pharisees seem to adjust their normally strict reading of Torah in the interests of political pragmatism.

Rescuing Israel from Hellenization

Explaining why a movement like the Pharisees arose at this particular point in Jewish history requires a closer look at what was going on in the nation. By the second century BCE the Jews' understanding of who they were—of their significance and place in the universe—was anchored to temple, territory and Torah. Jews were the people whose God dwelt in the Jerusalem temple, who themselves occupied the land promised to their ancestors, and who alone among the nations knew the will of the one God through their Scripture. That threefold identity was mangled when the northern portion of the land (including Samaria and Galilee) was overrun by the Assyrians in the eighth century BCE. Then it was nearly extinguished when the Babylonians finished off the southern portion, including the destruction of Jerusalem and the temple, around two centuries later. What did it mean now to be Israel, the people of the one true God when he had been rousted by pagan gods and his house demolished? What did it mean to be the seed of Abraham when they had no more control over the promised land, and many could no longer even live there? Did all of this call into question the reliability of the word of this God? And just as importantly Jews would be asking, what must we do, how must we live, if we are to once again walk in the way of Yahweh's blessing? Since our problems seem to have come as a result of our own abandonment of our God and his ways, what will a truly repentant and obedient people look like?

Now stir in Hellenistic culture with the fourth century coming of Alexander the Great and his successors to the land of Israel and the entire eastern Mediterranean.

> Colonies of Greek soldier-settlers were established and cities were founded on Greek patterns. The gymnasium, stadium, hippodrome, theatre, and celebration of Greek festivals spread the Greek way of life. Coinage followed the Attic standard. Greek language spread, and with it Greek literature and education.... Greek became the language for commerce, government, and literature. Greek culture came to hold sway throughout the eastern Mediterranean, at least in the cities and upper levels of society, among the Jewish aristocracy as well as among other peoples.[10]

---

10. Ferguson, *Backgrounds of Early Christianity*, 379.

As with any minority culture, different Jewish groups found different ways to get along with the dominant Hellenistic culture. The moneyed elite, among whom were the aristocracy and many leading priests, tended naturally to seek the preservation of their power and status. These, of course, would push the boundaries of accommodation. Why not educate our sons in the Hellenistic schools? We can teach them Torah in the evening at home. We should seek to get along with the political rulers; after all, how else can we hope to gain some helpful influence on behalf of our Jewish people?

On the other end of the spectrum would be those who remembered and held fast to the Israel of old. They would remember that in better days God chose their leaders, not some foreign power. Once we could stand proudly before others as Israel, with our distinctive language and customs like circumcision, food regulations, and resting one day out of seven. The new ways threaten all of that and must be vigorously resisted without compromise, even violently if need be.

And, of course, there were the bulk of the common folk who found themselves caught somewhere in between. They saw the wisdom of seeking to make the best of a bad situation by going along (within limits). After all, hadn't Jeremiah himself told the exiles in Babylon to settle down, get normal jobs, raise their families in the new situation and to "seek the peace of the city" where they now found themselves (Jer 29:7). Yet, they recognized the danger of going too far and losing touch with all that had made them who they were, God's people Israel. This same struggle has been repeated in culture after culture throughout much of human history, with the same varied responses. And as you readers probably know from experience, these disagreements about how far to bend and accommodate are hardly quaint armchair chats; they are deep-seated disagreements, full of emotion, sometimes resulting in the division of families and societies as we will see in the next phase.

This was the situation when we arrive at the period which saw the rise of the Pharisees. Following Alexander the Great's sudden death (323 BCE), his huge kingdom was administered by his generals and their successors. The Ptolemies, headquartered in Egypt to the south, ruled over Palestine first (301–198 BCE), followed by the Seleucids, headquartered in Syria to the north (198–167 BCE). Although this was a period of relative political peace for Palestine, the cultural tensions noted above continued to bubble. They exploded in the 160s–170s BCE. Three issues in particular powered this explosion. First, who would be high priest? This was of supreme importance, since in the absence of a Jewish king, it was the high priest who was effectively the chief administrative officer representing the Jews in the Hellenistic empire. According to the prophet Ezekiel, the choice of a high priest was to be limited to those descended from Zadok, of the line of Aaron; thus, these were called Zadokite priests.[11] So far so good, until Jason, the brother of the high priest, Onias III, bribed the Seleucid ruler, Antiochus IV (Antiochus Ephiphanes), and got himself appointed high priest instead. This Jason was then outbid and ousted by Menelaus, who was not even a Zadokite; thus, had no biblical right to the office. This initiated a long chain of questionable high priests. Of course, for some pious Jews this was too much to bear. The monks at Qumran, themselves largely priestly folk, were so incensed they refused to enter the Jerusalem temple and have anything to do with those they now viewed as "wicked priests."[12]

Josephus's three groups are fairly clearly present in this priestly controversy. The Sadducees were made up of leading priests and nobles, who saw value in accommodation with the Hellenistic rulers. They were headquartered in Jerusalem, managed the temple and its services, and were powerbrokers for the nation. The Qumran community as noted stood against them. As we will see, the Pharisees apparently took a more pragmatic attitude, at times joining with those who rejected a particular high priest due to non-Zadokite lineage; at other times acquiescing to a non-Zadokite high priest as we saw above in the Eleazar episode.

Added to this priesthood issue was a second one, money, or taxation. Whoever had authority from the Seleucid rulers to collect taxes had it made. Menelaus, mentioned above, belonged to the Tobiad family who had this taxation power. The Seleucids were eager to find the highest bidder, since they were under financial pressure from the menacing Romans and also needed to finance ongoing conflict with the Ptolemies in Egypt. Thus, when this extreme hellenizer, Menelaus, who seemed less concerned with preserving the character of Jewishness, offered a bigger bribe, and indicated Antiochus could help himself to the temple's treasures, the die was cast. As too often happens, the rich got richer, the taxes got heavier, and the poor got the short end.

But the issues that really touched off the powder keg were the cultural, the lifestyle issues which came to a head in the Maccabean revolt.

> In those days certain renegades [the powerful elites and many of the high priestly caste] came out from Israel and misled many, saying, "Let us go and make a covenant with the Gentiles around us, for since we separated from them many disasters have come

---

11. Cf. Ezek 40:46; 43:19; 44:15; 48:11.

12. "some of the Qumran scrolls refer regularly to the 'wicked priest' (*hakkōhen haraša'*), which is almost certainly a play on the title 'high priest' (*hakkōhen harōš*)." Grabbe, *Judaic Religion*, 80.

upon us." This proposal pleased them, and some of the people eagerly went to the king, who authorized them to observe the ordinances of the Gentiles. So they built a gymnasium in Jerusalem, according to Gentile custom, and *removed the marks of circumcision*, and *abandoned the holy covenant*. They joined with the Gentiles and *sold themselves to do evil*. (1 Macc 1:11–15)

Then the king wrote to his whole kingdom that all should be one people, and that all should *give up their particular customs*. All the Gentiles accepted the command of the king. Many even from Israel gladly adopted his religion; they *sacrificed to idols and profaned the sabbath*. And the king sent letters by messengers to Jerusalem and the towns of Judah; he directed them to follow customs strange to the land, to forbid burnt offerings and sacrifices and drink offerings in the sanctuary, to *profane sabbaths and festivals, to defile the sanctuary and the priests, to build altars and sacred precincts and shrines for idols, to sacrifice swine and other unclean animals, and to leave their sons uncircumcised*. They were to make themselves abominable by everything unclean and profane, so that they would *forget the law and change all the ordinances*. He added, "And whoever does not obey the command of the king shall die." (1 Macc 1:41–50)

Notice how observable lifestyle issues—circumcision, modesty, purity regulations, observance of Sabbath and food customs—mark out who is true to God versus one who has "abandoned the holy covenant."

In the face of this mortal attack on historic Jewish identity, the decisive act of loyal resistance occurred in the small Judean village of Modein. A local priest, Mattathias, refused to obey the government officials and sacrifice to pagan gods. Instead, he killed a fellow Jew who intended to commit such idolatry and he cut down one of the royal officers for good measure (read 1 Macc 1–2 for this gripping story). Having done this, "Mattathias cried out in the town with a loud voice, saying: 'Let every one who is zealous for the law and supports the covenant come out with me!'" (1 Macc 2:27) Although Mattathias would live only a year longer, he had five sons, one of whom, Judas, nicknamed Maccabeus (probably meaning "hammer"), took the military reigns in what would come to be called the Maccabean rebellion. Judas's brothers and successors, the Hasmoneans (named after an ancestor Hashmon), seized political power. This was the beginning of about a century of Jewish semi-independence, as a succession of Hasmonean high priests and rulers took advantage of the ebb and flow of Seleucid power in the region. In 164 BCE the daily burnt offering in the temple was resumed, leading to a new Jewish festival, Hanukkah, the feast of dedication (John 10:22) or lights.

Although this century of semi-independence began as a protest against the Hellenistic corruption of Israel's law and loyalty to their God, by its end the anti-Hellenistic leaders, the Maccabee-Hasmoneans, had succumbed to the allures of Hellenistic privilege. Priestly appointments were now given as political plums. Ruling families looked more and more like worldly potentates. Concern for keeping Torah among the well-to-do fell to all-time lows. Amidst this chaotic and fluid situation we find the beginnings of the Pharisees. This chronological point for their beginnings finds confirmation in Josephus's *Antiquities* (13.171–173) as we detailed when examining that passage above.

Hasidim and Scribes

In order to fill out this picture of Pharisaic beginnings in the Maccabean period, we should relate them to two other groups named around this same period.[13] One group are the Hasideans or *hasidim*,[14] the "pious." Immediately after Mattathias initiated the revolt, he was pursued into the wilderness and his forces were attacked. They refused to fight on the Sabbath day and most were slaughtered. Mattathias and the survivors made a critical decision, "Let us fight against anyone who comes to attack us on the sabbath day" (1 Macc 2:41).

> Then there united with them a company of Hasideans, mighty warriors of Israel, all who offered themselves willingly for the law.... And Mattathias and his friends went around and tore down the altars; they forcibly circumcised all the uncircumcised boys that they found within the borders of Israel. They hunted down the arrogant, and the work prospered in their hands. They rescued the law out of the hands of the Gentiles and kings, and they never let the sinner gain the upper hand. (1 Macc 2:42, 45–8)

These *hasidim* were noted for their devotion to Torah ("offered themselves willingly for the law"), and at this stage allied themselves with the

---

13. The reconstruction from this point forward entails some speculation, but is generally accepted. Davies, "Hasidim," 127–40; also Kampen, *The Hasideans*, [more speculative].

14. In the OT, *hasid* referred often to a pious or godly person (Ps 12:1; 32:6; Mic 7:2; etc.). From this same Hebrew term will later come the name of the group we know as Hasidic Jews.

Maccabees politically and militarily.[15] This coalition sought to restore Israel's ancient identity marks: they "circumcised all the uncircumcised boys" and "rescued the law out of the hands of the Gentiles."

This same group shows up a few chapters later, now in the company of "scribes," but taking a position quite different from the Maccabean leaders. In the mid-160s BCE the Syrian overlords had deposed the high priest, Menelaus, replacing him with "the ungodly Alcimus" (1 Macc 7:9), a non-Zadokite and confirmed Hellenizer. The Maccabees opposed this flagrant intrusion. A group of scribes and Hasideans were, however, willing to seek peace.

Then a group of scribes appeared in a body before Alcimus and Bacchides to ask for just terms. The Hasideans were first among the Israelites to seek peace from them, for they said, "A priest of the line of Aaron has come with the army, and he will not harm us." Alcimus spoke peaceable words to them and swore this oath to them, "We will not seek to injure you or your friends." So they trusted him; but he seized sixty of them and killed them in one day.... (1 Macc 7:12-16) Already a fracturing of the Maccabean coalition was evident.[16] While Judas Maccabee continued to oppose Alcimus, these scribes and Hasideans, who had earlier been solidly pro-Maccabean, have apparently dropped out of that rebellion now that some of their religious concerns have been satisfied.

In this last passage we saw a second new group, scribes, closely aligned with, though not necessarily equated with, the Hasideans. In the **Second Temple** Jewish world, scribe was a broad term encompassing a literate class of copyists, secretaries to civil administrators, document preparers as well as teachers and sages. Similar to the socio-economic level of Pharisees, scribes were neither at the top nor the bottom, but somewhere in the realm of mid-level bureaucrats and retainers, usually dependent on the wealthier classes for their employment.[17] It would be a mistake, however, to think of them only as technical assistants. In line with the biblical model of Ezra the scribe and the developments evident in Ben Sira, scribes could also be teachers, sages and

> The Second Temple period ran from approximately 516 BCE (construction of the new or Second Temple after the destruction of Solomon's temple in 586 BCE) to 70 CE (destruction of Herod's temple).

---

15. 2 Macc 14:6 portrays the Hasideans as integral to the Maccabean resistance from the start, rather than joining later.

16. The story is told differently in 2 Maccabees. There all the followers of Judas Maccabee are Hasideans (14:6), and they do not split over Alcimus.

17. See esp. Saldarini, *Pharisees, Scribes, and Sadducees*, ch. 11, "Social Roles of Scribes," 241-76.

Torah-experts in their own right.[18] Thus, we see quite a significant overlap in the status and roles of the Torah-devoted *hasidim*, the more literary scribes, and the Pharisees. Though the sparse evidence does not allow firm conclusions, it was probably from the ranks of these early pro-Hasmonean pious folk, like the *hasidim* and scribes, that the Pharisees arose.

What's in a Name ("Pharisees")?[19]

Our earliest documentary evidence comes from the first century CE when the Gospels and Josephus referred to them in Greek as *pharisaioi*. Traditionally this Greek appellation has been thought to derive from the Hebrew and Aramaic root *prš* meaning to separate, interpret, or specify. The noun plural *perushim* could then refer to those who separated, or perhaps who interpreted or specified.[20] Yet, even if the sense was "the separated ones," this still leaves us with several options for its precise nuance. From what did they separate? Was it a positive term in the sense of separation from sinners or impurity, thus within the general orbit of "holy"? This would fit well with the Maccabean origins we traced and with the stress on purity we will see repeatedly. Or was it meant negatively by their opponents, as in those who separate themselves from others on whom they look down haughtily, i.e., "holier than thou"? This is what non-Pharisees might have called Pharisaic separatists. Or perhaps separated from "us," from Israel, i.e., heretics or apostates? The term was, in fact, used often this way in the Talmud. All of these are serious possibilities capable of finding ancient texts which used the term in any of these senses. Or did we get off on the wrong track by focusing on "separation"? Thus, some favor "to interpret" or "to specify" for *prš* and conclude the name meant "the specifiers," as in those who specify in careful detail what the commandments mean. This would correspond well with the stress on their *akribeia* or precision as we will note shortly. Although we cannot attain full certainty at present, I will follow the majority who hold that Pharisees means "separated ones." This could be a positive epithet or negative, depending on who was using it and for what purpose. When Jesus addressed people as "Pharisee, hypocrite," that's clearly negatively loaded. But when Paul claimed "as to the law, a Pharisee," that was his Jewish badge of honor. It was probably this sense of

---

18. Rivkin, "Scribes, Pharisees," 139–40.

19. Helpful review of evidence and options in Saldarini, *Pharisees, Scribes, and Sadducees*, 220–25.

20. See esp. Baumgarten, "Name of the Pharisees," 411–28. For caution against reliance on etymology, see Morrison, "What's in a Name?"

separation from perceived apostates and sinners that began to be used at some point after the Maccabean events.[21]

Summary of Pharisaic Origins

From the few hints we have it seems most likely the group we refer to as Pharisees began sometime in the mid-second century BCE in connection with the Maccabean struggle against Hellenism over Israel's true identity. Against those who would erase the covenantal marks of circumcision, Sabbath observance and lawful foods, these devoted pious folk, these *hasidim*, stood firm and would not join the compromisers. Their very name, Pharisees, the separate ones, testified to this unwillingness to join with impurity and lawlessness. Instead, they would hold firm to Torah's ways.

---

21. Deines suggests the name originally referred negatively to their separation from the Hasmonean movement, then began to be used positively for separation from impurity and careful interpretation (Jos), and finally fell into disuse (Mishnah). Deines, "Pharisäer," 2:1456–57.

CHAPTER 2

Josephus and the Historical Development of the Pharisees

FOR OUR LOOK AT Pharisaic beginnings in the previous chapter we had only a couple of Josephan references. Fortunately, for the subsequent development of the movement into the first century CE we have several, some of which are duplicates (see table below). Although not many in number, these will yield significant pointers to the character of the movement.

Table: Texts in Josephus mentioning Pharisees
(chronologically ordered)

Content	Date	War	Antiquities	Life
Description of three schools of thought	160s BCE		13.171–173	
John Hyrcanus, Eleazar, and Pharisees	134–104 BCE		13.288–298	
Alexander Jannaeus and Salome Alexandra	76–67 BCE	1.110–114	13.400–432	
Pollion, the Pharisee, and Herod	37–4 BCE		15.3–4	
Pollion and Samaias refuse oath of loyalty to Herod	c. 20 BCE		15.370	
Intrigues in Herod's court	37–4 BCE	1.571	17.41–45	
Description of three schools of thought	6 BCE	2.119–66	18.11–22	

Content	Date	War	Antiquities	Life
Josephus's personal experience with Pharisees	56–60 CE			10–12
Josephus, Pharisees, and others seek to dissuade populace from revolt against Rome	66 CE	2.411–418		21
Some Pharisees and others seek to have Josephus removed from military command	66–70 CE			189–198

Following the mid-second century beginnings reviewed in the previous chapter, we must wait nearly a century for another mention during the reign of Queen Salome Alexandra. This occurs in two versions, a short one in *J.W.* 1.110–114 and a much longer narrative in *A.J.* 13.400–432. We will focus on the shorter narrative in *War* first, then examine the modifications in the longer *Antiquities* version.

Powerful Pharisees during Queen Alexandra's reign (*J.W.* 1.110–114; *A.J.* 13.400–432)

The early portion of *War* recounts the 100-year history of Jewish conflicts from the Maccabees to Alexander Jannaeus (c. 170–70 BCE). The Pharisees are not mentioned, and thus play no role in *War* until the story of Alexander's widow, Salome Alexandra, who reigned as queen from 76–67 BCE. He portrays her positively overall in 1.107–109. Similar to the Pharisees, she had a "reputation for piety [*doxan eusebeias*]" and "was, indeed, the very strictest observer [*ēkribou malista*] of the national traditions [*tou ethnous ta patria*, lit. of the customs of the fathers]." In connection with her reign, Josephus brings the Pharisees onto the stage (1.110–114). His description of their activities revolves around how they related to and affected Alexandra's reign. That is, the focus is not really on the Pharisees but on Alexandra. They disappear immediately, only to reappear about 70 yrs. later in Herod's reign (see below on *J.W.* 1.571 and 2.119, 162–166).

> Beside Alexandra, and growing as she grew, arose the Pharisees, a body of Jews with the reputation of excelling the rest of their nation in the observances of religion, and as exact exponents of the laws. To them, being herself intensely religious, she listened with too great deference; while they, gradually taking advantage of an ingenuous woman, became at length the real

administrators of the state, at liberty to banish and to recall, to loose and to bind, whom they would. In short, the enjoyments of royal authority were theirs; its expenses and burthens fell to Alexandra. She proved, however, to be a wonderful administrator in larger affairs.... But if she ruled the nation, the Pharisees ruled her. (*J.W.* 1.110–112)

A reader might initially think Josephus wished to portray the Pharisees quite positively. They are the "real administrators of the state" and obtain the "enjoyments of royal authority." Like Alexandra, but surpassing her, they have a reputation for piety (Gk. *dokoun eusebesteron*, lit. seem to be the most pious) and are known as "exact [*akribesteron*, lit. most precise] exponents of the laws." However, each of these seemingly positive notes carries a negative twist. Their political power turns out on closer reading to be *undue influence* ("taking advantage," they "ruled her"), which led to the dishonorable execution of numerous "distinguished" and "eminent" men (1.113–114). The LCL translation of 1.110 obscures this negative tone concerning their rise to power. Instead of its innocuous "growing as she grew, arose the Pharisees," the LCL marginal note is more on target ("grew up beside her into power"). Mason agrees, "Literally, 'grew up beside into her power' (like suckers around a tree)." That is, they "encroach[ed] on her authority parasitically."[1]

We will examine the matter of their reputation for piety and scrupulous exposition of the Jewish laws in more detail in the next chapter on Pharisaic character, but for now several of the Greek terms and phrases need to be unpacked to discern what exactly Josephus wished to say about their role at this stage in their history.

> [T]he Pharisees, a body of Jews with the reputation of excelling the rest of their nation in the observances of religion, and as exact exponents of the laws (1.110)

First, a "body [*syntagma*]" of Jews is probably too mild as a translation. When referring to a group of people, Josephus nearly always used *syntagma* in the pejorative sense of a gang or cabal.[2] After this opening negative tone, he acknowledges their reputation [*dokoun*] for piety; but does Josephus

---

1. Mason, "Josephus's Pharisees: The Narratives," 9. Additional negative tones about their political power include: Alexandra listened to them, but "with too great deference"; they had the "enjoyments of royal power" but "its expenses and burthens [sic] fell to Alexandra."

2. "a gang of women . . . created new disturbances (*J.W.* 1.568); see Mason, *Flavius Josephus on the Pharisees*, 84–85.

agree with this popular perception?[3] Shortly before this account he had told of Alexander Jannaeus, who exhibited "apparent moderation of character" (*J.W.* 1.85), but this reputation was repeatedly shown to be false (1.85–106). Then came Salome Alexandra who also had a "reputation for piety [*doxan eusebeias*]" as well as "strict observance" of laws and customs (*J.W.* 1.108). In her case the reputation proved to be largely deserved. Thus, when Josephus next introduces the Pharisees with a "reputation," the reader naturally asks if they will be found deserving of this reputation or not. What follows demonstrates the falseness of the claim, at least in the eyes of Josephus. They "take advantage" of the pious queen, enjoy the benefits without the burdens of power, and put to death those esteemed by others. In the case of these Pharisees, appearances are deceiving.

In *Antiquities* Josephus gives a much more detailed version of this same story (*A.J.* 13.400–432). This time he prefixes comments about the dying Alexander's instructions to his wife-successor regarding the Pharisees:

> Thereupon [Alexander] advised her to follow his suggestions for keeping the throne secure for herself and her children and to conceal his death from the soldiers until she had captured the fortress. And then, he said, on her return to Jerusalem as from a splendid victory, she should yield a certain amount of power to the Pharisees, for if they praised her in return for this sign of regard, they would dispose the nation favourably toward her. These men, he assured her, had so much influence with their fellow-Jews that they could injure those whom they hated and help those to whom they were friendly; for they had the complete confidence of the masses when they spoke harshly of any person, even when they did so out of envy. (*A.J.* 13.400–402)

The Pharisees are portrayed as immensely influential among the Jewish populace ("they had the complete confidence of the masses"). In view of his impending death Alexander had advised his wife to "yield a certain amount of power to the Pharisees" and to "not take any action . . . without their consent" (*A.J.* 13.404–406). Thus, the Pharisees and the populace will favor her and will grant him a grand burial. After Alexandra appointed her eldest son as high priest,

---

3. The sense of *dokoun* (vb *dokein*) is crucial here. Although it can mean someone "thinks, considers" they themselves are something (e.g., pious), it can equally refer to how someone appears or seems to others, i.e., their reputation. This latter sense was widespread in ancient Greek literature (LSJ) and in Josephus (e.g., in childhood he was "gaining a reputation [*dokōn*] for an excellent memory and understanding," *Life* 8), and is the sense favored almost universally for our passage by commentators and translators.

> she permitted the Pharisees to do as they liked in all matters, and also commanded the people to obey them; and whatever regulations, introduced by the Pharisees in accordance with the tradition of their fathers, had been abolished by her father-in-law Hyrcanus, these she again restored. And so, while she had the title of sovereign, the Pharisees had the power.... [They] in no way differed from absolute rulers. (A.J. 13.408–409)

This, however, will be the only time Josephus portrays the Pharisees as playing such a politically powerful role in the nation.

Once again, we see reference to these Pharisaic "regulations [*nomimoi*]" which derived from "the traditions of their fathers [*kata tēn partōan paradosin*]" which were already introduced in A.J. 13.288-298. He does not give us more detail about them here, but we will examine them more carefully below as well as in the Gospels' reference to the "tradition of the elders" (Mark 7:3, 4, 5).

In the *War* version, Josephus had mainly praise for Alexandra in spite of her weaker gender. For whatever reason, Josephus is much less sanguine about her in this later version. He disapproves of a woman's reign over Israel (A.J. 13.417), though he does retain muted praise of her almost manly capabilities (A.J. 13.430) and keeping the peace (A.J. 13.432). As in the previous account in *War*, the Pharisees remain troublemakers ("throughout the entire country there was quiet except for the Pharisees," A.J. 13.410), particularly by having others, persons of substance and virtue, put to death. Here they seem particularly opportunistic. Although they were not known as great supporters of her husband, once the fix was in with Alexandra, "by their eulogies they so greatly moved the people to mourn and lament that they gave him a more splendid burial than had been given any of the kings before him" (A.J. 13.406). Thus, in the end, neither Alexandra nor the Pharisees come off very well in this account.

Wary Participants: Herod and the Pharisees (A.J. 15.3–4, 370; 17.41–45; J.W. 1.571)

Pharisees appear again in connection with Herod (37–4 BCE) when we meet "Pollion the Pharisee and his disciple Samaias" (A.J. 15.3-4). During Herod's siege of Jerusalem (37 BCE) in order to solidify power as king of the Jews, these two had advised the Jerusalemites to capitulate to him. Somewhat later Herod would demand a loyalty oath of his Jewish subjects, and these two individuals, plus "most of their disciples," show up again, but this time they are not so favorable toward Herod and refuse to take the oath (A.J. 15.370).

Although Herod "persecuted in all kinds of ways" those who opposed him, he let Pollion and Samaias and their Pharisee disciples off with lesser punishment due to their earlier favorable behavior toward him. One of these two appears in one further, earlier episode though he is not there explicitly called a Pharisee (*A.J.* 14.172–176). This earlier incident took place while Herod was still governor of Galilee under his father, Antipater, and the Romans (47–37 BCE). It recounts the appearance of Herod "with his soldiers around him" before the Jewish council (Sanhedrin) on charge of murder. All are understandably fearful, but are still leaning toward conviction. One man, however, Samaias,[4] himself "upright" and "superior to fear," calls Herod out and declares him guilty according to the law. Yet, simultaneously he predicts Herod's future ascent to greater power, including his brutality against the political and religious leaders. This prediction apparently gains the Pharisee lasting favor in Herod's estimation.

These brief notices reveal several things about the Pharisees in the Herodian period. In spite of the affirming prophecy (Herod will rule) and their readiness to turn the city over to him, one could hardly say they were pro-Herod. The prophecy paints a gloomy and brutal picture of the future tyrant, they refuse to take the oath of loyalty, and Samaias not only affirmed Herod's guilt at trial but did so in highly unflattering terms (Herod seeks "to save himself by outraging justice" and is "putting his own interests above the law").

Of particular interest is the presence of an influential Pharisee in the Sanhedrin during Herod's time.[5] If accurate, this suggests the Pharisees did have some presence in the leading councils in Jerusalem just before the NT period. It portrays them as principled men (upright, fearless, refuse the oath), concerned with justice and the Jewish law. Samaias here is even credited with prophetic ability. His advice to capitulate at Herod's advance on the city may point to a certain pragmatic bent. Each of these stories points to some sort of special relationship between Herod and the Pharisees, perhaps a wary acknowledgement of the other's dangerous power.

The next mention of Pharisees comes while narrating intrigues in Herod's court and family 37–4 BCE (*J.W.* 1.571; *A.J.* 17.41–45). The Pharisees were exercising influence over some of the female family members and took the side of those opposing Herod ("they were obviously intent upon

---

4. *A.J.* 15.3 says it was Pollion, not Samaias, who made these statements. In addition, the MSS show variation in which name to use and its spelling. Many scholars remain skeptical of the historical value of these accounts, since the names are so confused and the parallel in *J.W.* 1.208–211 makes no mention of Samaias at all.

5. The text is ambiguous as to whether Samaias was present as an onlooker or a member, and the MSS vary between Samaias referring to the council as "you" or "us."

combating and injuring" him). Herod hears "that the Pharisees had corrupted some of the people at court." He then put the leading elements of these Pharisaic opponents to death along with those household members who had been listening to them. An inserted historical flashback explains this relationship of the Pharisees to these opposing family members (*A.J.* 17.42–43). At an earlier point in Herod's reign some 6,000 Pharisees had refused to take the oath of loyalty and were assessed a large fine (*A.J.* 15.370; *J.W.* 1.571). This fine was, however, paid by the wife of Herod's brother, who is now one of the conspirators in the palace intrigues. This explains why these conspirators and the Pharisees now join forces. In addition, the flashback asserts the Pharisees were able to foretell the future, and had prophesied that this benefactress and her offspring would take over Herod's throne, a prediction which, however, proved to be false.

A number of items about the Pharisees during the Herodian period are either confirmed or introduced in this passage. As usual their commitment to the exact interpretation and observance of ancestral traditions [*exakribōsei tou patriou kai nomōn*] is stressed (*A.J.* 17.41). Josephus in this case, however, gives this normally positive trait a negative cast by saying they were "haughty" or "took undue pride in" this exact observance.[6] We see again their involvement in national politics. However, unlike their earlier political power under Salome Alexandra, now they have to seek power through palace intrigues with other family members. The Pharisees have quite a history with Herod and in this case they stand opposed to him and pay dearly for it. Although they hobnob with the elites, their inability to pay their own fine hints at socioeconomic status somewhere below the wealthy elites.

Of particular interest is the mention of their total number, "over 6,000." This is the only specific indication anywhere of their numerical size. For comparison, Josephus credits the Essenes with 4,000 practitioners.[7] If we accept an estimate of 800,000 for the Palestinian Jewish population at the time, Pharisees constituted less than 1 percent of the total. However, if one adds the many "less vociferous supporters and sympathizers" who listened to the Pharisees, as well as the influence shown by Josephus's account of them in circles of power, then "Pharisaism constituted a very significant force in Herod's Judaea."[8]

---

6. On this negative tone in *mega phronoun*, see LSJ, s.v. *phroneō*, II.2.b.
7. *A.J.*.18.20; same number in Philo, *Quod Omnis Probus Liber Sit* 75.
8. Schaper, "Pharisees," 419.

Pharisees as One of the Three Jewish Philosophies
(J.W. 2.119–166; A.J. 18.11–25)

Moving on about ten years in his history (ca. 6 CE), Josephus comes now to the story of Judas the Galilean. Judas was a revolutionary who objected to paying Roman tribute since God alone should be lord and who founded a "fourth philosophy" (A.J. 18.9). "This man was a sophist who founded a sect of his own, having nothing in common with the others" (J.W. 2.118). This provides Josephus the opportunity to explain to his Roman readers that such zealotry, such anti-Roman revolutionary sentiment, was not typical of the three main Jewish schools of thought: the Essenes, the Pharisees and the Sadducees. Thus, he breaks off the historical narrative to give a lengthy description of these philosophies (J.W. 2.119–166).[9] We noted a shorter, parallel account earlier (A.J. 13.171–173).

J.W. 2.162–163, 166	A.J. 18.12–15
... the Pharisees, who are considered the most accurate interpreters of the law, and hold the position of the leading sect, attribute everything to Fate and to God; they hold that to act righteously or otherwise rests, indeed, for the most part with men, but that in each action Fate co-operates. Every soul, they maintain, is imperishable, but the soul of the good alone passes into another body, while the souls of the wicked suffer eternal punishment. The Pharisees are affectionate to each other and cultivate harmonious relations with the community.	The Pharisees simplify their standard of living, making no concession to luxury. They follow guidance of that which their doctrine has selected and transmitted as good, attaching the chief importance to the observance of those commandments which it has seen fit to dictate to them. They show respect and deference to their elders, nor do they rashly presume to contradict their proposals. Though they postulate that everything is brought about by fate, still they do not deprive the human will of the pursuit of what is in man's power, since it was God's good pleasure that there should be a fusion and that the will of man with his virtue and vice should be admitted to the council-chamber of fate. They believe that souls have power to survive death and that there are rewards and punishments under the earth for those who have led lives of virtue or vice: eternal imprisonment is the lot of evil souls, while the good souls receive an easy passage to a new life. Because of these views they are, as a matter of fact, extremely influential among the townsfolk; and all prayers and sacred rites of divine worship are performed according to their exposition. This is the great tribute that the inhabitants of the cities, by practicing the highest ideals both in their way of living and in their discourse, have paid to the excellence of the Pharisees.

---

9. Josephus typically refers to these groups with the term *hairesis*, which does not mean heresy, but a school of thought, a party or faction (Paul is of the Pharisaical "party" in Acts 26:5). Sometimes he will substitute *philosophia*, since Jewish groups could be most easily described to Greco-Roman outsiders as some type of philosophical teaching and way of life like Stoicism.

Since we will give considerable attention to many elements of these descriptions when we discuss the character of the Pharisees (chs. 3–5), we need now only note those elements important for tracing their historical development. They continue their existence into the common era as a coherent, identifiable form of Jewishness. Although some still seem willing to take up arms against foreign encroachment like their Maccabean forebears,[10] Josephus wishes to make clear they are not revolutionaries, but are more like philosophical movements such as Stoicism or Epicureanism. They are, in fact, willing to seek accommodation with Roman power. We see again the mention of their accuracy (*akribeia*) in Torah interpretation along with their popular appeal. Here the latter is tied to their theological views, probably immortality and eternal rewards in particular. In matters of Jewish praxis ("manner of life") their teaching "prevails over all," i.e., particularly over the Sadducees. Elsewhere, Josephus makes clear how unpopular the Sadducees were in these matters (*A.J.* 18.17). Since the Jewish manner of life revolved around how to properly keep the biblical commandments, we may assume this implies the Pharisees' interpretations regarding Torah obedience were widely acknowledged.[11] This may explain why Jesus' Torah disputes were typically with Pharisees, and receives confirmation in Jesus' statement, "The scribes and the Pharisees sit on Moses' seat; therefore, do whatever they teach you and follow it" (Matt 23:2–3). In a final comparison, the Pharisees are affectionate and harmonious versus the boorish and rude Sadducees.

Of particular importance for our estimation of the Pharisees' historical development and influence is the notice that they "hold the position of the leading sect" (*J.W.* 2.162). At this stage in Jewish history Josephus is aware of numerous existing factions, each of which intertwines politics and religion in differing ways. But in what sense does he think the Pharisees are the "leading sect"? The Greek phrase is open to differing interpretations. They could be the most important or influential, the most numerous, or the oldest (i.e., first to develop). Or it could even mean they "lead astray the first school of thought [i.e., the Essenes]," and thus are not really the chief

---

10. Whereas the account of the Zealots in *War* mentioned only Judas the Galilean as ringleader (*J.W.* 2.117–118), *Antiquities* mentions a second ringleader, Saddok, a Pharisee (*A.J.* 18.3, 9–10).

11. Popular acknowledgment does not equate with careful practice. The village farmer might acknowledge the Pharisees' Sabbath restrictions on work, but still plow his field on Sabbath when constrained by rain and weather. This is not unlike modern Christians who might agree with their pastor that one ought to attend church every Sunday, yet on occasion still enjoy sleeping in.

sect at all.[12] Preferable in my view is the translation, the Pharisees "take for themselves [the position of] the leading school."[13] Thus, Josephus does not claim they are, in fact, the leading group, but only that *they arrogate to themselves a leading role*. Nor is this contradicted by the way he puts things in *Antiquities*. The LCL translates "they are, as a matter of fact, extremely influential" (*A.J.* 18.15). This is incorrect and should be translated "they happen [*tynchanousin*] to be the most persuasive." The verb *tynchanō*, repeated in the following parallel line, gives not Josephus's unqualified affirmation but speaks of their popularity as something that just happens to occur, almost as a matter of chance, not as a regular or deserved characteristic.

Pharisees Oppose the Jewish Revolt (*J.W.* 2.411–418)

The final mention of Pharisees in *War* occurs in the narration of events leading to the war of 66-70 CE, and lays the blame upon revolutionary-minded Jews, above all Eleazar, son of Ananias the high priest. He forbade accepting gifts from foreigners, thus leading to the cessation of the twice-daily sacrifices for the emperor. Josephus is concerned in *War* to distance post-70 Judaism, particularly its leaders and populace (including, of course, himself), in the eyes of Rome from such rebellious, anti-Roman actions. Thus, he narrates how "the principal citizens . . . with the chief priests and the most notable Pharisees" opposed this anti-Roman policy and sought to dissuade the populace (2.411–418), but they could not overcome those following the revolutionaries.

The Pharisees are not identified as members of the high priestly caste, nor as belonging to the "principal citizens" of Jerusalem/Judea, i.e., the wealthy and influential elites. That is, they are portrayed as part of the lay populace, the *dēmos*, somewhat lower in socio-economic status than "principal citizens," but probably not of the lower classes since they are invited to share power. They do, as we have seen elsewhere, exercise political influence. Their influence in this text appears secondary to the chief priests and notable citizens, so they are not the leading political element. They are in favor of a policy of appeasement and are distanced from any revolutionary fervor. How much of this distancing is due to Josephus's aim to portray

---

12. So Mason, *Flavius Josephus on the Pharisees*, 128–32.

13. Mentioned by Saldarini, *Pharisees, Scribes, and Sadducees*, 111n11. This is supported by the probable sense of the verb used here, *apagō*, which more commonly means "take for oneself" (LSJ). It can be used in the sense "lead away" or even "divert [from the subject]" (thus Mason's suggestion, cf. previous note) but does not mean "hold the position of" as in the LCL translation.

Jewish leadership this way, and how much is historically accurate, is difficult to say. In any case, he portrays some "leading Pharisees" positively and as in favor of accommodation with the Roman authorities.

A final mention of the Pharisees in Josephus's works is found in *Life* 189–198,[14] where he recounts the attempt by John of Gischala in Galilee and others in Jerusalem to remove Josephus from his military command in Galilee during the revolt of 66–70 CE. He repeats what we have heard numerous times before: the Pharisees "have the reputation of being unrivalled experts in their country's laws," or more literally, "they appear to excel all others in precision [*akribeia*] with regard to ancestral customs [*peri ta patria nomima*]." Of particular interest, Josephus narrates a joint political venture of his enemies. This group included some Pharisees from lower social positions (Jonathan and Ananias), one Pharisee, Simon of Jerusalem, from "a very illustrious family," another Pharisee, Jozar, from a priestly family, and chief priests, Ananus and Jesus. This confirms the picture we have gained elsewhere from Josephus that Pharisees were sometimes involved in high-level political deliberations, and seem to have been from lower social positions, but can also include the occasional illustrious lay as well as priestly families.

History of the Pharisees: A Synthesis

After their probable beginnings in connection with the mid-second century BCE Maccabean uprising, we find the Pharisees more developed and influential with the populace and in ruling circles by the rule of the Hasmonean John Hyrcanus (134–104 BCE). Their good relations with Hyrcanus soured when a troublemaker, Eleazar, insinuated slander regarding his mother, and the king switches to the Saducean side.

The Pharisees and the Sadducees grow as populist political lobby groups. In addition, the Pharisees had become popular Torah interpreters whose legal customs [*nomima*], based on traditions not explicitly found in the written Torah, had been widely adopted. So popular were they and their teachings that Hyrcanus's revocation of them resulted in "the hatred of the masses for him" (*A.J.* 13.296). Further, their influence was with the masses, the bulk of common Jews, farmers, merchants, traders, manual laborers, etc., while the Sadducees had a hearing among the well-to-do and powerful.

Moving on some decades to the mid-first century BCE, we find the Pharisees gaining real but apparently short-lived political power during the reign of the Jewish queen Salome Alexandra. Their widespread popularity

14. He briefly noted the presence of "leading Pharisees" along with priests in *Life* 21.

remains undiminished ("they had the complete confidence of the masses"). This popular influence, rather than wealth, heritage or official position, is the basis of their political power in higher circles. If Josephus is to be believed in these accounts, the Pharisees were not immune to motives of revenge (they had their enemies among the upper class put to death) and petty opportunism (they gave Alexandra's husband, who had been no great friend of theirs, a splendid funeral). As we will hear repeatedly, so here it is particularly as precise expositors of biblical law that they are renowned.

During the Herodian period (latter half of first century BCE) much of the picture we have seen continues unchanged. The Pharisees are still known especially for their exact interpretation and observance of Torah in line with ancestral traditions (*A.J.* 17.41), as well as for their upright lives (*A.J.* 14.172). They are also known for ability to predict events, though in one important case their prophecy fails. They continue to be involved in national political affairs and have entrée to the Herodian court as well as Jewish decision-making bodies (Sanhedrin), though not necessarily as official members. Socio-economically they remain broadly within the retainer class, administrators, educators, scribes, who are neither poor nor wealthy (though some Pharisees may have gained some wealth). The single numerical estimate of their size (6,000) suggests they remained a small portion of the total population, but large enough to function as power-brokers for the larger populace.

Their relationship with Herod and his regime is variable. They appear fundamentally as troublemakers opposed to him, warning against him in the public council meeting, castigating his behavior, refusing to take the loyalty oath he demanded of everyone, stirring sedition and generally "combating and injuring" Herod (*A.J.* 17.41). Yet, they view his rule as ordained and confirmed by their own predictions, even if as punishment on the nation. For this acknowledgment Herod favors the Pharisees in some cases, exempting them from harsher punishment when they refuse to vow loyalty (though he did fine them substantially). Yet, this favor has limits. When they engage in conspiracy against him, he has many of them put to death.

When we arrive, finally, at the period of the Jewish revolt against Rome (66–70 CE), we find the Pharisees still influential in public life and with the masses; so much so that Josephus felt the need to "engage in public life" in accord with their teachings. The center of Josephus's description of them still focuses on their "precision [*akribeia*] with regard to ancestral customs [*peri ta patria nomima*]" (*Life* 191). They are still found in a variety of socio-economic levels, including some of priestly descent. At least a few Pharisees belong to upper-class families in Jerusalem. One of these, Simon ben Gamaliel, has an influential voice in the main Jerusalem leadership council

(Sanhedrin), and is even able to give directions for actions in Galilee. Josephus differentiates Pharisees from Zealots, indicating that the Pharisees were more prepared to find accommodation with Roman domination (*A.J.* 18.11–25). However, the Pharisees were almost certainly co-conspirators in this revolt in spite of Josephus's attempt to distance them.[15]

---

15. He claims, after all, to conduct his public life in accord with the Pharisees, and is the general for the revolt in Galilee. See Sanders, *Judaism: Practice and Belief,* 386.

Part 2

Character of the Pharisees

CHAPTER 3

Distinctives in Josephus

UNLIKE THE PREVIOUS TWO chapters, which focused on history, the next three chapters answer the question, what sort of people were these Pharisees? What were their beliefs and convictions? What sort of lifestyles did they lead? We will utilize mainly the explicit material in Josephus, but we will also note where this intersects with the picture in the NT, and will cautiously bring in confirming or modifying echoes from the DSS and rabbinic literature.

First, we will gather what our Jewish sources seem to agree on as to what the Pharisees looked like, especially what made them stand out to these observers. This will highlight their *distinctives*. However, if we stopped with distinctives our portrait would be skewed. Any portrait focused only on distinctives runs the risk of failing to notice all that this sub-group shared with its larger social circle. Since Pharisees were first of all Jews, we will also incorporate in chapter 5 what was common to most Jews of the period, including Pharisees. Although they were *distinctive* Jews, they were still distinctive *Jews*.

Precision in Interpreting and Obeying Torah

Numerous times Josephus spoke of the *akribeia* of the Pharisees.

- exact exponents [*akribesteron*] of the laws (J.W. 1.110)
- considered the most accurate [*met' akribeias*] interpreters of the laws (J.W. 2.162)
- priding itself on its adherence to [*ep' eksakribōsei*] ancestral custom (A.J. 17.41)

- have the reputation of being unrivalled experts [*akribeia*] in their country's laws (*Life* 191)[1]

This word refers to "strict conformity to a norm or standard," and thus "exactness" or "precision."[2] In relation to the Pharisees, Josephus used it to refer both to their interpretation of the Jewish laws as well as their observance of them. That is, their interpretations of commandments were precise, exact, and specific. When we come to Jesus' disputes with Pharisees, as well as what we find in rabbinic literature, we will see that many interactions revolved around *how to specify the implications* of a commandment. For instance, did the command to rest on Sabbath still allow one to rescue an animal stranded in a pit or not (see ch. 7)? This more precise spelling out of the meaning and implications of a commandment was called *halakhah* (more on this later).

Not only their interpretation, but equally their personal adherence to the commandments was described with *akribeia*. This could, of course, simply parallel the precision in interpretation. That is, they spelled out the implications of the commandments more thoroughly, and thus, their own practice would be more exacting than others. It could also, however, refer to their *intention* to obey. That is, they were more serious about obedience, more intent on conforming their daily lives *exactly* to the divine will. They were the truly pious and devoted, as also Paul claimed (Gal 1:14).

A couple of clarifications of this Pharisaic *akribeia* are in order. First, it was not only the Pharisees whom Josephus considered to exhibit *akribeia*. He used this word group (including related verbs and adjectives) 134 times and for many different people.[3] This does not mean, however, that the Pharisees were just one among many as to *akribeia*. Though not the exclusive practioners of *akribeia*, Josephus's Pharisees were clearly at the top of the list; they were "more exact [*akribesteron*]" than others (*J.W.* 1.110).

Second, and importantly for our attempt to reconstruct the genuine Pharisees, *akribeia* was a positive trait. Honorable characters possessed it, dishonorable ones did not. It was not used to mean picayune nitpickers, people who focused on insignificant details while missing the big picture. Remember where this concern for *akribeia* arose . . . in the fight for preserving

---

1. Although not explicitly called Pharisees, many view those who objected to the stoning of James, the brother of Jesus and "who were considered . . . strict [*akribeis*] in observance of the law" (*A.J.* 20.201) to be Pharisees. Baumgarten, "Name of the Pharisees," 413 and n9. A few additional texts may possibly refer to Pharisees with *akribeia*, though we cannot be certain (*J.W.* 1.648; *A.J.* 19.332; 20.43).

2. BDAG, LSJ.

3. Josephus himself (*Life* 9), Queen Salome Alexandra (*J.W.* 1.108, "the very strictest observer"), Jews in general (*Ag. Ap.* 2.149), two scholars, Judas and Mattathias (*J.W.* 1.648), Eleazar (*A. J.* 20.43), priests (*Ag. Ap.* 1.29, 32, 36, 54), et al.

the Jewish way of life in the Maccabean rebellion. Those who were careful to follow God's ways were protecting Israel's identity and future from those who would throw it away for Hellenistic pottage. Their concern for scrupulous law observance arose not from the question, "How do we save our souls?" but from the question, "How do we preserve our people?"

We will want to recall all this when Jesus calls the Pharisees "blind guides" who "strain out a gnat but swallow a camel" (Matt 23:24). Whatever fault he was trying to pinpoint in these Pharisees, it was the not the positive *akribeia* for which the movement was generally known. And it certainly did not imply they were legalists and hypocrites. When giving his defense before King Agrippa, Paul himself put forward as a proof of his good character, "I have belonged to the strictest [*akribestatēn*] sect of our religion and lived as a Pharisee" (Acts 26:5).

Committed to the "Traditions of the Fathers"

Alongside Pharisaic accuracy or *akribeia* in handling Torah, we also noticed repeated mention of their commitment to what Josephus called ancestral customs, regulations, or traditions of the fathers:

> regulations, introduced by the Pharisees in accordance with the tradition of their fathers (*A.J.* 13.408);
>
> priding itself on its adherence to ancestral custom (*A.J.* 17.41);
>
> excel all others in precision with regard to ancestral customs (*Life* 191).

What exactly were these regulations and traditions? Could these be the Pharisaic "traditions" Jesus criticized ("you break the commandment of God for the sake of your tradition," Matt 15:3)? How did they differ from the laws of Moses?

Josephus employed a number of different words for these traditions or regulations.[4] Most frequently he spoke of them as *nomima*, which refers to what is "conformable to custom, usage, or law" (LSJ). They are also *paradosis*, a tradition,[5] and *nomoi* (laws or customs). And he can speak of them as *patria*, as ancestral ways. Each of these terms retains its slightly different nuance, but Josephus used them more-or-less synonymously to refer to the same body of Pharisaic customs or laws. In quite a number of instances he combined

---

4. For details, see Mason, *Flavius Josephus on the Pharisees*, 100–106, 230–40.

5. Note also the frequent use in these contexts of the related verb *paradidōmi*, "to pass along [as tradition]."

these terms with some reference to "fathers" or "ancestors" [*patera*]. Thus, "The Pharisees had passed on to the people certain regulations [*nomima tina paredosan*] handed down by former generations [*ek paterōn diadochēs*]" (*A.J.* 13.297), or more literally "from a succession of fathers."

This brings us to a second question, who were these ancestors, these fathers? On the one hand, it seems clear from *A.J.* 13.297 cited above that they were not identified with the writers of Scripture.

> The Pharisees had passed on to the people certain regulations handed down by former generations and <u>not recorded [*ouk anagegraptai*] in the Laws of Moses</u>, for which reason they are rejected by the Sadducean group, who hold that only those regulations should be considered valid which were written down (in Scripture) [*nomima ta gegrammena*], and that those which had been handed down by former generations need not be observed. (*A.J.* 13.297)

Yet in other instances, Josephus seemed to muddy the waters and these ancestral laws were nothing other than the Mosaic laws. In one example of this, the Pharisees were "a group of Jews priding itself on its adherence to ancestral custom [*tou patriou*] and claiming to observe the laws [*nomōn*] of which the Deity approves" (*A.J.* 17.41).[6] For a Jew like Josephus, these *nomoi* approved by the God of Israel can be nothing other than the Mosaic legislation.

Mason's resolution of this tension breaks the impasse.

> Although Josephus identifies the *nomoi* of the Jews with the Mosaic Law, he evidently sees that Law only through the filter of post-biblical tradition and current practices familiar to him, which he finds already implicit in the Law.[7]

These "post-biblical tradition and . . . practices" were the ancestral traditions and regulations he attributed to the Pharisees.[8] They were the Pharisaic interpretations and applications of the Mosaic laws, and thus, for those who agreed with these interpretations, *already implicit in the Torah*, yet not explicit. Thus, there is a sense in which they were different

---

6. This coalescing of ancestral traditions and Mosaic laws is even clearer if we follow codices W, E and some Latin MSS which omit *kai* (and), thus merging "ancestral custom" and "laws of which the Deity approves" into a single entity: "the ancestral laws of which the Deity approves."

7. Mason, *Flavius Josephus on the Pharisees*, 100.

8. Mason argues further than the linguistic connection of *nomima* and *patera* ("traditions of the fathers") probably represents the Pharisees' own language about their teaching. Mason, *Flavius Josephus on the Pharisees*, 101–3.

from Torah (its implications or application), yet also contained in the words given by Moses.

Who then, exactly, were these fathers in the "traditions of the fathers"? Josephus can use "fathers [*patera*]" or "our fathers" in the same way as generally in Jewish literature, to refer to the exodus generation, the characters in the patriarchal narratives, those who returned from exile; in short, "to all the Jews and Israelites of past generations."[9] However, in *A.J.* 13.297 and 408 he seemed to have a more specific Pharisaic "traditions of the fathers" in mind.

- regulations [*nomima*] handed down by former generations [*ek paterōn*] (297a)
- regulations [*nomima*] . . . handed down by former generations [*tōn paterōn*] (297b)
- regulations [*nomimōn*] introduced by the Pharisees in accordance with the tradition of their fathers [*tēn patrōan paradosin*] (408)

While these texts could simply refer to the traditional Mosaic legislation, two factors suggest he had something more specific in mind. First, these were highlighted by Josephus here as specifically *Pharisaic* traditions, not the customs and laws common to all Jews. The Pharisees have handed these traditions on to the populace (*A.J.* 13.297), whereas the Mosaic legislation was already known. And, second, these regulations came lit. "from a succession of fathers [*ek paterōn diadochēs*]" (297a). The concept of preserving a legitimate chain of tradition to the founders was important to Greek philosophical schools such as those of Plato, Epicurus, etc.[10] We also know from rabbinic literature that such a chain of rabbinic teachers was reputed to stretch back to the first century and even beyond ("Rabbi X said to Rabbi Y"). Since such language was not typical for Josephus, it is entirely possible that this reflects the language of Josephus's Pharisees themselves. Their own claim was that their teachings, their Torah interpretations, had an equally august heritage, stretching back to Moses himself through a "succession of fathers."[11]

---

9. Mason, *Flavius Josephus on the Pharisees*, 232. See, for example, *J.W.* 5.377–405.

10. Turner, "Note on 'Succession' Language," 197–99; cited in Mason, *Flavius Josephus on the Pharisees*, 235.

11. One additional Josephan passage belongs in this discussion, but the lack of clarity in its translation and interpretation has usually sidelined it. The LCL translates *A.J.* 18.12:

> They follow the guidance of that which their doctrine has selected and transmitted as good, attaching the chief importance to the observance of

This leads us to a third question . . . Are these Pharisaic traditions the Oral Torah spoken of in rabbinic literature? Judaism, at least since the time of the Mishnah and Talmud, has believed in a dual Torah. The Written Law is contained in the Hebrew Tanakh, the Christian OT. The Oral Law are the traditions given by Moses but not written down. The classic Talmudic text for this is m.'Abot 1.1.

> Moses received the Torah from Sinai and handed it on to Joshua, Joshua to the Elders, the Elders to the Prophets; and the Prophets handed it on to the men of the Great Assembly.[12]

There is little dispute that later Jewish tradition held to such an unwritten, oral Torah, but is this what Josephus had in mind when speaking of Pharisaic traditions? This has been a long-held point of view, and would seem to be confirmed by the Gospel accounts where Jesus contrasts the Pharisaic "traditions of the elders" with the "commandment of God" (Matt 15:1–9).[13] However, upon closer inspection the evidence no longer bears this out.[14]

---

those commandments which it has seen fit to dictate to them. They show respect and deference to their elders, nor do they rashly presume to contradict their proposals.

This seems not to deal with the traditions of the fathers and brings in a second issue, respect for elders. However, it would be better translated:

> They follow the authority of those things that their teaching deemed good and handed down;
>
> They regard as indispensable the observance of those things that it saw fit to dictate.
>
> Out of honor they yield to those who go before them in age,
>
> Nor are they inclined boldly to contradict the things that were introduced.

The first two lines speak of their "teaching [*logos*]," i.e., their tradition, which has been "handed down [*paredōken*]." The last two speak of honoring and not contradicting these very traditions introduced by "those who go before them," i.e., their ancestors or fathers. This last point will be contrasted with Sadducees who "dispute with the teachers of the path of wisdom that they pursue" (A.J. 18.16). For this translation and interpretation, see Mason, *Flavius Josephus on the Pharisees*, 288–93.

12. Cited in Neusner, *Pharisees*, 14–15. See also b. 'Erub. 54b which stresses the oral transmission.

13. Supporters of finding rabbinic "oral law" already in Josephus and the NT include: Rivkin, *Hidden Revolution*; Gerhardsson, *Memory and Manuscript*, 21–32; Hengel, *Judaism and Hellenism*, 1.173–175.

14. Those rejecting the concept of Oral Torah for the early Pharisees include: Sanders, *Jewish Law*, 97–130; Neusner, *Torah*; and esp. now, Jaffee, *Torah in the Mouth*.

The key text is the passage from Josephus quoted already above (*A.J.* 13.297). It seemed to contrast regulations which *were written down* with those *not written down*. That is, the objection of the Sadducees had to do with the *form* of the laws and traditions; were they written laws or unwritten (i.e., oral) laws?[15] However, as several have suggested, and as Mason has now convincingly demonstrated, the issue in this passage is not over the *form* of the traditions, written or unwritten, but over whether they were "recorded in the Laws of Moses."[16] That is, they were not found *explicitly* in the written laws of Moses. This is the sense in which they were "not written." The Sadducees objected because they wanted to stick closer to the explicit words of the Pentateuch and viewed the Pharisaic interpretations, which were not found explicitly written therein, as invalid. *Not written* meant *not explicitly found in* rather than *orally transmitted*.

To summarize: The Pharisees were known for, and themselves prized, their particular interpretive traditions of the Mosaic commands. These they called the "traditions of the fathers" or "of the elders." For Pharisees these regulations were little different than the explicit commands from Moses since, as far as the Pharisees were concerned, these implications were already present in the original commands. These traditions had not been recently thought up, but passed along reliably via a "succession of fathers" (*A.J.* 13.297). It was these traditional customs that the Pharisees taught to the populace, but which had been abolished by Hyrcanus, then re-instated by Queen Salome Alexandra (*A.J.* 13.408). And it was these traditions that the Sadducees rejected since they were not explicitly "recorded in the Laws of Moses" (*A.J.* 13.297). We concluded further that this Pharisaic tradition was not yet viewed as an authoritative Dual or Oral Torah as it would be in rabbinic literature, i.e., as divinely revealed on Sinai and passed along only orally.

Distinctive Doctrines

Fate vs Human Freedom

> The Pharisees . . . say that certain events are the work of Fate [*heimarmenēs*], but not all; as to other events, it depends upon ourselves whether they shall take place or not. (*A.J.* 13.172)

---

15. "They were laws that had been transmitted in unwritten form." Rivkin, *Hidden Revolution*, 41.

16. Mason, *Flavius Josephus on the Pharisees*, 242–3; also Neusner, *Rabbinic Traditions*, 2.163, 177. The LCL addition to the translation above in parenthesis of "in Scripture" suggests the same point.

Whereas the other two descriptions of the three major Jewish schools (*J.W.* 2.163; *A.J.* 18.13) included the issue of "fate" as one among several that differentiated the three, the description in *A.J.* 13 made "fate" the sole issue of interest. For that reason we will focus on this passage, and bring in the other two passages for additional illumination.

Fate [*heimarmenē*] was a common and central term to ancient philosophy, referring to "the belief that things are brought about, of necessity, by set causes or impersonal powers."[17] Reflection on fate was particularly connected with Stoicism, and Josephus made an explicit comparison between the Pharisees and the Stoics (*Life* 12). The difficulty here, of course, is that Josephus and the Pharisees were Jews. Their belief was not in an impersonal deterministic "Fate," but in a personal God. Thus, although Josephus used the language of fate, and may himself have been influenced by Stoic reflections, most interpreters doubt that he has here simply abandoned Jewish belief in the God of Israel. While it is true that *A.J.* 13.172 might have sounded more secular, this was not true for the parallel descriptions. *J.W.* 2.163 says the Pharisees "attribute everything to Fate *and to God*," and *A.J.* 18.13 brings "God's good pleasure" into their empowerment of the human will.[18]

When Josephus used the language of fate, it was not far from the Bible's language of divine providence. When reporting King Agrippa's words at death, he referred to this as due to "fate [*heimarmenē*]" and equally as his "lot as God wills it" (*A.J.* 19.347). And when speaking of the coming Roman attack on Jerusalem he spoke equally of this as "fate" and as God's determined condemnation (*J.W.* 6.109). In fact, divine providence [*pronoia*] is found even more often in Josephus than fate. During the Maccabean rebellion, for instance, all Jonathan's victories were "by God's providence [*pronoia*]" (*A.J.* 13.163).[19]

Josephus set up a clear spectrum of views regarding fate/providence with the Sadducees and Essenes on the ends, and the Pharisees in the middle. The Essenes appear more deterministic, all is predestined.

---

17. Klawans, *Josephus and the Theologies of Ancient Judaism*, 46.

18. Scholars have suggested different models for relating Josephus's Jewish and Greek philosophical ideas. Perhaps he remained a thoroughgoing Jew and did not actually believe in Fate, but merely clothed his discussion in Greek philosophical language. Or, did he actually imbibe deeply of the philosopher's stream and of the widespread ancient belief in destiny, but sought some sort of synthesis? And however we resolve this particular question for Josephus himself, what of his portrayal of the Pharisees and Fate? Did he accurately portray their position? On the academic debate, see Mason's appendix, "Scholarly Interpretations of Josephus on Fate and Free Will," in Mason, *Flavius Josephus on the Pharisees*, 384–98.

19. On *pronoia* in Josephus, see Attridge, *Interpretation of Biblical History*, 71–78.

> Fate is the mistress of all things, and . . . nothing befalls men unless it be in accordance with her decree. (*A.J.* 13.172)
>
> [They] leave everything in the hands of God. (*A.J.* 18.18)

The Sadducees, on the other hand, "do away with Fate, holding that there is no such thing and that human actions are not achieved in accordance with her decree, but that all things lie within our own power." (*A.J.* 13.173; also *J.W.* 2.166). The Pharisees in the middle "say that certain events are the work of Fate, but not all; as to other events, it depends upon ourselves whether they shall take place or not" (*A.J.* 13.172). In *A.J.* 18.13 Josephus calls this a "fusion [*krasin*]," a mixing or blending of divine and human agency. In *J.W.* 2.163 he says human action "rests . . . for the most part with men, but that in each action Fate co-operates," lit. "assists."

It is always difficult to judge Josephus's accuracy from this distance.[20] We know that he was ready to adjust facts to convince his Roman audience and to strengthen the image of the Jewish people. In this instance, however, his portrayal of Pharisees as blending divine and human agency, as holding both to the sovereignty of the divine will and to the efficacy of human volition, seems to line up with hints from other quarters.[21] Rabbi Akiba was reputed to have said, "All is foreseen, but freedom of choice is given."[22] And in another rabbinic saying, "Everything is in the hands of God except the fear of God."[23]

Resurrection (Immortality of the Soul?) and Post-Mortem Reward and Punishment

One of the mainstays of Pharisaic doctrine was their belief in resurrection and post-mortem rewards and punishments. This was paired with Sadducean non-belief in the same.

---

20. For a more skeptical view on the historical value of Josephus's characterization of fate and the schools, see Mason, "Josephus's Pharisees: The Philosophy," 41–66.

21. As to his evaluation of the other two groups, the Essenes/Qumran community does appear to have been deterministic (e.g., 1QS 3:15-17; 11:10-11). See VanderKam, *Dead Sea Scrolls Today*, 76–78, 109. Our knowledge of the Sadducees is meager. Saldarini may be correct that their rejection of fate in Josephus may actually refer to their denial of "apocalyptic intervention in world history," thus "stressing human control over life." Saldarini, *Pharisees, Scribes, and Sadducees*, 304.

22. m. 'Abot 3:15. Cited in Sanders, *Judaism: practice and belief*, 419.

23. b. Nid. 16b; b, Ber. 33a; cited in Mason, *Flavius Josephus on the Pharisees*, 207.

(Pharisees)

Every soul [*phychēn*] . . . is imperishable, but the soul of the good alone passes into another body [*sōma*], while the souls of the wicked suffer eternal punishment (*J.W.* 2.163).

They believe that souls have power to survive death and that there are rewards and punishments under the earth for those who have led lives of virtue or vice; eternal imprisonment is the lot of evil souls, while the good souls receive an easy passage to a new life. Because of these views they are, as a matter of fact, extremely influential among the townsfolk . . . (*A.J.* 18.14).

(Sadducees)

As for the persistence of the soul after death, penalties in the underworld, and rewards, they will have none of them (*J.W.* 2.166).

The Sadducees hold that the soul perishes along with the body (*A.J.* 18.16).

Josephus himself apparently accepted these Pharisaic tenets (*J.W.* 3.374-5; *Ag. Ap.* 2.218), and he asserts in the *Apion* passage this was the general view of the Jewish populace. It was, in fact, partly "because of these views" that the Pharisees were popular among the common people. This particular distinction over resurrection doctrine between the two groups finds confirmation in the NT (Mark 12:18 par.; Acts 23:8). A few rabbinic texts may attest belief in bodily resurrection (e.g., m. 'Abot 4:22), but their Pharisaic connection is unclear, and the rabbis generally showed little interest in the topic.[24]

Even with this general affirmation, there remain, however, a couple of important related issues to address.[25] First, is Josephus testifying to a Pharisaic belief in bodily resurrection of the person, or to something more akin to a Greek immortality of the soul ("souls have power to survive death") or even to reincarnation ("the soul of the good . . . passes into another body")? He clearly takes up the Hellenistic language common to immortality and reincarnation,[26] and contemporary Jewish views were widely varied, including bodily resurrection and reincarnation.[27] But was this how Pharisees

---

24. Avery-Peck, "Death and Afterlife in the Early Rabbinic Sources," 243–66.

25. See esp. Mason, *Flavius Josephus on the Pharisees*, 156–70.

26. A soul is *aphtharton* (imperishable, indestructible) and can *anabaioun* (live anew), both terms used by Plato in speaking of reincarnation and soul-immortality. On ancient views in general, see Moore, *Ancient Beliefs*.

27. See Nickelsburg, *Resurrection, Immortality, and Eternal Life*.

spoke of their doctrine, or was it Josephus's way of recommending Jewish views to a Greco-Roman audience? The more likely conclusion is that Pharisees believed in some sort of personal, embodied survival of death.

Second, whichever version was Pharisaic, it was not the typical Hellenistic reincarnation or metempsychosis. Rather than an inevitable cycle of death and reincarnation, the version Josephus portrayed was ethically driven. It was "the soul of the good" that enjoyed a positive outcome, while evil souls suffered eternal punishment or imprisonment (i.e., no re-embodiment).

Politically Engaged

Josephus portrayed the Pharisees as a politically engaged group though only minor players in the larger political drama. This may have been due in part to his literary aims; that is, he wished, especially in *War*, to explain to a Roman audience the nature and extent of Jewish *political* blame for the anti-Roman revolt. Beneath that, however, seemed to lie a substratum of historical events.

During the reign of Queen Salome Alexandra (76–67 BCE), they sought and gained a remarkable degree of power. This, however, was the only period where Josephus portrayed them as possessing the official exercise of national political power.[28] At other times a few Pharisees were portrayed as present in circles of power, but on the whole they exercised *popular* influence. This influential, though not official, position in Jewish society appears to have remained the case into the first half of the first century CE, since Josephus aligned himself with the Pharisees to further his public life (*Life* 12). This political influence without official position remained their situation to the time of the Jewish revolt (66–70 CE; cf. *Life* 189–198).

If we are correct in seeing the Maccabean-era *hasidim* as their predecessors, this would also paint them as politically involved at their very origins. We have to keep in mind that ancient political involvement cannot be separated from social and religious motivations. Thus, alongside the Maccabees they sought political change, but their motivation was religious. They resisted movements toward Hellenization because this threatened central elements of Jewish identity such as circumcision or Sabbath-keeping (1 Macc 1). Like the Qumran community they opposed some high priestly appointments that were both religious and political moves.

28. Rivkin, on the other hand, painted the Pharisees *throughout Josephus's works*, both in politics and in Torah interpretation, as the dominant force. Sadducees and even Herod had to bend to their power and scholarly authority. Rivkin, *Hidden Revolution*.

A related question may prove important for our later examination of the NT Pharisees: What was their role in the Sanhedrin? Acts 5:34 places a Pharisee named Gamaliel in an influential role in the Jerusalem "council [*synhedrion*]" and Acts 23:6 pictures Sadducees and Pharisees together in this same council. Josephus, likewise, portrayed the Pharisee Samaias (or Pollion) in this governing Jewish council at the time of Herod (*A.J.* 14.172–176; 15.3–4, 370). Our sources, however, are not clear that a well-defined Sanhedrin had become a stable governing institution already by this time. It is clear that "through much of the Second Temple period, the high priest was the chief representative of the community to the ruling empire," and that he "was assisted through most of this time by an advisory body called variously (in Greek) the *gerousia* (senate), *boule* (council), or *sunedrion* (from which comes the Hebrew Sanhedrin)."[29] Thus, there was most likely some sort of advisory body in Jerusalem to which belonged Pharisees at different times and in different strengths. However, against the impression left by older reference works, Pharisees were not—certainly not *always*—a majority in such a body.

We cannot wrap up the question of Pharisaic political involvement without engaging, at least briefly, the thesis of Jacob Neusner. While the Pharisees in Josephus's *War*, according to Neusner, "were a political party, active in the court affairs of the Maccabean state," by the first century at the instigation of Rabbi Hillel they had abandoned politics to become a "pure food club."[30] By this last phrase he means "a table-fellowship sect . . . characterized by stress on careful tithing and maintenance of the cultic purity laws outside of the Temple, in their own homes."[31] Neusner argues that the Gospels support this picture, since controversies often occur over meals and regarding issues of purity, but not over issues of political governance. In addition, he urges, the rabbinic writings support this view, since topics related to purity issues come up as Pharisaic while typical political issues do not.[32] On their political involvement, we disagree mainly with Neusner's contention that the Pharisees *drop out of politics* in Josephus's writings after the Hasmonean period. If he meant simply "abandoned overt, official political control," we would agree. However, he seems to want to portray them as more of a quietistic, inward-looking pietist group, simply uninterested in influencing national policy. We have

---

29. Grabbe, *Judaic Religion*, 149.
30. Neusner, *From Politics to Piety*, 48.
31. Neusner, *From Politics to Piety*, 14; also 90–92.
32. See Neusner, "Rabbinic Traditions about the Pharisees before 70 CE: An Overview," 297–311.

argued that they did continue to exercise political influence, but through popular persuasion rather than official position.[33]

Sanders has assembled a list of eight events narrated in Josephus which demonstrate clearly the continued political engagement of the Pharisees as a group.[34]

1. Two Pharisees, Pollion and Samaias, advised the leaders to open the gates when Herod beseiged Jerusalem (*A.J.* 15.3).

2. Pollion and Samaias (or 6,000 Pharisees according to the second account) refused the loyalty oath to Herod and continued their intrigues against him via their influence over the women in Herod's court (*A.J.* 15.370; 17.41-45).

3. Contined court intrigues by Pharisees leading to the death "of the Pharisees who were most to blame" (*A.J.* 17.43-45; *J.W.* 1.571).

4. Near the end of Herod's life two teachers instigated an act of rebellion (pulling down Herod's golden eagle over the temple gate). Although not identified as such, evidence points to their Pharisaic identity (*J.W.* 1.648-655; *A.J.* 17.149-167).

5. Judas the Galilean, aided by Saddok the Pharisee, led a brief insurgency at the time of the census (6 CE; *J.W.* 2.117; *A.J.* 18.4).

6. Just before the outbreak of the revolt (66 CE), chief priests sought the aid of "leading Pharisees" to quiet the populace and pacify the Roman procurator (*J.W.* 2.411; cf. also *Life* 20-23).

7. During the war, chief priests sought an alliance with Simon ben Gamaliel, member of a leading Pharisaic family (*J.W.* 2.563; 4.159).

8. A committee sent by the Jerusalem leadership to investigate Josephus in Galilee was made up of three Pharisees (one of priestly descent) and a priest (*Life* 189-98).

Influential in Social and Religious Spheres

Readers of the NT Gospels may be forgiven for envisioning the typical Pharisee as a grumpy, narrow-minded person who liked to gripe about the mass of commoners, the *am ha-aretz*. Josephus's Pharisees could hardly be

---

33. This is not far from Sanders's position, who agrees with Neusner that the Pharisees no longer exercised political "control," but disagrees regarding their popularity and influence in public life. Sanders, *Judaism*, 399-404, and ch. 21 "Who Ran What?"

34. Sanders, *Judaism*, 384-87.

more different! He regularly comments on their popularity with the bulk of the Jewish population.

- "so great is their influence with the masses that even when they speak against a king or high priest, they immediately gain credence" (*A.J.* 13.288).
- "the Pharisees have the support of the masses" (*A.J.* 13.298).
- the Pharisees had power "to dispose the nation favorably toward" Queen Salome Alexandra and "had the complete confidence of the masses" (*A.J.* 13. 401–2).
- Even Josephus, though not himself a convinced Pharisee, conformed his public life to Pharisaic regulations since these were the most widely recognized and approved in the populace (*Life* 12).[35]
- Even the Sadducees had to bend to Pharisaic wishes, "since otherwise the masses would not tolerate them" (*A.J.* 18.17).

Rather than being stand-offish, they belonged to the more common class of people and "cultivate harmonious relations with the community" (*J.W.* 2.166). And, if we are correct as to their origins in the Maccabean period, they shared with the broader population the common love of Israel's heritage and distinctives.

What may come as a real surprise is that it was specifically the Pharisaic regulations that were so popular with the masses, especially since Jesus is often understood to refer to them negatively as "heavy burdens" laid on others (Matt 23:4). When Hyrcanus was persuaded to desert the Pharisees and to "abrogate the regulations which they had established for the people," the result was not relief but "the hatred of the masses for him and his sons" (*A.J.* 13.296). Josephus gives one hint as to the reason for their popularity ... their teaching on resurrection and the afterlife which gave hope beyond this hard life (*A.J.* 18.15), but otherwise does not explain why these regulations were so popular. Another hint may lie in the DSS. We will examine these hints in more detail in the next chapter, but suffice it to say for now, the Pharisaic regulations made obedience to the law, particularly to its purity rules, easier, more reachable for the common non-priestly Jewish person. For this reason the stricter Qumranites called them "seekers of smooth things," i.e., they sought the easier way of obedience. Josephus himself may give a hint in this direction when he said Pharisees "are naturally lenient in the matter of punishments" (*A.J.* 13.294).

---

35. For this understanding, see above pp. 4–5.

Josephus also commented on the Pharisees' influence over the praxis of piety among the populace.

> They are, as a matter of fact, extremely influential among the townsfolk; and all prayers and sacred rites of divine worship are performed according to their [the Pharisees'] exposition. This is the great tribute that the inhabitants of the cities, by practicing the highest ideals both in their way of living and in their discourse, have paid to the excellence of the Pharisees. (*A.J.* 18.15)

So influential were they, says Josephus, that the Sadducees in priestly office "submit . . . to the formulae of the Pharisees, since otherwise the masses would not tolerate them" (*A.J.* 18.17). Precisely which practices are in view with these "prayers and sacred rites of divine worship" is not clear. Since these focused on practices "among the townsfolk," this probably did not have to do with temple praxis.[36] Priests lived throughout Israel "among the townsfolk," so it may be that Josephus had various forms of practical piety in mind which may have in some way involved priests, such as prayers, vows,[37] purification pronouncements and ceremonies, etc. This Josephan text has been used regularly to point to Pharisaic control of synagogue life. This view has now been abandoned, since it fits neither with Josephus's own synagogue statements,[38] nor with NT evidence of synagogue organization.[39]

This might be an appropriate place to make a comment about what sort of individuals Pharisees might have been. Were they honest and upright, or devious and two-faced? The fact that they were widely popular militates against the idea that they were as a group bald-faced hypocrites. Groups who gain such a following have to prove themselves worthy of such popular trust and adulation. And especially if they were known for teaching the will of God, they would themselves need to be substantial exemplars of this teaching. Previously we observed that the Pharisees were

---

36. Rabbinic texts like b. Yoma 19b (speaks of temple priests' fear of and submission to the Pharisees) are often cited as parallels. Sanders marshals evidence against the idea that Jerusalem priests would be guided by Pharisaic rules. Sanders, *Judaism*, 395-99. In addition, this idea that Sadducees submitted to Pharisaic regulations is missing in the earlier *War*, and may be an intentional exaggeration; Meier, *Marginal Jew*, 3:297.

37. The word used here for "prayers [*euchōn*]" can also mean vows.

38. Krause, *Synagogues*, 198-99. On leadership in ancient synagogues, see Levine, *Ancient Synagogue*, ch. 13, "The Sages and the Synagogue" (466-98). He states plainly, "the truth of the matter is, the Pharisees had little or nothing to do with the early synagogue" (41).

39. The synagogue leader (*archisynagōgos*) in Mark 5:21-23, 35-43 is not identified as a Pharisee, nor the one in Luke 10:13-17. Pharisees appear regularly in synagogues in the Gospels, but are never referred to as having control.

fundamentally interested in righteousness, virtue, and pleasing God. In fact, Hyrcanus viewed them as his worthy religious guides. "He begged them, if they observed him doing anything wrong or straying from the right path, to lead him back to it and correct him" (*A.J.* 13.290). Although Josephus himself had his doubts, he acknowledged their reputation as "more pious" (*J.W.* 1.110) and as reflecting on how to "act rightly [*dikaia*] or otherwise" (*J.W.* 2.163). The Pharisee Samaias was considered "upright [*dikaios*]" and "righteous [*dikaiosynē*]" by both friend and foe alike (*A.J.* 14.172, 176). Yet, there was also a hint of pride and haughtiness as far as Josephus was concerned (*A.J.* 17.41). Thus, the Pharisees end up looking like we might expect of a serious religious movement, deeply and authentically committed to their principles, to their God and heritage, yet quite humanly capable of pettiness and occasional hypocrisy. We will want to recall this picture when Jesus calls them hypocrites.[40]

Lifestyle and Standard of Living

This is not really a "distinctive," but such information is essential to our portrait.

> The Pharisees simplify their standard of living, making no concession to luxury. (*A.J.* 18.12)

The Greek of this text is difficult and open to alternate translations.

- "they live meanly, and despise delicacies in diet" (Whiston)
- "their lifestyle is one of restraint (or "they disparage the accoutrements of life"); they do not yield at all to the softer side" (Mason)

Such simplicity of lifestyle makes sense for the Pharisees if, as we have noted at several points already, they were by-and-large not high up the socio-economic scale. That they avoided luxuries finds confirmation in later rabbinic tradition.[41] Jesus does charge (some of) them with loving money (Luke 16:14), but we will argue such generalization was typical of his invective (ch. 14 below). Of course, this depiction of the "average"

---

40. At the same time, we should remember that Josephus himself seems to doubt their authenticity; he views them as hypocrites. See on *dokeo* in *J.W.* 1.110 above (pp. 18-19 and n3). On this see, Liebowitz, "Hypocrites or Pious Scholars?," 54-55.

41. One tradition quotes the Sadducees as saying, "It is a tradition amongst the Pharisees to afflict themselves in this world; yet in the world to come they will have nothing." *Avot de Rabbi Natan* 5; cited in LCL *Josephus, A.J.* 18.12 (p. 10, n. "b"). Josephus may also be adjusting his description of the Pharisees to align them in austere behavior with Stoics (see *Vita* 12).

Pharisee does not ignore that there also existed the occasional wealthy, connected, or priestly Pharisee. The Pharisee Simon ben Gamaliel, for instance, came from "a very illustrious family" and was party to decision-making at the highest levels during the revolt (*Life* 190–192). Another, Jozar, was of priestly descent (*Life* 197).

The bulk of the Pharisees had to work alongside other Jews for a living, but we have little evidence for their typical occupations.[42] By the time of the Gospels some Pharisees were functioning as professional scribes, and thus worked with documents and in other lower-level administrative positions. Josephus, however, seems to portray Pharisees and scribes as non-overlapping groupings, though this may be simply the result of limited interest in such detailed social descriptions. Since Pharisees were known for Bible teaching, some Pharisees may have earned a living by teaching. However, what we know of Jewish education at this time (no public schools or mandatory education; something largely for the elite) would indicate that this would not likely have been the source of support for very many. The fact is, we do not know much about their day-to-day lives. It is possible that some were farmers, carpenters, workers in leather goods (Paul), hired hands, etc., but we cannot say with any certainty. Saldarini thinks it most likely they were part of the "retainer" class, mostly "officials, bureaucrats, judges and educators."[43] Such retainers formed the nexus between the small elite classes ruling the nation and the large mass of peasants, farmers, etc.

From what little evidence we have, Pharisees will have married and raised families, and engaged socially with other Pharisees as well as with other Jews. There does not appear to have been an official "Association of Pharisees" with membership lists, dues, requirements, etc.[44] Rather, being a Pharisee was more a matter of personal conviction and lifestyle, involving especially a commitment to maintaining Israel's distinctiveness as a nation devoted to God and Torah. While this commitment might be said to characterize all Jews to some extent, Pharisees made this more central to their lives ("more pious") and passed on a body of traditions regarding Torah-interpretation and -praxis.

Readers should be forewarned that, some of my descriptions above, especially those regarding their power and influence and their place in society, run counter to what will be found in many standard reference

---

42. Saldarini, *Pharisees, Scribes, and Sadducees*, 284–85.

43. Saldarini, *Pharisees, Scribes, and Sadducees*, 284, also 41–42. This revises earlier views which saw Pharisees as "merchants, artisans and peasants." Jeremias, *Jerusalem in the Time of Jesus*, 259. Somewhat differently, Baumgarten assigns them more toward the "middling" elite end of the spectrum. Baumgarten, *Flourishing of Jewish Sects*, 42–51.

44. On these private associations or *haburoth*, see ch. 8, pp. 104–5.

works.⁴⁵ There one can read that the Pharisees controlled many aspects of daily, synagogue, national and temple life, and that they were most often urban artisans who kept to themselves in private purity associations. Most of these conclusions were based on evidence from the later rabbinic sources. Developments in rabbinic studies have led scholars to treat these sources more critically regarding their value for describing pre-70 CE Pharisees (see next chapter).

Where Were They Located?

Our sources are all agreed that Pharisees were present and active in Jerusalem, as one might expect for any Jewish group seeking to influence Israel. A number of scholars, however, are convinced there was no significant Pharisaic movement in Galilee, where the Synoptic Gospels locate most of Jesus' interaction with them.⁴⁶ This would, of course, be highly significant for our study of the Pharisees and Jesus. Further investigations have, however, concluded for some Pharisaic presence in first century Galilee. Freyne has a thorough treatment of the question.⁴⁷ He thinks they were most likely present in Galilee during the first half of the first century, but they were not in authority in civil or religious spheres. They were competing like other groups and like Jesus of Nazareth for the allegiance of the populace. As Saldarini summarizes, the Pharisees in Galilee were a "minor social force."⁴⁸

In preparation for our study of Pharisees in the NT, it might be helpful at this point to summarize some of the findings that will show up again in the Gospels. The Pharisees:

- believed in resurrection;
- were known for *akribeia* vis-à-vis Torah;
- were known for unwritten traditions of the fathers;
- were popular and influential with the masses;
- were sometimes related to the scribal and priestly classes;
- had some political influence;
- had regional presence (both in Jerusalem and Galilee);

---

45. I am thinking here of more popular volumes such as Jeremias, *Jerusalem in the Time of Jesus*; Edersheim, *Life and Times of Jesus the Messiah*; or Schürer, *History of the Jewish People in the Age of Jesus Christ*.
46. Murphy-O'Connor, *Paul: A Critical Life*, 56–59; Smith, *Jesus the Magician*, 157.
47. Freyne, *Galilee, Jesus, and the Gospels*, 198–218.
48. Saldarini, *Pharisees, Scribes, and Sadducees*, 293; cf. also 291–93.

- were of varied socio-economic status;
- were known for righteous lives; yet, also exceptions—haughty, opportunistic—were known.

CHAPTER 4

Echoes in the DSS and Rabbinic Literature

IN PREVIOUS CHAPTERS WE have mainly mined the works of Josephus. There are, however, additional Jewish voices that may shed light on the Pharisees, both before and after the NT period. These will be our focus in this chapter as we seek to compile a picture of the Pharisees from within Judaism. To round out our picture, we will also explore in the next chapter their character as Jews who shared much with other Jews.

Pharisees in the DSS

The scrolls, first discovered in 1946/1947 in numerous caves around the northern end of the Dead Sea, testify to the beliefs and practices of a sectarian Jewish group in the couple of centuries prior to the Christian era. It is now commonly thought they were part of the larger Essene movement mentioned by Josephus, but who, unlike other Essenes, had chosen to live in desert isolation in a closed community.[1] The discovery revolutionized our understanding of late Second Temple Judaism. Prior to this, scholars were aware of some diversity among Jews; they knew from Josephus there were Sadducees, Essenes, Pharisees, and Zealots. However, all but the Pharisees were considered small groups with little influence on Judaism as a whole. Leading reference works spoke of Judaism of this period (200 BCE–70 CE) as a fairly monolithic entity, and of Pharisees as characteristic of this normative Judaism. The scrolls gave a window into a

---

1. Debate continues over whether the Qumran community and its library can be equated with the Essenes known from Josephus, or even whether every scroll represents the group's distinctive views (e.g., Jubilees). Since our appeal will be only to texts acknowledged as "sectarian," we will use interchangeably such terms as "Qumran community," "Essenes," "sectarians," etc.

quite different Jewish religious world . . . one filled with highly opinionated groups, passionately opposing one another and challenging others' right to even bear the name "Jew."[2]

When coming to the DSS in search of Pharisees one could initially think we've hit a dry hole, since Pharisees are not found explicitly in any of the writings. On closer inspection, however, the Pharisees may be in view in a few texts after all, but in disguise as it were. A group surfaces numerous times under the designation "seekers after smooth things." We can be fairly confident that the Qumran sectarians had the Pharisees in view when using this moniker.[3] The phrase itself (Heb. *dorshē ha-ḥalaqōt*) indicates those who seek, investigate, or study [*d-r-sh*] smooth, slippery, or flattering things [*ḥ-l-q*]. Most scholars take "smooth" as a negative trait referring to interpreters or interpretations found by others to be flattering or too easy. The origin of this negative label is most often traced to Isa 30:10-11, where the Israelites say to the prophets of Yahweh, "Do not prophesy to us what is right; speak to us smooth things." At Qumran this may have been seen as a "punning reference" to the Pharisees, since a change of only two Hebrew letters produces the pun; the *dorshē ha-halakhōt* [seekers of correct behavior] become the *dorshē ha-ḥalaqōt* [seekers of smooth things].[4]

Six DSS passages use this phrase. The first five yield a fairly consistent picture of a group opposed by the Qumran community, but without enough details to secure an identification as Pharisees. The sixth points more clearly to the ancient Pharisees as these "seekers of smooth things."

> [T]hey sought easy interpretations [*darshū baḥalaqōth*], chose illusions, scrutinized loopholes, chose the handsome neck, acquitted the guilty and sentenced the just, violated the covenant, broke the precept colluded together against the life of the just man, their soul abominated all those who walk in perfection, they hunted them down with the sword and provoked the dispute of the people. (CD, I.18-21)[5]

Obviously the sectarians were opposed to these people who were also Jews ("violated the covenant, broke the precept"), and these "easy" folk were no friends to the Qumranites ("abominated all those who walk in perfection

---

2. A good introduction is VanderKam, *Dead Sea Scrolls Today*.

3. Saldarini calls this interpretation "common in the literature but not certain." Saldarini, *Pharisees, Scribes, and Sadducees*, 279. Some scholars have perceived Pharisees under additional monikers such as "builders of the wall," "sages" and "Ephraim/Manasseh," but these have not garnered widespread support.

4. Sanders, *Judaism: practice and belief*, 382, and 532n1.

5. Translations from García Martínez, *Dead Sea Scrolls Translated*.

[= DSS community])." The mention of "loopholes" is of particular interest in light of the *halakhic* disputes we will examine in a moment. Jesus also criticized the Pharisees for finding loopholes around the commandments (see on Mark 7:9–13, pp. 114–16). The next three passages reinforce this image of a Jewish group which interpreted the commandments in a way the sectarians viewed as smooth, easy or too lenient.

> I have turned into an ardent spirit against all the interpreters of flat[tering] things [*dorshē ḥalaqōth*]. (1QH X.14–15)

> You have freed me from the zeal of the sowers of deceit, from the congregation of the interpreters of flattering things [*dorshē ḥalaqōth*]. (1QH X.31–32)

> The interpretation of the word, for the last days, concerns the congregation of those [looking] for easy interpretations who are in Jerusalem [. . .]. (4QpIsa^c (4Q163) frg. 23 II.9–10)

Again we note these are not scattered individuals but a group, a "congregation." They are charged with deceit or being "lying interpreters,"[6] and are, in fact, zealous in this regard. In one text they are placed specifically in Jerusalem. The next passage portrays the opposition in stark terms; these "seekers of smooth things" look to "destroy" the Qumranites.

> These are the congregation of Those Looking for Easy Interpretations, who [. . .] seek to destroy [the members of the Community . . .] by their fervor and their animosity . . . . (4Qcatena (4Q177) frag. 9 II.12–13)

Numerous elements in these passages could fit well with what we have discovered in Josephus about the Pharisees: their lenience or "easy interpretations," their zeal, their attention to detail viewed by others as finding breaks or loopholes in the law. However, the "seekers of smooth things" have been described in general enough terms to apply to other Jewish movements, but in the sixth passage some details are given that point strongly to the Pharisees.

> Its interpretation [Nah 2:13] concerns the Angry Lion [who filled his den with a mass of corpses, carrying out rev]enge against those looking for easy interpretations [*dorshē haḥalaqōth*], who hanged living men [from the tree, committing an atrocity which had not been committed] in Israel from ancient times . . . . (4QpNah (4Q169) frgs. 3+4, I.6–8)

---

6. So Vermès, *Dead Sea Scrolls in English*, s.v. II.31.

According to nearly all interpreters, "the Angry Lion" was the Hasmonean Alexander Jannaeus, who c. 88 BCE suffered a betrayal by Pharisees and "had eight hundred . . . crucified in the midst of the city" (J.W. 1.85-98; A.J. 13.376). Thus, these "looking for easy interpretations" are, indeed, our Pharisees.[7]

Following this pointer come several additional instances of "seekers of smooth things."[8] In each a prophetic judgment from Nahum is applied to the Pharisees. The thunderous, angry judgment of the God of Israel will fall upon them; they are no better than the Ninevites! This is no staid Bible discussion. The "easy interpreters" are leading Israel astray and will be destroyed in the final cataclysm. When Jesus thunders against the Pharisees for misleading "these little ones" and calls them a brood of vipers with no part in the kingdom of God, we may want to remember how much he sounds like these angry Essenes.

Halakhah: Central to Qumran and the Pharisees

Before leaving the DSS, we should note carefully a concept central to the sect's critique of the Pharisees, one which will also play a significant role when we come to Jesus and the Pharisees. *Halakhah* (also spelled *halakha, halaka* or *halacha*) comes from Hebrew *halakh* meaning "to walk." *Halakhoth* (pl.) are guidelines spelling out how Jews are to walk or behave in line with the biblical commandments. For example, one of the Ten Commandments requires Israel to rest and not work on the Sabbath. But this leaves myriad unanswered questions. Will I break this command if I cook a meal, take a five-mile hike, play tennis, perform a heart surgery, etc.? Some might say this is being far too picky, but pious Jews would respond, "Do you desire to keep God's commands, to do his will, or not?" If one truly desires to follow God's desires, facing these detailed, everyday life questions is unavoidable. To do otherwise would be tantamount to saying "I don't care" to God, or thinking "God doesn't really care whether I obey or not"; neither of which was an option for a serious Jew.

One can easily imagine, *halakhoth* would multiply since the commandments tended in most cases to be fairly general and new situations would arise requiring a decision. One was told to tithe of one's produce, but does one count only what was harvested or should one pay a tithe also on what was

---

7. Supporters of this interpretation include VanderKam, "Pharisees and the Dead Sea Scrolls," 228-33; Dimant, "Jewish Writings," 511-12; and Horgan, *Pesharim*, 160-62. Against this wide-spread identification, see Doudna, *4Q Pesher Nahum*, 654-74.

8. 4QpNah (4Q169) II.2, 4; III.3, 7.

left in the field? Does this count every type of produce? What if I receive a bushel of apples from a neighbor who is not so observant? Am I now consuming untithed produce?[9] And how do we resolve conflicts between commandments or principles themselves? We noted already the conflict between "do not work" and preserve life. As you might imagine, not everyone agreed with a particular resolution. Some were stricter and some more lenient in their interpretation. Different groups cultivated their own body of traditional *halakhoth*, and these differentiated them, often in visible ways, from other groups. As Schiffman concludes, Judaism was "halakho-centric."[10]

Again, this was not merely a matter of crossing t's and dotting i's correctly, such decisions touched on the central identity of the people of God, the Jews. They were the people of the God who spoke to Moses on Sinai. Shaping their lives according to Yahweh's will was what they were all about. And *halakhah* was that shape. We will be reminded of this when listening to Jesus castigate the Pharisees for their rules and traditions, their shape, while introducing his own: You have heard (i.e., their *halakhah* says), but I say . . . .

It should not surprise us to find the DSS community jousting with other Jewish groups over the correct *halakhah*.

> [W]e see halakhic issues at the center of Jewish sectarianism in the Second Temple period. Halakhah and its theoretical underpinnings separated the various sectarian groups from one another. As the various movements sought to define themselves, they, in turn, intensified their differences in interpretation of Scripture and in the attendant practices that they followed. For this reason, Jewish legal issues must stand at the center of all discussions of sectarianism in Second Temple times.[11]

It is now generally recognized that *halakhic* disputes lay at the heart of much of the Qumran community's disagreement with and separation from other Jewish groups. This quite often had to do with issues of ritual purity. One scroll, 4QMMT or the "Halakhic Letter," outlined numerous such areas of dispute. For instance, Torah stipulated that a leprous person was not to eat sacred food until he/she was clean (cf. Lev 13–14, 22). The *halakhah* in MMT said this occurred after sunset on the eighth day (B 71–72). They were polemicizing against a group holding a different

---

9. I can still remember similar debates among Christian financial advisors as to whether one's tithe should be on the pre-tax "gross" income, or if the after-tax "net" would suffice.

10. Schiffman, *Halakhah at Qumran*, 13.

11. Schiffman, *Qumran and Jerusalem*, 5; and ch. 19, "The Pharisees and their Legal Tradition according to the Dead Sea Scrolls," 321–36.

position. From the Mishnah we know some rabbis said the cleansing was valid *before sunset* on the eighth day (m. Neg. 14:3). Something like this was probably behind this particular purity dispute in MMT. Another dispute concerned the purity of liquids poured from an impure vessel into a pure one, something that would have been very important when filling the many ritual purification pools. MMT said such liquid must be considered impure (B 55-58). The Mishnah points out a group who held the opposite (m. Yad. 4:7; m. Ṭehar. 8:9). In each case, the opposing group held a more lenient stance.[12] It is such *halakhic leniency* that seemed to be at issue in calling this group "seekers of smooth things." And we might remember that Josephus also spoke of the Pharisees as being known for leniency (A.J. 13.294) as well as for their exactness (*akribeia*) in interpretation.

Regulations for Sabbath behavior were also found in the DSS and reveal clearly the *halakhic* disagreements among Jewish groups over such questions.

> No-one is to walk in the field to do the work which he wishes on the sabbath. He is not to walk more than one thousand cubits outside the city. No-one is to eat on the sabbath day except what has been prepared; and from what is lost in the field, he should not eat. And he should not drink except of what there is in the camp. (CD X.20-23)

The thousand cubit Sabbath walking limit was followed here by the sect.[13] Later rabbis appealed to Num 35:2-5 and sometimes extended this to two-thousand cubits (m. Soṭah 5:3; m. Yoma 6:4-5), since the Numbers text mentioned both a one-thousand and two-thousand cubit limit. This may seem arcane and picayune to us today, but such careful attention to the commandments spelled the difference between keeping and breaking the law of God, and thus the difference between pleasing and angering God.

The CD text cited above also mentioned what one may prepare and eat on the Sabbath. Since food preparation was clearly "work," most Jewish groups frowned on doing this on the Sabbath and insisted that Sabbath food be prepared ahead. Some dispute remained, however, over whether eating fallen fruit was allowed, requiring no "preparation." While the sect seemed here to allow this, some later rabbis were more cautious (m. Pesaḥ. 4:8). This particular *halakhic* disagreement will arise again in the Gospels when Jesus' disciples pick and eat grain in a field on the Sabbath (Mark 2:23-28 par.; pp.

---

12. On these allegedly Pharisaic *halakhoth* in 4QMMT see Hultgren, *From the Damascus Covenant to the Covenant of the Community*, 287-90.

13. See Schiffman, *Halakhah at Qumran*, 90-98.

91–94). Whether the problem was "harvesting" or "preparing" (i.e., rubbing the husks), Jesus appeared to follow an even more lax *halakhah*.

Pharisees in the Rabbinic Writings: Mishnah and Talmud

Movie buffs may remember the scene in Yentl where Barbara Streisand's character, impersonating a male student, is in the Yeshiva surrounded by other students at small tables with large books. At each table students are bent over the large volumes, loudly disputing the meaning of each line, each word. They are studying the Talmud. The Talmud is immense; you won't read it in a night, not even in a month. The standard Soncino edition runs to 26 volumes. It is the primary text for Jewish theology and religious law (*halakhah*). The Talmud is not really a book in the sense of literature with an author. It is a collection of traditions which were passed along orally, including sayings, scripture commentary, rehearsal of debates, etc. Many of these were anonymous, while others had a name attached ("Rabbi XYZ said . . ."). The Talmud consists of 1) the Mishnah, a collection of the early Jewish oral traditions written down about 200 CE, 2) the Tosefta, written around 300 CE, a supplement to the Mishnah with additional oral traditions, stories, etc., and 3) the Talmud, a larger corpus which includes additional commentary, sayings, stories, etc., and which has come down in two forms, the Palestinian (or Jerusalem) Talmud (prob. completed c. 500 CE) and the Babylonian Talmud (prob. completed c. 600 CE).[14]

Earlier studies of the Pharisees assumed that the rabbis behind the Mishnah were themselves essentially Pharisees.[15] When the Jerusalem temple was destroyed by the Romans in 70 CE, according to the reigning scholarly hypothesis, many of the surviving rabbis gathered at Jamnia (or Yavneh) and began to re-order Judaism around Torah rather than the temple. The Sadducees/priests no longer had a place of authority and employment, and the Essenes and the Zealots had disappeared, so the Pharisees were the only ones left to define the new post-destruction Judaism. Their heirs carried on the oral traditions now enshrined in the Mishnah and Talmud. As we mentioned, some sayings had a name attached, which seemed to "prove"

---

14. The terminology referring to these bodies of literature is somewhat fluid. Sometimes, Mishnah can refer to any oral saying rather than the now-written Mishnah, and Talmud can be used for the entire body of rabbinic literature. If this sounds a bit confusing, welcome to the world of Talmudic studies. For an accessible introduction, see Young, *Meet the Rabbis*, ch. 6 (Introduction to Early Jewish Writings).

15. Classic studies in this vein are: Schürer, *History of the Jewish People in the Time of Jesus Christ*, 2.10–28; R. Travers Herford, *Pharisees*; Moore, *Judaism*, 1.56–92.

this (e.g., Hillel, Gamaliel), but the assumption was applied liberally to the anonymous sayings, as well.

On the basis of such assumptions, scholars discovered in the Talmud a wealth of information about the Pharisees, including the following.

- obsessed with minor details of purity
- enforced priestly purity among non-priestly Jews
- mostly laymen with no scribal education (though the leaders and influential members were scribes), mostly merchants, artisans and peasants, and some priests
- theologically they were "legalists," i.e., one's relationship with God was founded upon one's level of legal obedience to commandments[16]
- attached great importance to meritorious works of supererogation
- dominated Jewish religious praxis among the common folk as well over the Sadducees, and determined the liturgy even of the priests and sacrifices in the temple
- held a majority in the Sanhedrin
- controlled the synagogues
- had two main schools, a conservative or strict one (Shammai) and a more liberal one (Hillel)
- lived in small closed communities (*haburōth*) and would not eat or gather with gentiles and non-Pharisees, whom they considered ritually unclean
- were very popular among the common people, yet viewed them with disdain as ignorant of the Law and unclean since they did not tithe properly or observe Pharisaic purity rules; in fact Pharisees avoided business dealings, marriage and hospitality with non-Pharisees
- common meal Friday evenings
- strict rules of admission for entry to community (one month or one year probationary period)
- had to marry and practice a trade (e.g., Paul's leatherworking)
- prodigious memorizers of Torah
- observed fixed hours of prayer
- had to be 40 years of age to be ordained as a rabbi

16. They sought to "perfectly observe the law and have therefore a claim to the promises"; Schürer, *History of the Jewish People*, 2.24.

- believed their oral traditions were as authoritative as Torah itself since they originated with Moses' spoken word on Mount Sinai

How and Why That Changed

It was particularly the work of Jacob Neusner in the 1970s that led to a wholesale re-evaluation of using rabbinic literature in this way.[17] He demonstrated to the satisfaction of most scholars that we cannot take the attributions in this literature at face value. When, for example, a text reads "the sages said," or even more specifically "Rabbi Akiba said," we cannot take this as proof that such oral tradition was present or prominent in the first century. Such traditions grew over time, added details (such as specific names), imputed later practices to earlier times, etc.

Most of the things listed above that we thought we knew about the Pharisees were built on this shaky foundation. For example, there has been ongoing debate regarding Paul's marital status. When he said, "To the unmarried and the widows I say that it is well for them to remain unmarried as I am" (1 Cor 7:8), did this imply he was never married, married but not living conjugally, married then divorced, or married then widowed? The Talmud was brought into this debate. Rabbi Eliezer (c. 90 CE) was reputed to have said a prospective rabbi should marry before ordination.[18] The attribution of the ordination ruling to a late first-century (Pharisaic?) rabbi may be accurate, or it may simply reflect the reigning later practice now given authority by attaching an authoritative earlier name to it. And what does one do with the contrary positions and examples found also in the Talmud?[19] Thus, it turns out we don't really "know" that first-century Pharisees/rabbis had to marry early. The best we can say is, "such a position seems to be consistent with some later rabbinic praxis."

Thus the earlier easy equation—rabbinic tradition = Pharisaism—that yielded so much supposed information about the historical Pharisees has had a very large question mark placed over it.[20] This certainly doesn't mean the rabbinic literature is useless in our quest; but on how exactly to employ

17. Neusner, *Rabbinic Traditions about the Pharisees*.

18. For the relevant Talmudic passages, see StrB, s.v. 1 Cor 7:1–8.

19. Those who read German might enjoy the spirited back-and-forth on this question between Jeremias, "War Paulus Witwer?," 310–12, and Fascher, "Zur Witwerschaft," 62–69.

20. It is likely that the post-70 rabbis were not even interested in identifying as Pharisees and promoting the sort of sectarian strife characterizing pre-70 Judaism. See Cohen, "Significance of Yavneh," 27–53.

it, there is at present no consensus. Some are what we might call minimalists, convinced that we can find very little of the early Pharisees with any certainty.[21] Others are not quite so ready to throw in the historical towel.[22] I find myself generally in agreement with these critical non-minimalists, but because of the continued uncertainty I will use rabbinic sources primarily for *illustrative* purposes. That is, Talmudic debates may give examples of the sorts of disputes and interests we find clearly in other sources (e.g., Gospels, DSS). On occasion they may even be used *suggestively*, i.e., they may suggest a reason or further detail to a poorly understood issue. The minimalists will not like this, but as long as we remember the fine line we're walking here and don't let too much hang on this, I think we can proceed.

---

21. Neusner is convinced "the historical value of the rabbinic traditions of pre-70 Pharisaism is not apt to be considerable," Neusner, *Pharisees*, 6. Much pre-Hillelite Pharisaic interest "was simply obliterated," Neusner, *Pharisees*, 257. Also, Stemberger, *Jewish Contemporaries of Jesus*.

22. Similar to my approach is, Kazen, *Scripture, Interpretation, or Authority?*, 71–72. See also Sanders, *Jewish Law*, 184–236 (he uses Neusner's accepted early-strata passages on purity issues, but thinks they *do* reflect first-century realities).

CHAPTER 5

Common Identity with Other Jews

OUR EXAMINATION THUS FAR has concentrated on what *distinguished* Pharisees from other Jews, in the writings of Josephus, the DSS, and the Talmud. This is helpful, and has usually been the focus of studies on the Pharisees. However, it carries an inherent danger . . . the Pharisees look different from most other Jews. This, in fact, is a gross error. *The Pharisees shared with most other Jews immensely more than what differentiated them.* They both believed in the God of Israel as the only true God, in Israel as his chosen people through Abraham and Moses, in Torah as God's guidance for his people, in the Jerusalem temple as the place of his earthly presence, and on and on. While Pharisees may have thought themselves more "scrupulous [*akribeia*]" in many respects, first and foremost they were Jews. To overlook this, as has often been done unwittingly in studies of the Pharisees, is to fail to really understand them. It is to their shared Jewishness we now turn.

Common Judaism

Was there, however, such a thing as "common Judaism," practices and beliefs shared by most Jews, whether common people, priests, Essenes, etc.? Some scholars have abandoned the singular "Judaism" in favor of the plural "Judaisms." There was never, they argue, a monolithic religious entity named "Judaism." Rather, there were multiple Jewish groups, movements and tendencies. While their convictions may have overlapped, these groups differed significantly, as did the way they practiced their Judaisms. And, perhaps most importantly, they often excluded other Judaisms from even being considered a valid Judaism.

The modern debate over Judaism (sg.) versus Judaisms (pl.) got some impetus from E. P. Sanders's work, who held that in spite of diversity over many issues, Jews of nearly all stripes held to what he called "covenantal nomism," and had quite a large palette of shared beliefs and practices.[1] Some Jewish and Christian scholars quickly pushed back, stressing the differences which they felt Sanders had underplayed.[2] This book is not the place to carry on that debate in detail, so allow me to cut to the chase.[3] Along with E. P. Sanders and many others, I still think there is value in speaking in the singular of "Judaism" in and around the first century. This is certainly not meant to deny that there were serious differences among the many sub-groups; so serious that some of them refused to even recognize other groups as "real Jews." Nevertheless, my argument is that there was a sense of Jewishness common to most of these groups.[4] Even when rejecting the Jerusalem priests as wicked and calling them "gentiles," the DSS still viewed them as obligated to Jewish covenantal requirements, something not demanded of non-Jews. It is precisely because Qumran considered these apostate priests to be Jews that they engaged in such heated debate and critique with them.

What follows, then, is a brief description of some elements of Jewishness held in common by most Jews in the first century. It does not encompass every aspect of Jewish thought and praxis, but primarily those which appear to have greatest relevance to the question at hand . . . who were the Pharisees, what sort of Jews were they?

God, the One and Only

"Hear, O Israel: The LORD is our God, the LORD alone."
(Deut 6:4)

Judaism is not a creedal religion, but if it had a central creed, this would be its text. It would be hard to imagine an ancient Jew whose heart would not be roused by hearing these words, which were repeated daily in homes everywhere. Bits of this text were carried as a reminder in small boxes strapped to forearms and foreheads and placed in the doorposts of

---

1. Sanders, *Paul and Palestinian Judaism*, and Sanders, *Judaism*. Sanders's position on Judaism has been strengthened and affirmed by many, including Dunn, *Partings of the Ways*.

2. For example, Neusner, *Judaic Law*, and Carson et al., *Justification and Variegated Nomism, Vol. 1, Complexities*.

3. A helpful overview of the debate (siding largely with Sanders) is Stemberger, "Was There a 'Mainstream Judaism,'" 189–208.

4. A "fundamental similarity" in outlook and ideology in spite of rampant sectarianism according to Baumgarten, *Flourishing of Jewish Sects*, 55–58.

the home (Deut 6:7–9).[5] A host of common convictions arise from this statement, the Shema.[6]

The only true God is the God of Abraham, Isaac and Jacob, the God who brought Israel out of Egypt, the God who gave Moses his Torah on Sinai. Israel is to be passionately committed ("you shall love...") to this God alone, and to abhor the worship of any other god. This lies at the root of the widespread abhorrence of idolatry and "graven images" in ancient Judaism.[7]

Israel, His Graciously Chosen People

This God is "*our* God." That is, he is the God who chose a small and weak slave nation in Egypt to be his people, his treasured possession among all the nations. This choosing, this election, was not based on this tiny people's strength, character or achievements, but on this God's lovingkindness, his grace.

> It was not because you were more numerous than any other people that the LORD set his heart on you and chose you—for you were the fewest of all peoples. It was because the LORD loved you and kept the oath that he swore to your ancestors, that the LORD has brought you out with a mighty hand, and redeemed you from the house of slavery, from the hand of Pharaoh king of Egypt. (Deut 7:7–8)

At its very foundations, Judaism has always been a religion of grace.

Torah, His Protective Guidance

This God who chose this people did not leave them to find their own way, but gave them his guiding wisdom, his Torah, his law.[8] For Jews this was not

---

5. A *mezuzah* (lit. "doorpost") is a small decorative case containing a small bit of Torah such as the Shema, and affixed to the doorpost in obedience to Deut 6:9 ("write them on the doorposts"). The *tefillin* or phylacteries, were small leather boxes containing a bit of Torah and strapped to forearms or foreheads during prayers (Deut 11:18).

6. The shorthand "Shema" comes from the opening of the Hebrew text: *shema yisrael* (Hear, O Israel).

7. Life in the Roman Empire confronted Jews with many difficult decisions in this regard. For example, could a Jew handle and use the Roman coinage which contained human images? Apparently, Jews had devised ways to accommodate to this reality, as seen in the story of Jesus, the Pharisees and the coin for taxes, Matt 22:15–22.

8. Although Bibles normally translate *torah* as "law," the central meaning is teaching, guidance, instruction, as any good Hebrew lexicon reveals. It does, of course, contain

just for the religious part of life, but it governed *all of life*, it was a complete *way of life*.

> Religion governs all our actions and occupations and speech; none of these things did our lawgiver leave unexamined or indeterminate. (*Ag. Ap.* 2.171)

God's gifts—grace, election, deliverance, blessing, commandments—require the appropriate human response: loving obedience. These words precede the Shema:

> Now this is the commandment—the statutes and the ordinances—that the LORD your God charged me to teach you to observe in the land that you are about to cross into and occupy, so that you and your children and your children's children may fear the LORD your God all the days of your life, and keep all his decrees and his commandments that I am commanding you, so that your days may be long. Hear therefore, O Israel, and observe them diligently, so that it may go well with you, and so that you may multiply greatly in a land flowing with milk and honey, as the LORD, the God of your ancestors, has promised you. (Deut 6:1–3)

And these instructions follow immediately after:

> You shall love the LORD your God with all your heart, and with all your soul, and with all your might. Keep these words that I am commanding you today in your heart. (Deut 6:5–6)

This relationship of grace and obedience in Judaism is what Sanders described as "covenantal nomism," in which "'covenant stands for God's grace in election . . ., 'nomism' for the requirement of obedience to the law (*nomos* in Greek . . .)."[9]

Let's pause here for just a moment, since getting the relationship right in Judaism between the divine gift (grace) and the human response (love, obedience) will be crucial to our study of the Pharisees. Traditionally, the Pharisees (and often the whole of ancient Judaism) have been portrayed as legalists, those who saw divine grace as the response to human achievement. One kept commandments *in order to earn* God's favor and blessing.

---

commandments and prohibitions, but its central significance is not as a legal list of do's and don'ts, but as the guiding and protecting wisdom of God for how Israel is to conduct her life in this world.

9. Sanders, *Judaism*, 262; further 262–78. His original presentation of covenantal nomism is found in Sanders, *Paul and Palestinian Judaism*, 419–28, esp. 422–23.

And, so traditionally, Jesus opposed this legalism with grace. God loved the undeserving, the sinner.

This caricature of Jewish soteriology has always been opposed by Jewish thinkers, and has now been largely abandoned by other students of the Bible. Replacing it has been some version of what E. P. Sanders referred to as "covenantal nomism." Simply put, God's election of puny Israel forms the foundation of all Jewish hopes. The great act of unearned salvation in Jewish soteriology is his deliverance of the nation from slavery in Egypt. The gift of the Torah through Moses guided the nation in its newly granted relationship with Yahweh. Like all healthy divine-human relationships, God's gift called for the receiving partner to respond in gratitude, love and obedience. This keeping of the law did not establish or earn that relationship, but neither was it an optional matter. The genuine partner will walk in God's ways, not in their own. Put in terms more familiar to Christian theology, Israel is saved by grace through faith (= loyalty) and judged according to her deeds.[10]

If we have given Judaism a fair shake to this point, and if we are correct that Pharisees stood on this same common ground with other Jews, then Jesus' disputes with Pharisees will most likely not have been over grace versus legalism. They did not disagree over the relationship of grace and works, but over something else. It will be our task in studying the Gospels to ask what exactly was the point of their disagreement, if not what we traditionally thought it was?

The Temple, His Holy Dwelling on Earth

> "whoever swears by the sanctuary, swears by it and by *the one who dwells in it*" (Matt 23:21)

Prior to the destruction of Herod's temple in 70 CE, Judaism had been a temple-based religious system, at least in the few centuries leading up to and including the first century. Although Jews certainly could meet with God outside Jerusalem, could pray and listen to him elsewhere than in the temple, it was only in the Jerusalem temple that God actually dwelt, where his glory rested upon the altar, where priestly mediation for the nation through sacrifice could take place, where cleansing and forgiveness could be formally carried out in the presence of Aaronic priests and Levites.

This did not mean, of course, that there was no Jewish critique directed against the temple, or at least against aspects of the temple system. The

---

10. The literature on covenantal nomism has grown immensely since Sanders's work in 1977. For a concise introduction with further bibliography, see Yinger, *New Perspective on Paul*, esp. 9–12.

OT prophets could be scathing in this regard (Mic 3:11–12; Jer 25:6). Numerous texts in the DSS railed against the Jerusalem priesthood and they refused to worship or sacrifice in that polluted house. And Jesus sounded the same notes of judgment upon the temple and its officials ("not one stone will be left upon another," Luke 21:6). But apart from a possible few exceptions, such critique was not against the temple *per se*, but against corruption and abuses associated with it.[11]

Priests and Levites

Priests and Levites existed to serve the temple, preparing and offering the sacrifices, hearing confessions, carrying out cleansing rituals, conducting the temple liturgical services, etc. Their roles were hereditary belonging to the tribe of Levi (thus, Levites) and to one particular Levite, Aaron, whose descendants inherited the priesthood.

Most priests and Levites had temple duty only one week every twenty-four, plus during the three pilgrimage festivals. Some lived year-round in Jerusalem, especially those who belonged to the aristocracy, while many lived throughout the country. In all these places they were often community and synagogue leaders, administrative and religious scribes, teachers of the law and judges. An inscription found in 1913 with the ruins of a first-century synagogue building speaks of one such priest's activities.

> Theodotus the son of Vettenus, priest and ruler of the synagogue, son of a ruler of the synagogue, son's son of a ruler of the synagogue, built the synagogue for reading of the law and for teaching of the commandments.[12]

Their acknowledged role as leaders, nationally and locally, is attested in numerous Jewish texts.

> In his commandments he [Moses] gave him [Aaron] authority and statutes and judgments, to teach Jacob the testimonies, and to enlighten Israel with his law. (*Sir.* 45:17)

> [The law] assigns the administration of its [the nation's] highest affairs to the whole body of priests, and entrusts to the supreme high-priest the direction of the other priests. . . . to

---

11. Possible exceptions might include the building of an alternate Jewish temple in Egypt (Leontopolis), the rejection of "all temples" in *Syb. Or.* 4:25, and the replacement of the earthly sanctuary and priesthood with a "better" one in the NT letter to Hebrews.

12. Cited in Sanders, *Judaism*, 176; taken from Deissmann, *Light from the Ancient Near East*.

[these priests] he entrusted the ordering of divine worship as their first charge . . . . this charge further embraced a strict superintendence of the Law and of the pursuits of everyday life; for the appointed duties of the priests included general supervision, the trial of cases of litigation, and the punishment of condemned persons. (*Ag. Ap.* 2:186–87)

Since it pertains directly to our view of first-century Pharisees, readers should be aware of a debate related to what I have just said about the leadership and teaching roles of priests in first-century Palestine. A long-standing consensus contends that the Pharisees had taken over as law-teachers and magistrates, displacing the priests.[13] Priests and Sadducees had to bend to the authority of Pharisees in synagogues, in determining purity, and in Torah interpretation. Sanders showed that this view is without sufficient evidence, most of which comes from rabbinic literature and reflects a post-70 situation where, indeed, priests had lost power.[14] In the first century, some priests adhered to Pharisaic tradition, others, probably more of them, to Sadducean leanings, and all competed with supporters of Herod and the Romans, and with each other for influence among the populace.

Tithes and Taxes

One of the areas of dispute between Jesus and the Pharisees concerned tithes and taxes (e.g., Luke 11:42). Both parties showed a commitment to the general system of Jewish tithes and temple taxes and general acquiescence to the taxes levied by Rome and its underlings such as Herod, but disagreed on the particulars.

OT instructions concerning tithing can be found in many places (e.g., Lev 27; Num 18; Deut 18). These various instructions overlapped or even stood in tension with one another. In addition, "first fruits" were to be given which provided non-sacrificial food for priests. By the first

---

13. See, for example, Jeremias, *Jerusalem in the Time of Jesus*, 264: "high priests, however unwillingly, had to fulfil the liturgical ceremonies according to the Pharisaic interpretation . . . the complete calendar . . . was fixed according to Pharisaic reckoning," and the Sadducean priests were in many respects "powerless." Also, Schürer, *History of the Jewish People*, 1.179: "the greatest amount of influence was already practically in the hands of the Pharisees, with whose demands the Sadducees were obliged, however reluctantly, to comply. . . . The Sanhedrim was by this time *practically* under the predominant influence of the Pharisees."

14. Sanders, *Judaism*, 170–82. Instone-Brewer concurs: "there is nothing to substantiate the later rabbinic assertions that the priests acted in accordance with Pharisaic rulings," Instone-Brewer, "Temple and Priesthood," 202.

century varied attempts to combine these confusing regulations led some to require more than a single tithe in a year and to include different items under the requirements.[15]

Tithing also had a connection to purity regulations, since some tithed items were "holy," i.e., set aside for sacrifice or priestly consumption. Rather than trot a calf or drag a cart of grain from a village to Jerusalem, an option was to sell the item in the village and later spend the money in Jerusalem, or consume it oneself (and reimburse later). In these cases, however, it was important that this sacred food be handled in purity. For the particularly scrupulous, this created problems, since the neighbor selling the food might not have observed purity precautions. In addition, Jews empire-wide were liable for an annual temple tax of a half-shekel (about 2 days wages for a day-laborer).

Torah, Synagogue, Sabbath, and Prayer

These would have been common elements of Jewish piety in the first century. Probably twice daily pious Jews recited the Shema and perhaps the Ten Commandments. Constant reminders of Torah and the covenant were found on doorposts and worn on forearms and foreheads. Since most first-century Jews were not literate, they did not read the Bible, but they would have been thoroughly imbued with the stories, thought, and language of Torah through home instruction and weekly Sabbath gatherings where public reading of Torah was an essential element.[16] Philo testifies to the glad and non-burdensome character of this Torah-centric life for most Jews.

> God . . . demands nothing of you which is either oppressive, or uncertain, or difficult, but only such things as are very simple and easy. (Philo, *Spec. Laws* 1.299–300; trans. Yonge)

Personal and communal prayers were also a central element of common Jewish piety. Although finalized at a later period, many of the Eighteen Benedictions probably reflect the sorts of prayers uttered by Jews during the first century, giving us a window into common piety.[17]

---

15. For details, see Sanders, *Judaism*, ch. 9, "Tithes and Taxes," 146–69.

16. "The most important element was the *congregation* [Gk. *synagogē*], which assembled to worship, listen to the scriptural readings, and participate in instruction and prayer." Ma'oz, "Synagogue of Gamla," 41.

17. Heinemann, *Prayer in the Talmud*, 26–29. Cited in Sanders, *Judaism* 204.

> Graciously favour us, our Father, with understanding from thee,
> And discernment and insight out of thy Torah.
> Blessed art thou, O Lord, gracious bestower of understanding.
>
> Behold our afflictions and defend our cause,
> And redeem us for thy name's sake.
> Blessed art thou, O Lord, Redeemer of Israel.
>
> Have compassion, O Lord our God, in thine abundant mercy, on Israel thy people,
> And on Jerusalem thy city,
> And on Zion, the abode of thy glory,
> And upon the royal seed of David, thy justly anointed.
> Blessed art thou, O Lord, God of David, Rebuilder of Jerusalem.
>
> We thank thee, Our God and God of our fathers,
> For all the goodness, the lovingkindness, and the mercies
> With which thou hast requited us, and our fathers before us.
> For when we say, 'our foot slips',
> Thy mercy, O Lord, holds us up.
> Blessed art thou, O Lord, to whom it is good to give thanks.

Echoing this spirit is one of the prayers found at Qumran.

> I give you [thanks, Lord,]
> because you have taught me your truth,
> you have made me know your wonderful mysteries,
> your kindness with [sinful] men,
> your bountiful compassion with the depraved of heart.
> Who is like you, Lord, among the gods?
> Who is like your truth?
> Who, before you, is just when judged? [. . .]
> All the sons of your truth
> you take to forgiveness in your presence,
> you purify them from their sins
> by the greatness of your goodness,
> and in your bountiful mercy,
> to make them stand in your presence,
> for ever and ever. (1QHa XV (= VII).26–32)

Circumcision

Circumcising male children eight days after birth was clearly stipulated in Torah and failure originally carried severe penalties ("cut off from his people") since it amounted to a violation of Israel's fundamental covenant with God (Gen 17:12-14). The foundational significance of this rite for Jewish identity was lastingly reinforced in Maccabean times when some tried to eliminate it, provoking armed resistance. Even non-Jews recognized that circumcision belonged centrally to Jewishness. It was practiced almost universally by Jews, as is clearly witnessed in the NT.[18]

Food Laws

Even today non-Jews recognize that many Jews eat only certain "kosher" foods, those allowed by the laws of *kashrut* (foods permissible for consumption). This may seem burdensome to those outside the observant community, but for most observant Jews it poses no great difficulty. The laws governing such foods are found largely in Lev 11 and Deut 14. Certain types of animals are forbidden (pigs, birds of prey, most insects, etc.) as are the main fatty parts and the blood of allowable animals. For one growing up in this culture in ancient Israel, keeping such regulations became second-nature. Transgressing would in most cases have required a considered intention to violate ancient custom.

Purity Laws

Concern for ritual purity was another element of common Jewish piety, and one which will be largely unfamiliar to most of us reading this book. Since numerous conflicts between Jesus and the Pharisees revolved around this issue, we will reserve for later the explanation of many details (e.g., why did Pharisees stress hand-washing), and will here simply introduce the general concept.

Contracting ritual impurity was in most cases not a matter of committing a sin. Thus, childbirth, menstruation, and genital discharges rendered one unclean temporarily. The main consequence was temporary

---

18. Philo mentions some allegorizers who may have abandoned the physical rite in favor of its symbolic meaning, but he himself does not agree (*Migration* 89-93). In the NT, pious Jews consistently practice the rite, including the associated sacrifices (Luke 1:59 [John the Baptist's parents]; 2:21 [Mary and Joseph]; Acts 21:21; Rom 2:25; 3:1-2; Phil 3:5).

inability for temple contact or with food destined for priests (i.e., in tithes), although sexual relations were to be temporarily stopped, as well. Cleansing from such impurity required a visit to the temple with the prescribed sacrifices (Lev 12:1–8; 15). However, alongside this grew up cleansing procedures which could be carried through outside Jerusalem, usually involving immersion in or sprinkling with water. John 2:6 mentions "six stone water jars for the Jewish rites of purification, each holding twenty or thirty gallons," and the proliferation of *miqvaoth* or ritual pools throughout the land testifies to the widespread observance. As we will see in Jesus' disputes with Pharisees, there were disagreements over how far to carry this. For instance, should one avoid contact with less scrupulous Jews or unclean persons, lest one also be made unclean (Pharisees), or could one eat in a "sinner's" home and minister to the unclean (Jesus)? In any case, the basic validity of the purity rules seems not to have been in dispute, since Jesus also instructs those cleansed to follow the proper rites with a priest (Mark 1:44 par.; Luke 17:14).[19] As noted earlier, this is an area where Pharisees differed from other Jews, not by denying this temple purity connection, but by extending it to daily life. Many of Jesus' conflicts arose over applications of this Pharisaic extension.

The Heart of It All: Love and Mercy

Some of us grew up hearing that Christianity represented a God of love, while Judaism knew only a God of wrath and retribution. Jesus said "do unto others," while Judaism said "an eye for an eye." Actually, it would be hard to find anything further from the truth. One will find divine wrath and retribution in the OT, as well as aching love and mercy . . . the same has to be said of the NT.[20] So, how did Jews put this together?

John Goldingay uses the image of dominant and secondary personality traits to describe divine love and wrath.[21] In the OT, as also in Judaism, love is God's primary trait, while wrath is a real, but secondary trait. God's punishment extends to several generations, but his lovingkindness to the

---

19. Neusner doubts that the masses kept the purity laws. Neusner, *Reading and Believing*, 54. Against this see, Sanders, *Judaism*, 229–30. Some see confirmation of non-observance in the Pharisees' comment in John 7:49 ("this crowd, which does not know the law"), but that refers more likely to the failure of the masses to keep the commandments *as interpreted by the Pharisees*.

20. See, for example, Tasker, *Biblical Doctrine of the Wrath of God*.

21. Goldingay, *Israel's Faith*, 165–70.

thousandth generation (Exod 34:6-7). As Lamentations phrases, his anger is not "from the heart," not from his deepest primary motivation.

> For the Lord will not reject forever. Although he causes grief, he will have compassion according to the abundance of his steadfast love; for he does not willingly [lit. from his heart] afflict or grieve anyone. (Lam 3:31-33)

This primacy of love and kindness, both divine and human, has always characterized Jewish thought.[22] The Jewish scribe in Mark 12:28-34 applauded Jesus' answer that the chief commandment was to love God and love the neighbor. And Rabbi Hillel was reputed to have said the message of Judaism could be summed up with, "That which is hateful to you, do not do unto others" (b. Šabb. 31a). Later, the rabbis would term mercy "the right hand" of God, i.e., his dominant trait.[23] The centrality of love and mercy is not what differentiates Jews and Christians, nor did it differentiate Jesus from Judaism, or from the Pharisees.

---

22. See now Levenson, *Love of God*.
23. Schechter, *Aspects of Rabbinic Theology*, 322-23.

Part 3

New Testament Portrait: Disagreements with Pharisees

CHAPTER 6

Jesus and the Pharisees: Introductory Matters

As WE TURN TO the Gospels we need to remind ourselves that Jesus and the twelve disciples shared what we are calling common Judaism with the Pharisees and with the common Jews we will meet at every turn. Jesus and his followers were not part of a new religion, but were first and foremost Jews practicing Judaism. This should make us alert to the fact that whatever the core of their disagreements, it was not about whether to be Jews. No one at this stage on the "Christian" side was saying "You need to stop being Jewish and become Christian."[1] No, their disagreements were about *what kind of Jew they thought one should be*. And for reasons we will discover, the way of being Jewish taught by Jesus came into severe conflict with the way of being Jewish promoted by Pharisees.

The Historical Problem with "Christianity"

What I just said might lead some to think I want to somehow downgrade Christianity. Far from it. Instead, I want to bring what we today call "Christianity" into sharper historical focus and to understand our founding document, the NT, more accurately. For many centuries now, Christianity and Judaism have been clearly distinct and separate religions. For a Christian to become Jewish, or vice versa, has meant leaving the former religious affiliation and joining a new one. *This was not how things worked in the first century*. Jews who followed Jesus did not "become Christians" in the sense of leaving their Judaism and joining a new and different religion. Of course,

---

1. By the second century some church leaders were, in fact, saying that one could not practice Judaism *and* be a follower of Jesus (e.g., Ign *Magn.* 10:2–3).

they did become followers of Jesus the Jewish messiah, but they remained as Jewish as they had always been. The earliest disciples continued temple-centered worship (Acts 2:46; 3:1–4:4; 5:17–26, 42; 21:26–36; 22:17; 24:18; 25:9) and Paul still submitted to synagogue discipline (2 Cor 11:24). In fact, there was as of yet no new and distinct religion called Christianity. There were Jews who adhered to Jesus the messiah and followed his teachings, and there were Jews who adhered to Moses and various traditional ways of following the God of Israel and did not accept that Jesus of Nazareth was the Jewish messiah; but they were all Jews.

In the mid-first century the term "Christian [Gk. *christianos*]" was just beginning to be heard (Acts 11:26; 26:28; 1 Pet 4:16), but was a term used by outsiders for "partisans of Christ." It did not yet refer to a well-defined religious movement, and was not yet a term of self-reference among Jesus followers. No one yet defined themselves as a "Christian."[2]

What Sort of Jew Should We Be?

So, once again, Jesus was not criticizing the Pharisees (or Sadducees, scribes, etc.) for adhering to Judaism and, instead, proposing Christianity. No, he was criticizing *their way of practicing Judaism*, and was proposing instead *his way of practicing Judaism*.

The Pharisees were well-known for their *akribeia*, their exactness or precision in the interpretation of the Mosaic laws as well as in their carrying out of these interpretations. We noted when discussing Pharisaic *akribeia* earlier, that other Jews also cared about being accurate, but apparently not quite to the degree pursued by the Pharisees.[3] In a number of the disputes between Jesus and the Pharisees they argued about the precise or exact meaning of Torah (e.g., on divorce). Like most Jews, Jesus cared about *akribeia*, too,[4] but he tempered it in ways that made his interpretation and praxis significantly different from that of the Pharisees. He didn't seem as concerned with ritual purity or Sabbath violations. In the eyes of the stricter Pharisees, he was not merely less precise; he was breaking the commandments and misleading Israel. And in the eyes of Jesus the Pharisees' traditions, which focused so much on precise interpretation and praxis, resulted in them being the ones who broke the commandments and were "blind guides."

---

2. See the helpful overview by Wilkins, "Christian," 1:925–26.

3. According to Josephus, the Pharisees were "more accurate [*akribesteron*]" than others (*J.W.* 1.110).

4. Matt 5:17–20.

These disputes over how to properly practice Torah bring us to *halakhah*. As we explained in ch. 4, the way of life, the "walk [Heb. *halakh*]," that a group developed out of its particular reading of Scripture was their *halakhah*. The Pharisaic "traditions" mentioned in the Gospels contained such *halakhah*, more detailed explanations of what the Mosaic law required. Jesus demonstrated and taught a different *halakhah*, a different "walk" based on the Mosaic instructions. He healed regularly and gladly on the Sabbath, let his disciples pluck and eat in the grainfields, and dined with sinners. These *halakhic* disagreements formed a key element of what separated the Pharisees from Jesus.[5] As Meier summarizes, "the historical Jesus is the halakic Jesus."[6] And these *halakhic* issues were not just of interest to scholars, experts or leaders; to be a common Jew seeking to be faithful to God and his covenant meant to live according to some *halakhah*, some understanding of what the commandments actually required in the many varied situations of life. "At the time of Jesus, everyone would have lived according to a halakha."[7] The question was "whose *halakhah*"? So, in addition to questions of "precise" interpretation, their disputes, highlighted in the chapters that follow, often revolve around the resulting *halakhah*, the way of life being taught to Israel.[8]

Mixed in with these disagreements over *akribeia* and *halakhah*, we will find that Jesus and the Pharisees also disagreed fundamentally over time; that is, what time is it on God's eschatological clock? Jesus' proclamation centered on this: "The time is fulfilled, and the kingdom of God has come near" (Mark 1:15). The clock is striking midnight and a new day is dawning in God's dealings with Israel and the world. The time of Israel's redemption, her release from foreign oppression, and of creation's bondage to sin and decay, is dawning. As Jesus announced in Capernaum, the time has come "to proclaim release to the captives and recovery of sight to the

---

5. The classic instance of *halakhic* disagreement in the Gospels is the divorce pericope (Mark 10:2–12; Matt 19:3–12). It is well-known that Jewish teachers differed over *whether* and *in which cases* divorce was allowable, and rabbinic sources even suggest a distinction between liberal Hillelite *halakha* ("for any cause," cf. Matt 19:3) and more restrictive Shammaite views. Thus, when the Pharisees asked "Is it lawful . . . to divorce?" they were posing a classic *halakhic* question. On background and interpretation, see Instone-Brewer, *Divorce and Remarriage*; Kazen, *Scripture, Interpretation, or Authority?*, 195–282; and Sigal, *Halakhah of Jesus*, 105–44.

6. Meier, *Marginal Jew*, 4:8.

7. Kazen, *Scripture, Interpretation, or Authority?*, 32.

8. A few have argued that Jesus had no interest in *halakhah*; e.g., Westerholm, *Jesus and Scribal Authority*. His attempt, however, to theorize a "statutory" view of law (Pharisees) versus "the attitude of the heart" (Jesus) reflects an outdated view of law in Judaism.

blind, to let the oppressed go free, to proclaim the year of the Lord's favor" (Luke 4:18–19). To some degree, the Qumran community agreed. But, as far as we know, most of the Pharisees (and the Sadducees) did not. In their minds, God was still at work in and for Israel in the same way he had been for some centuries. This was the time during which Israel must sustain her faithfulness to God's ways in the midst of foreign temptation; for the Pharisees this meant observing carefully their way of life, their *halakhic* traditions. The disagreement over time will crop up especially in the parables, but also in some of the interpretive disputes.[9]

At the root of all these disagreements over *akribeia*, *halakhah*, and time, lays *the* crucial divisive issue: the disagreement over authority, or more precisely over who was authorized by God to instruct Israel. The Pharisees were widely recognized authorities in Torah praxis and interpretation (Matt 23:2–3). As we saw in the chapters on their history and character, they enjoyed popularity and influence among the masses. Others, like the Essenes, the Sadducees, the Zealots, or the partisans of Herod vied for this influence, but for varying reasons, none of them had much chance of rivaling the authority of the Pharisees.[10] But charismatic prophets, healers, and preachers did pop up now and again with a chance at drawing off a following.[11] Then came another, Jesus, who "taught them as one having authority" (Mark 1:22). And he backed up this authority to teach with authority and power to heal, to cast out demons, and to forgive (Mark 2:10; 3:15; Matt 9:1–8). This question of Jesus' authority would finally play a central role in his arrest and trial (Mark 11:28). And this new prophet-teacher who came with such authority was popular. Crowds followed him around Galilee, even into Jerusalem itself. Thus, in many of the disputes between Pharisees and Jesus this question of his authority will become central. Who is he to be teaching and acting this way? What does he mean by mysteriously aligning himself with the "son of man" who has authority to heal, forgive, act like David, adjust Sabbath *halakhah*, etc.? Jesus' claim to authoritatively lay out Israel's path at this critical moment brings him into direct conflict with the Pharisees, who also lay claim to guiding Israel in the right way. Note carefully, in none of this is Jesus opposing Judaism, Moses, Torah, or the *halakhic* keeping of the commandments. He is as committed to these as are

---

9. Thus, when justifying his non-fasting praxis, Jesus claims "the bridegroom is with them" (Matt 9:15).

10. For most common Jews, the Qumran community was too isolated, the Sadducees too compromised, the Herodians only half-committed to Israel, and the Zealots too radical.

11. See esp. Hanson and Horsley, *Bandits, Prophets, and Messiahs*.

the Pharisees (and other Jews). They disagree over what that commitment should look like and over whose teaching is from God.

In the bulk of the chapters to follow, we will examine the Gospel conflicts between Jesus and Pharisees by categories: Sabbath conflicts, ritual purity conflicts, food conflicts, etc. In most of these cases we will focus on one of the Synoptic accounts, but we will bring in the other Synoptics for the full picture.

What's a "Synoptic" Gospel?

Having just mentioned the word "Synoptic," it may help some readers to explain that term a bit further. Three of the four Gospels—Matthew, Mark, and Luke—parallel one another in remarkable ways. They include many of the same stories and sayings, sometimes in the same order, and sometimes with almost exactly the same wording. Thus, they may be "viewed together," in parallel, or "Synoptically" (from Gk. *syn* [with] + *optikos* [view]). The Gospel of John does not belong to the Synoptic Gospels, because his account is so different from theirs, containing few of their stories, parables, actions, etc.

The major Synoptic problem is to explain how it came to be that these three accounts are so very similar, down to the very wording in many cases, and yet so very different. For a long time now, the majority view, which I will largely follow here, is that Mark was written first, and that Luke and Matthew both consulted Mark's account while composing theirs. This explains a fair amount of the similarity in content, order and wording. But Luke and Matthew also had access to additional sources, sometimes resulting in material not found in Mark, thus some of the differences.[12]

More recently, however, the role of non-written, oral tradition has begun to play a greater role in explaining the similarities and differences among the Synoptics. That is, rather than envisioning Matthew composing his Gospel at a desk with Mark, Q, and M spread out before him, and then cutting and pasting like a good newspaper editor, it may be that much of the similarity and difference he reflects was already present in the memories and oral traditions he and others in his circle treasured. This oral-tradition view need not exclude the previously dominant literary view; the reality

12. Since some of this non-Markan material found in both Matt and Luke is so similar in content and wording, one of these sources must have been written and used by both. It is referred to as Q (for German *Quelle* = source). Matthew and Luke each had unique material we will call M (Matt) and L (Luke). Most scholars consider all of these to have been written sources, certainly Mark, but also Q, M, and L. For this traditional Synoptic solution, see Stein, "Synoptic Problem," 784–92.

probably involved some blending of both. This blended view will be taken in what follows.[13] One consequence is that I will not often use language like "Matthew changed . . .," since that assumes Matthew was looking at another (written) version like Mark, and then consciously and intentionally omitted or changed something (referred to by scholars as "redaction" or "editing"). Instead, in many cases it may be just as likely that Matthew did not omit or redact anything, but simply reproduced the version of the saying or story as it was told in his circles.

The bottom line of all this is that we will want to take each Gospel seriously, rather than dumping them all into a blender, hitting "Hi-speed," and then seeing what homogenized product results.[14] No, each of them, Matthew, Mark, Luke, and, of course, John, is a unique transmitter of the memories of Jesus available to them. My own conviction is that each of the unique and differing accounts was so intended by God—"inspired," in theological language.

Four Versions of the Pharisees

Some readers may be surprised to learn that each of the four Gospels presents the Pharisees somewhat differently. As we will see, they use differing terminology and even differ in regards to how positively or negatively the Pharisees appear. What follows is a brief overview of each Gospel's distinctive portrayal of the Pharisees.

The Gospel of Mark

We begin with Mark, since his Gospel is considered by most the earliest (65–70 CE). Mark mentions Pharisees twelves times in nine different episodes.[15] They are unmistakably opponents from the start. After preaching, healing, and casting out demons around Galilee (ch. 1), Mark relates a series of five controversy stories (2:1—3:6). Four of these explicitly involve Pharisees, and the fifth likely does, as well.[16] By the fifth conflict (3:1–6), the tension between Jesus and the Pharisees has grown intense. The latter

---

13. See esp. Dunn, *Jesus Remembered*, 192–254; and Dunn, "Altering the Default Setting," 139–75.

14. Marshall, *Portrayals of the Pharisees*.

15. 2:15–17, 18–22 (2x), 23–28; 3:1–6; 7:1–8 (3x); 8:11–13, 14–21; 10:2–9; 12:13–17.

16. The first conflict mentions only "scribes" explicitly (2:6), but the ensuing mention of "scribes of the Pharisees" (2:16) may suggest the scribes in the first episode were also "of the Pharisees."

now are looking for an occasion to accuse Jesus and conspire against him to "destroy" him, while Jesus is angry at their "hardness of heart." This early opposition will continue right up to Jerusalem (12:13). Mark, however, unlike Matthew, does not involve the Pharisees in the arrest and trial. That role belongs to the chief priests, scribes, and elders.

The Pharisees criticize Jesus for eating with "sinners," for "working" on Sabbath, for failure to fast, and failing to cleanse hands. They also challenge his authority and dispute with him about divorce law and paying taxes. Although the question about taxes has a clear political dimension, most of the conflicts revolve around Jewish Torah praxis. Since Mark's account most likely has a non-Jewish audience in mind, he includes parenthetical explanations of these Jewish points of *halakhah* (e.g., 7:3–4) or "tradition(s) of the elders" (7:3, 5).

In many ways the scribes rival the Pharisees in Mark's Gospel as Jesus' opponents, which raises the question of their identity and their relationship to the Pharisees. Scribes are mentioned more often (21x) and crop up in thirteen episodes.[17] Sometimes scribes are themselves Pharisees (2:16), sometimes they are closely paired with Pharisees ("Pharisees and scribes," 7:1, 5), sometimes they are the primary conflict partners with Jesus (2:6; 3:22; 9:11, 14; 12:28, 38), and sometimes they are paired with priests and elders (11:18, 27; 14:1, 43, 53; 15:1, 31; also 8:31; 10:33). This last combination is largely due to the scribes' involvement with the chief priests and elders in the final conflict in Jerusalem, whereas Mark has the Pharisees disappear from these proceedings.

Who Were the NT Scribes?

In largely illiterate societies, those who could read/write were important and were granted higher status. Such were scribes throughout the ancient Near East. They were akin to what we call a "secretary," including not only writing skills and dictation (like an office secretary), but equally advising roles and mid-level government offices (like a cabinet secretary). Scribes were well-known in the Jewish world, such as Baruch and Ezra, and Josephus uses the term "for officials at all levels from village to royal court."[18] The ideal scribe was a combination of scholar, teacher,

---

17. 2:1–12, 15–17; 3:20–27; 7:1–8; 9:14–29; 11:15–19, 27–33; 12:28–34; 14:1–2, 43–50, 53–65; 15:1–5, 21–32.

18. Saldarini, "Scribes," 1013; see his entire article for a good overview, 1012–16.

Torah-expert and manager-leader, though scribes filled a wide variety of roles, and were not simply Torah-experts.[19]

Hence, "scribe" was a professional designation, it described their task or job. Pharisee was more of a religious or party designation. One could be both a scribe and a Pharisee (Mark 2:16, "scribes of the Pharisees"; Luke 5:30, "Pharisees and their scribes"). There were also scribes more closely associated with Sadducees, priests or elders.[20] Luke's "lawyers" are nearly synonymous with scribes, but with the focus on their Torah-expertise (cf. Luke 11:46, 53).

Thus, scribes and Pharisees were overlapping designations.[21] Some, but not all, professional scribes aligned themselves with the party of the Pharisees. And some, but not all, of the Pharisaic persuasion were professional scribes.

The Gospel of Matthew

Matthew is usually dated a couple of decades later than Mark (c. 80–100 CE) and may have had access to Mark's Gospel as well as to other written sources. He included all of Mark's Pharisee and scribe incidents, but varied the labels in some cases.[22] Matthew also has additional Pharisee conflicts in non-Markan material,[23] thus providing a fuller picture than Mark's somewhat minimal coverage. Overall one would have to say Matthew brings the Pharisees more into the center of the conflict with Jesus than Mark had

---

19. For a helpful overview of various tasks undertaken by scribes, see Twelftree, "Scribes," 733–34. On the understanding of scribes taken in this study, esp. as broader than Torah-experts, see Schams, *Jewish Scribes*.

20. The combination of "elder, chief priests and scribes" shows up repeatedly in Jerusalem seeking Jesus' death (e.g., Mark 8:31).

21. Martin Pickup recognizes this overlap, but incorrectly limits the teaching function to scribes alone, and not non-scribal Pharisees. Pickup, "Matthew's and Mark's Pharisees," 72.

22. Mark's "scribes of the Pharisees" (2:16) is in Matt simply "the Pharisees" (9:11); Matthew has Pharisees rather than scribes accuse Jesus of collusion with Beelzebul (Mark 3:22; Matt 9:34; 12:24); Mark's Pharisees (8:11) become Pharisees and Sadducees (Matt 16:1; cp. 12:38); Mark's "yeast of Pharisees and Herod" (8:15) is in Matt "yeast of the Pharisees and Sadducees" (16:6).

23. 3:7; 5:20; 22:34; 23:1–36 (woes to "scribes and Pharisees").

done.[24] Although others such as scribes, chief priests, etc. are still involved in conflict with Jesus (as in Mark), the Pharisees more often take center-stage in controversies with Jesus. This is particularly clear in the uniquely Matthean "seat of Moses" comment (23:2), the woes to "scribes and Pharisees" in ch. 23, and the notable involvement of Pharisees, unlike in Mark or Luke, in the events surrounding the arrest and crucifixion (21:45; 27:62). Matthew also highlights more than the other Synoptics that the conflict between Jesus and the Pharisees revolved around their differing teaching as to Israel's proper way of righteousness. Unlike the Pharisees whom John rejects for his baptism, Jesus comes for John's baptism "to fulfill all righteousness" (3:7–17). His first extended teaching is about "fulfilling" the law and prophets and aims specifically at a way of "righteousness" that "exceeds that of the scribes and Pharisees" (5:17–20). Only in Matt is the "leaven of the Pharisees" their "teaching" (16:12). And Matthew has the scribes, Pharisees and others address Jesus more often as "teacher" (8:19; 9:11; 17:24; 19:16). Finally, since Matthew's audience was probably more Jewish, he can omit Mark's explanations of Jewish praxis (e.g., Matt 15:1–3; Mark 7:1–6).

The Gospel of Luke

Written later than Mark (c. 70–90 CE), Luke tells us he had access to other written accounts of Jesus' life and message (1:1–4), possibly some form of Mark's Gospel. Luke's portrait of the Pharisees is considered by many to be "puzzling" or "enigmatic," as well as "very different" from Mark's and Matthew's.[25] In particular, these scholars think Luke is much more positive toward the Pharisees. Jesus dines in the homes of Pharisees (only in Luke; 7:36–50; 11:37–39; 14:1–6). They sometimes seem positively inclined toward Jesus (13:31; 19:39). Rather than lumping them all in a single pot like Mark does, Luke can differentiate that only "some Pharisees" were involved in certain conflicts (6:2). And rather than seeking to "kill" Jesus (Mark 3:6), Luke's parallel says they only looked for "what to do" (6:11). Like Mark, but unlike Matthew, Luke's Pharisees are not involved in the events surrounding the arrest and trial (though, according to Acts, Luke was aware that the Sanhedrin included Pharisees).

However, to say that Luke is "very different" toward Pharisees is hardly accurate.[26] They are still the clear and major opponents of Jesus prior to the passion week. Luke adds the devastating judgment, "they

24. So Pickup, "Matthew's and Mark's Pharisees," 89–108.
25. For example, Brawley, *Luke-Acts and the Jews*; and Sanders, *Jews in Luke-Acts*.
26. See, for example, Carroll, "Luke's Portrayal of the Pharisees," 604–21.

rejected God's purpose for themselves" by refusing John's baptism (7:30). They are still called hypocrites and lovers of money, and Jesus pronounces "woes" against them. Luke reproduces six of Mark's nine conflict episodes with Pharisees.[27] And he adds numerous negatively charged interactions with Pharisees not found in Mark.[28]

Luke is not so much different as differentiated in his portrayal. Whereas the Pharisees function as a more or less undifferentiated mass, as "flat" characters, in Mark and Matthew, Luke differentiates between some Pharisees and other Pharisees. On the whole they oppose Jesus and "reject God's purpose," but Luke lets us see that there were exceptions. This opens the door for his portrayal in Acts, where Gamaliel gives aid (5:34–39), Pharisees are included among the followers of Jesus (15:5), and one notable Pharisee, Paul, is a central Christian hero (23:6; 26:5).

Gospel of John

John's portrayal of the Pharisees has some striking differences from the Synoptics as well as considerable overlap.[29] The elements of similarity include:

- opposition to Jesus, including rejection of his message; yet there is also
- division over response to Jesus, that is some believe;
- criticism of Sabbath healing;
- the Pharisees were influential teachers; and they are
- absent from trial and crucifixion scenes (though involved in the arrest).

The differences, however, have spurred considerable debate. First, John consistently pairs Pharisees with the chief priests as the two groups who form the decision-making body for Israel (7:32, 45; 11:47, 57; 18:3). Gone are the scribes,[30] elders, and Sadducees. Their authority is not

---

27. He omits entirely the divorce conflict. Pharisaic presence is not explicit in the "taxes" episode (20:19ff), but those the scribes and priests send to test Jesus are described as "pretending to be righteous" (v. 20), which could refer to Pharisees.

28. Healing of the paralytic (5:17); Pharisees "rejected God's purpose for themselves" in not accepting John's baptism (7:29–35); incident with woman anointing Jesus takes place in Pharisees' home (7:36–50); "woes" (11:39–45; from Q); meal and sabbath-healing controversy in Pharisees' home (14:1–6); "lovers of money" (16:14); question re. when kingdom is coming (17:20–21); parable of Pharisee and tax-collector (18:9–14).

29. A good overview is in Saldarini, *Pharisees, Scribes, and Sadducees*, 187–98.

30. Scribes occur in 8:3, but this is part of a non-Johannine interpolation not found in the earliest MSS.

merely informal as in the Synoptics, but now formal, since they can send delegations of priests and Levites (1:24) and temple police (7:32; 18:3) and determine who is or is not allowed into a synagogue (9:22; 12:42). In John, the Pharisees seem to be in charge. Second, the Pharisees are predominantly headquartered in Jerusalem where most of their conflicts with Jesus occur. This is quite different from the Galilean focus in the Synoptics. This difference should not, however, be overplayed, since Jesus is also known to have been active in Galilee in John (e.g., 4:1–3; 7:1),[31] but it is a clear difference of geographical focus. Third, mostly gone are the *halakhic* disputes. Instead, the Pharisees, along with "the Jews" and the chief priests mainly interact with Jesus regarding his identity. For instance, in the Sabbath healing narrated in chapter 9, there is no argument over what Torah does or does not permit on Sabbath (central to the Synoptic narrative), but the opponents dispute over whether Jesus is a prophet from God or not. Nowhere do the Pharisees engage Jesus as a worthy teacher-competitor (as in the Synoptics), as an equal.

These differences are best explained by recognizing that John has shaped his narrative to a much greater extent than the Synoptics in light of his own later situation.[32] This is why he speaks even more often of "the Jews," referring sometimes to the Jewish populace, but most often to the Jerusalem leadership.[33] By the latter part of the first-century, when John's Gospel was finalized, groups like the Essenes, the Zealots, and the Sadducees had largely disappeared. Instead, the Pharisees and the priests remained with increasing influence. This was also a period of increasing antagonism between mainstream Judaism and the Jewish Jesus movement, leading eventually to an expulsion of Jesus-followers from synagogues. Thus, for John's late first-century audience "the Jews" were those spokespersons for Jewish leadership opposed to the Jesus movement. This means that some of the differences we noted above, especially the formal authority and the focus on Jesus' identity, tell us more about John's later audience and situation than the original situation in the 30s. For that reason, we will want to be more cautious in simply adopting John's perspective when describing the historical Pharisees.

---

31. According to 4:3 Jesus "went back once more" (NIV) to Galilee, hinting at earlier activity there. A weaker Gk MS tradition omits "once more [*palin*]," eliminating the idea that Jesus had earlier been in Galilee.

32. For this argument, made by many others, see Brown, *The Gospel according to John*, 1:lxx–lxxv; and Keener, *Gospel of John*, 194–228, 431–33.

33. See Von Wahlde, "Johannine 'Jews,'" 33–60.

Modern Study of Jesus and the Pharisees[34]

Earlier generations had it much easier. They knew who the Pharisees were (hypocritical legalists), and thus knew also how Jesus formed the perfect contrast. Now that we have a more historically accurate view of ancient Judaism and of the Pharisees (genuinely pious and covenantally non-legalistic), one that is not such a contrast to Jesus, the question as to their relationship and root disagreements is more complex. Of course, there are still plenty of scholars who see Jesus as unalterably and radically opposed to the Pharisees and their view of Torah-obedience, their *halakhah*.[35] If nothing more, a surface reading of the Gospels shouts this conclusion ("you hypocrites"). On the other side, and perhaps more surprisingly, more and more writers think Jesus was in many ways actually pretty close to the Pharisees. He, too, stressed the importance of radical obedience to Torah, even its jots and tittles (Matt 5:17–20). Some would go so far as to say he was himself a Pharisee, or at least a sympathizer to its aims.[36] Regarding the unmistakable opposition between Jesus and the Pharisees as portrayed in the Gospels, it was either exaggeration or an invention of the early church. This last point (invention) has become commonplace in studies of the Gospel Pharisees, so we will return to it below ("authenticity"). Somewhere between these two poles (complete disagreement, complete harmony) lies the position of this study. Jesus shared with the Pharisees (and with most other Jews) the vast majority of his beliefs and practice. He even shared with the Pharisees, in particular, a commitment to the careful interpretation of and obedience to Torah's commands. We find him disputing not over *whether* one should keep Sabbath, tithe produce, observe purity, etc., but over precisely *how* one should carry out these commandments; that is, over *halakhah*. Halakhic disputes could become ferocious, sometimes involving name-calling, exclusion, etc. This goes a long way toward explaining their conflicts, but not quite far enough. For one thing, Jesus was not crucified for *halakhic* disagreements. Yet, if we probe more deeply *why* Jesus opposed the *halakhah* of the Pharisees and they his, we may discover that these *halakhic* disputes arose from precisely the deeper concerns that would eventually

---

34. See now Sievers and Levine, *Pharisees*, which appeared too late for incorporation into this study.

35. "The historical Jesus was in reality both anti-Halachah and anti-Torah." Lambrecht, "Jesus and the Law," 77.

36. Best known here is Hyam Maccoby who argues carefully that Jesus was "a typical Pharisee," in fact "the most recognizable Pharisee in the whole of first-century Jewish literature." Maccoby, *Jesus the Pharisee*, quotations pp. 119, 141. See also Amos, *Hypocrites or Heroes?*, esp. 164–68.

lead to the cross. Here I will note once again these deeper disagreements, which I will try to fill out in the chapters to come.

- Jesus disagreed as to time. Now is when Israel's God is breaking into human history to restore and redeem his people. "The kingdom of God is at hand" (Mark 1:15).
- Jesus disagreed as to hermeneutic. The interpretive lens for understanding all the commandments is God's merciful nature and love for his human creation. "The Sabbath was made for human beings" (Mark 2:27).
- Jesus disagreed as to authority. Instead of the "tradition of the elders," his own teaching was the locus of authority. "But I say to you" (Matt 5:22).
- Jesus disagreed as to his own role and identity. God had authorized him to teach Israel his ways in these last days. "Something [i.e., someone] greater than the temple" and "greater than Solomon" is here (Matt 12:6, 42). He is the "son of man" who is "lord of the Sabbath" (Mark 2:28).

These last comments bring us to the crucial issue of the authenticity of the Gospel stories, their historical reliability. My own stance throughout this investigation is that these accounts do give us access to what Jesus of Nazareth in the early part of the first century said and did, and on the flip side, access to the Pharisees with whom Jesus interacted. Readers unfamiliar with the "quest of the historical Jesus" may react to the previous sentence with surprise that anyone would think otherwise.

> New Testament scholars do not, of course, accept the antagonism between the Marcan Jesus and the Jewish leaders as descriptive of "the historical Jesus," but rather as reflective of the subsequent struggles of the early Christian church and the Judaism from which it had just recently separated.[37]

In general these skeptical attitudes regarding historicity in the Gospels are connected with what is called form criticism and the quest of the historical Jesus. When passing along the stories about Jesus, the church of the latter decades of the first century so shaped and re-worded them for relevance to its own needs that it is nearly impossible to peel back these later editorial moves and get to the original words of Jesus. Thus, what we read in the Gospels does not tell us much about the historical Pharisees or Jesus. On one of the most crucial texts on Jesus and purity (Mark 7:1–23, Jesus "declared all

---

37. Malbon, "Jewish Leaders," 262.

foods clean"), John Meier concludes, "With the exception, then, of 7:10–12, nothing goes back to the historical Jesus."[38]

This is a widespread and influential position among NT scholars, and, if correct, would mean these chapters on the Gospel Pharisees are little more than a historical wild goose chase. As noted above, however, I am more confident that the Gospels do give us a reliable window into the actual conflicts between the Pharisees and Jesus. We are not alone in this more confident assessment.[39] "In spite of the polemic orientation of the texts, the value of the Synoptics as sources for the reconstruction of the Pharisees at the time of Jesus must be ranked as high."[40] True, the stories were not written down for decades, but were passed along orally, and we do have evidence that some of these later church situations did influence the telling of the stories.[41] But such understandable adjustments by a story-teller for his/her audience do not mean that the story as a whole was invented for later consumption.[42] Recent studies have shown that such oral traditions were characterized by stability in the core elements alongside variability in secondary elements.[43] Thus, the gist of the story or saying remains constant; ancillary details can vary. For example, it was still a story about a paralytic being lowered through a roof to be healed by Jesus, even if the roof details differed. To give another example, the story of Jesus healing a man with a withered hand in a synagogue in front of Pharisees is told in all three Synoptic Gospels (Mark 3:1–6; Luke 6:6–11; Matt 12:9–14). The core elements are constant: Jesus, man with withered hand, synagogue,

38. Meier, *Marginal Jew*, 4:413.

39. On the whole historical debate concluding for a position close to mine, see Blomberg, *Historical Reliability of the Gospels*.

40. Wilk, "Die synoptischen Evangelien," 107 (author's translation).

41. For example, Mark has the paralytic lowered by his friends through a thatched roof (2:1–12), whereas Luke's version (5:17–26), probably told among later Hellenistic audiences, envisions a tiled roof as in a Roman villa ("let him down . . . through the tiles," v 19). See McCown, "Luke's Translation," 213–16.

42. The form critical explanation that these Pharisee conflict stories were later inventions seems to me inherently unlikely. "So far as we know, healing on the Sabbath, and moreover in a synagogue, no longer played any role in the later 'Hellenistic' churches where, according to Bultmann, these scenes are supposed to have originated. And this holds all the more for tithes, gifts for the temple, handwashing, and other questions of ritual purity, as well as for other topics which Sanders enumerates. Conversely, burning issues [for the later church] . . . like circumcision, table fellowship with the uncircumcised, eating consecrated meat, and drinking libation-wine—are *not* addressed in the Gospels." Hengel and Deines, "E. P. Sanders's 'Common Judaism,'" 7, italics original.

43. Two helpful studies are Dunn, *Jesus Remembered*, 173–254, and Bailey, "Informal Controlled Oral Tradition," 34–54.

Sabbath, healing, question ("is it permissible"), Pharisees, resulting opposition. Ancillary details vary: Luke adds that Jesus was "teaching," that it was the man's "right" hand, and that scribes were also present; Mark includes the silence of the Pharisees, the anger of Jesus and the presence of Herodians; Matthew adds a saying about saving one's sheep.[44]

---

44. Some views of biblical inerrancy cannot tolerate such discrepancies and, thus, are forced to harmonize the differences. My own view is closer to what some term "inerrancy of intent" or "infallibility"; the author's intended point unfailingly gives us what the divine author wished to communicate. Thus, harmonizing the minor discrepancies is less important than discerning what the text is seeking to communicate.

CHAPTER 7

Never on Saturday: Disagreements over Sabbath Rules

JEWS RESTED ONE DAY out of seven, the Sabbath, which ran from Friday sundown to Saturday sundown. The law specified that they should do no work on this holy day. This was one of their most conspicuous behaviors and earned them scorn from their non-Jewish neighbors who saw this as laziness. For Jews, of course, this cessation of normal labor one day out of seven was a key sign of their identity as the obedient people of the one true God.

But even among Jews themselves there were differences about what "thou shalt do no work" actually meant. Jesus understood this differently than many of his Pharisaic compatriots. As far as they were concerned Jesus "does not observe the sabbath" (John 9:16). This surfaces in the Gospels especially over two issues: 1) Does plucking grain qualify as "work," and thus as a violation? 2) Does healing the sick qualify as forbidden Sabbath work?

Readers should be aware that Bible scholars hold widely differing perspectives on Jesus and the Sabbath.[1] Some dispute the historicity of these Sabbath incidents—Jesus was in full agreement with the Pharisees on this point and never broke Pharisaic Sabbath rules or had disputes about such. The Gospel stories are creations of the later church to explain why they didn't keep Sabbath like other Jews. Others think Jesus completely dispensed with Sabbath regulations, either because he rejected the Law altogether as any longer binding, or because he rejected ritual elements of Torah and kept only the moral principles. And still others, including this author, think Jesus did keep the Sabbath, but disputed with Pharisees over what exactly it meant to rest and not work on that day, i.e., over *halakhah*.[2]

---

1. Helpful overview in Bäck, *Jesus of Nazareth and the Sabbath Commandment*, 3–13.

2. See esp. Doering, "Much Ado about Nothing?," 217–41; Doering, "Sabbath Laws

The Gospels portray Jesus as a Sabbath-keeper. He visited the synagogue on Sabbath (Mark 1:21; 3:1; 6:2; Luke 4:31; 13:10). This was, in fact, his "custom" (Luke 4:16). This should be no surprise since communal Sabbath gathering was common to those serious about their Jewish faith, and Jesus would have appeared unacceptably deviant to neighbors and the common folk if he was regularly "skipping church." True, some opponents did accuse him of "breaking the sabbath" (John 5:18), but as we will see, this referred to breaking their particular Sabbath regulations, not to general disrespect of the Sabbath itself.

What's a Jew to "Do"? Plucking Grain on Sabbath

All three Synoptic Gospels tell this story of Jesus' hungry disciples in a grainfield on a Sabbath (Mark 2:23-28; Luke 6:1-5; Matt 12:1-8). In Mark's narrative this is the fourth in a collection of five controversy stories with scribes or Pharisees (2:1—3:6).[3]

1. Scribes accuse Jesus of blasphemy for telling the healed paralytic his sins are forgiven (2:1–12)
2. Pharisaic scribes object to Jesus eating with toll collectors and sinners (2:15–17)
3. Why Jesus doesn't fast like the Pharisees (2:18–22)
4. *Pharisees accuse Jesus of breaking the Sabbath by plucking grain (2:23–28)*
5. Pharisees angered because Jesus heals on the Sabbath (3:1–6)

Jesus and his disciples are traveling on the Sabbath and pass through grainfields. The disciples (not Jesus apparently) begin to pluck grain from the heads. Some Pharisees are present to see this, although we are not told how it is they happen to be present (traveling with Jesus? watching him?). They challenge Jesus regarding the disciples' action, which they claim is "not permitted" on Sabbath. Jesus, then, springs to his disciples defense.

What precisely was their alleged Sabbath violation?[4] The OT forbids "work" on Sabbath (Exod 20:8-11; Deut 5:12-16), and Exod 34:21 extends

---

in the New Testament Gospels," 207–53; and Doering, *Schabbat*.

3. Luke follows this sequence closely (5:17—6:11). Matthew splits the sequence, placing the first three controversies in ch. 9 (vv. 1–17) and last two in ch. 12 (vv. 1–14). Both differ from Mark at points regarding the identity of the opponents. On this Markan collection, see Dewey, *Markan Public Debate*.

4. Among the many suggestions are 1) the disciples were stealing the grain, 2) they

"work" to include planting and harvesting. Jews serious about obeying God couldn't stop with such general guidelines, of course. What about cultivating the field? (Jub 50:12 says "no.") What about eating right from the plant or stalk without "harvesting"? What about eating grain that falls on the ground? To this latter situation, Qumran's *Damascus Document* allowed it only if such grain was "lost [i.e., perished] in the field" (CD 10:22–23). The Talmud shows the later (post-70 CE) rabbis further systematizing thirty-nine types of forbidden work along with additional sub-types.[5]

As if all these possibilities aren't confusing enough, Luke's version may suggest the issue was food preparation, since he says they "rubbed them [the heads of grain] in their hands, and ate them" (6:1). While eating was allowed on Sabbath, food preparation was not (Exod 16; 35:2–3), for which reason Jews usually tried to prepare their Sabbath meals before sundown Friday. The Pharisees may have thought Jesus and his disciples failed to think ahead and get their Sabbath meal ready in time, and now on the Sabbath had to begin getting their meal ready.[6]

Thus, whichever of these options we find most convincing, the Pharisees' objection represented a fairly typical Jewish attempt to spell out the meaning of the Sabbath work-prohibition. The disciples were "plucking heads of grain," they were engaged in some form of reaping or Sabbath meal preparation considered by others to be a violation of the commandment. The Pharisees were certainly not unique in their concern, nor were they being picayune or legalistic. Like most serious Jews, they were trying to take obedience to God's will seriously. Nor were Jesus and the disciples ignoring the Sabbath prohibition, they simply understood its implications differently.

This episode is then primarily "a question of *halakha*, of what is legally permitted or prohibited."[7] The phrasing of the question points in this direction[8] as does the way Jesus responds. He takes the Pharisees' question of Sabbath *halakhah* seriously and, in good rabbinic fashion, poses a

---

were making a path (= work), 3) they were walking too far (= work), 4) they were consuming the new grain before the wave offering from it had been made. The Pharisees themselves focus only on "plucking grain."

5. On these and other Jewish Sabbath regulations relative to this "plucking" incident, see Doering, "Sabbath Laws in the New Testament Gospels," 208–20. For rabbinic rulings, see m. Šabb. 7:2; y. Šabb. 7.9b; and cf. Str-B 1.617.

6. Suggested by Kazen, *Scripture, Interpretation, or Authority?*, 101.

7. Lane, *Gospel according to Mark*, 115.

8. *Ouk eksestin* (not permitted) was the phrase widely used for such *halakhic* legal definitions. Josephus, for example, wished to write a book "concerning the laws, that is, why according to them we are permitted [*eksestin*] to do some things while we are forbidden to do others" (*A.J.* 20.268).

counter-example from Scripture.[9] "Have you never read what David did when he and his companions were hungry and in need of food? He entered the house of God, when Abiathar was high priest, and ate the bread of the Presence, which it is not lawful for any but the priests to eat, and he gave some to his companions" (Mark 2:25-26). This retort seems at first glance to deal more with permission to eat sacred foods than with Sabbath work and has led to all kinds of suggestions as to why Jesus would bring up this particular story.[10] Since Mark's conclusion focuses on Jesus' authority ("the Son of Man is lord even of the Sabbath," v. 28), it makes sense that Jesus would pick a story in which David had authority to bend Sabbath law in the interests of human need.[11]

Jesus moves from stating a Scripture precedent to a Scripture principle. "The sabbath was made for humankind, and not humankind for the sabbath" (Mark 2:27). Since a similar-sounding idea can be found in rabbinic sources,[12] the general sentiment humanizing Sabbath law was probably not new with Jesus, and the Maccabean relaxing of Sabbath law to preserve life in warfare points in the same direction (1 Macc 2:41). Jesus reminds his opponents that the very creation of Sabbath by God in the beginning was for the benefit of his human creation [Gk. *dia ton anthrōpon*, for the sake of humanity] and not the other way round.

So, if Jesus and many Pharisees agreed on the importance of Sabbath law and *halakhah*, and on Sabbath as created by God for the benefit of his human creation, where was the nub of their disagreement? Why did these Pharisees say "you can't do that on Sabbath," and Jesus respond, "yes, you can"? The answer lies in Mark's conclusion to the story. "So the Son of Man is lord even of the sabbath" (Mark 2:28). Christian theology has often seen this as Jesus' own claim to set the rules as the divine "Son of Man," the

---

9. Contra France who thinks Jesus means "to call in question the whole scribal industry of Sabbath-regulation." France, *Gospel of Matthew*, s.v. Matt 12:1-14.

10. E.g., David broke the law, so can Jesus. Human hunger trumps Sabbath rules.

11. Although neither the story in 1 Sam 21 nor Jesus' brief quotation of it refers to Sabbath, the bread David ate (the "showbread") was placed fresh every Sabbath in the holy of holies in the tabernacle (Lev 24:8). Some Jews later connected this and placed the David incident on a Sabbath (b. Menaḥ. 95b).

Matthew has Jesus add that Torah itself allows the temple priests to break the Sabbath work command (probably by their work of offering sacrifices), yet remain guiltless (12:5-6). And "something greater than the temple is here," i.e., Jesus as agent of the dawning kingdom of God. The point here in Matthew is essentially the same as that in Mark; Jesus is authorized to interpret the Sabbath command, and in this case to give mercy preference over sacrifice (Matt 12:6b).

12. "the Sabbath was delivered to you, not you to the Sabbath," Mek. Exod. 31:13-14; see also b. Yoma 85b.

Lord himself. As Yahweh incarnate, he is Lord of the Sabbath. This is certainly how the later Trinitarian church viewed matters, and may possibly be hinted at if this verse is Mark's own conclusion rather than the words of Jesus.[13] If, however, as I think more likely, this is Jesus' own conclusion, such a near Trinitarian claim almost certainly overstates Jesus' intent.[14] The Pharisees would hardly have let such a seeming blasphemy go without comment. Rather, in the Synoptics Jesus normally veils his self-revelations so that even at the very end, at his trial, the authorities are still trying to pin down who he is actually claiming to be (Mark 14:55–64). This "lord of the Sabbath" saying is likewise such a veiled expression. In Hebrew *bar enash* (lit. "son of a human being") can be synonymous with a human being as in Dan 7:13, but it can also be a figure invested with extraordinary authority as in Dan 7:14 ("To him was given dominion and glory . . . an everlasting dominion that shall not pass away"), and later verge on a messianic title. Likewise, "lord [*kyrios*]" could be heard as "sir" or "master," or as a reference to God himself. Jesus' response works quite well on the purely human level. David was a human being, a "son of man," and demonstrated how the Sabbath was for the benefit of people, not their harm. He was "master of the Sabbath" in that instance. Yet, in light of the consistent Synoptic pressure on Jesus from the Jewish leaders regarding his authority, Jesus' double-edged language contained a veiled claim to be the authoritative interpreter of the will of God, of Torah and the commandments.

How About Healing?

In addition to picking grain on the Sabbath, the Pharisees disagreed with Jesus over whether he should be healing people on the Sabbath.[15] A disabled man ("with a withered hand") is present in the local synagogue and Pharisees are "watch[ing] him to see whether he would cure him on the sabbath, so that they might accuse him" (3:2). Mark and Luke use a word for this "watching [*paratēreō*]" that could be translated "lie in wait for" and hints at their opposition from the start. This opposition reaches a climax at

---

13. So Lane, *Gospel According to Mark*, 118–19.

14. The question of Jesus' own Christology, his perception of his own role and identity, is far too large to engage in this book. For a balanced introduction to the issues, see Bird, *Are you the One who is to come?* Bird argues that Jesus understood his role and identity in messianic terms, even if he may not have referred to himself as "the messiah." And on the Trinitarian question—Did Jesus know he was divine?—see Wright, *Challenge of Jesus*, ch. 5, "Jesus & God" (96–125).

15. As elsewhere Luke has "scribes and Pharisees" united in opposition (5:21, 30; 11:53; 15:2).

the end of this pericope as the Pharisees "immediately conspired with the Herodians against him, how to destroy him" (Mark 3:6).[16]

Just as in the grain-plucking episode, the Pharisees want to catch Jesus violating the Sabbath work prohibition, or more accurately, to charge him with doing what their *halakhah* does not permit on the Sabbath. But what exactly was the Pharisaic viewpoint on this?[17] Healing *per se* was not a major topic of *halakhic* discussion.[18] Instead, numerous texts detail instances when saving life was permissible on the Sabbath, implying that apart from such an emergency situation these actions would not be permissible. We have already seen an early example of this when self-defense in war was deemed an allowable exception in Maccabean times (1 Macc 2:29-41). Dropping medicine in a patient's throat was allowed by some later rabbis (not all apparently) when there was any possibility of danger to life (m. Yoma 8:6), as was a midwife's effort to deliver a baby on Sabbath or the performance of a circumcision when the child's eighth day fell on a Sabbath.[19] One might prevent an animal's suffering on the Sabbath by providing food and water, but not do the work of lifting it from the pit.[20]

> Other groups, however, like the DSS community maintained stricter regulations.
> The wet-nurse should not lift the baby to go out or come in on the Sabbath. No-one should press his servant or his maidservant or his employee on the Sabbath. . . . No-one should help an animal give birth on the Sabbath day. . . . And if he makes it fall into a well or a pit, he should not take it out on the Sabbath. And any living man who falls into a place of water or into a place[21] (. . .), no-one should take him out with a ladder or a rope or a utensil. (CD XI.11-17)

---

16. Matthew and Luke omit the presence of the Herodians. Earlier commentators thought the Pharisees intended to seek a death penalty for Sabbath-breaking as in Exod 31:15 (so Jeremias, Pesch, et al.). By the first century, however, most groups sought ways to ameliorate this extreme penalty. See Collins, *Mark*, 207-8. More likely, any charge was simply intended to counter Jesus' growing popularity as a teacher by exposing him as a Sabbath-breaker.

17. See esp. Doering, "Sabbath Laws in the New Testament Gospels," 226-53.

18. "*No pre-Tannaitic source* apart from the Gospel tradition mentions healing at all as forbidden on the Sabbath." Doering, "Sabbath Laws in the New Testament Gospels," 228, italics original.

19. m. Šabb. 18:3; 19:2; cf. Str-B 1.623-29; 2.533-34.

20. "An animal that is fallen into a cistern — one may provide it with food where it is, lest it dies." (t. Šabb. 14[15]:3 [MS Vienna]); cited in Doering, "Sabbath Laws in the New Testament Gospels," 232.

21. 4Q268, fragment 3 reads "or a well."

For some, "intentional healing was considered forbidden, while 'by the way' cures, such as therapeutic side effects of nutrition, were approved of."[22] The very fact that these texts must detail *permissible healing actions* implies there were healing actions which were impermissible.

Thus, the precise contours of Pharisaic *halakhah* on this subject must remain somewhat unclear to us, but such a straightforward non-emergency healing on the Sabbath as we have in the Markan account would for many have been impermissible as seems clearly to be the case in the Markan incident.[23] Jesus' healing in the synagogue was intentional, and the man's life was not in danger.[24] His question, "Is it lawful to do good or to do harm on the sabbath, to save life or to kill?" (Mark 3:4), appears to intersect with this *halakhic* debate which focused on exceptions for preserving life.

As with the previous grain-field conflict (2:23–28), here also Jesus focuses on the freedom to do good ("to do good . . . to save life") on the Sabbath, rather than on the restrictive intent of the Sabbath command. In all these conflicts, the issue is not whether one must keep the Sabbath command (that is taken for granted by all parties), but over the proper interpretation of Sabbath-keeping (i.e., over what exactly is and is not covered, over *halakhah*).[25] It is not quite correct in my view to say Jesus "overrides" the Sabbath prohibition in cases of saving life or doing good. What he does is exercise authority to interpret the meaning of the commandment. His claim is that he is *not breaking the commandment* by his actions. It is no surprise that such a direct challenge to the Pharisees' *halakhah* and, thus, to their leadership of the people would meet with a hostile reaction.

This also explains the surprisingly harsh turn in this incident. Jesus' question to the Pharisees—"Is it lawful to do good or to do harm on the sabbath, to save life or to kill?"—is met with stony silence. If this had been nothing more than a typical *halakhic* debate, surely the Pharisees might have responded with something like, "Yes, it is sometimes permissible to preserve life on the Sabbath, but this situation does not rise to a life-threatening emergency." The Pharisees' silence and Jesus' resulting anger

22. Doering, "Sabbath Laws in the New Testament Gospels," 229. See m. Šabb. 14:3, 4; 22.6c; t. Šabb. 12[13]:8–13.

23. So Doering, "Sabbath Laws in the New Testament Gospels," 228–29. The synagogue leader in Luke 13:10–16, as well as the Pharisees in John 9:15–16, agree that Sabbath healing is impermissible. Some interpreters see no Sabbath violation, since Jesus did not "work" but merely spoke a word of healing to the man (Flusser, *Jesus*, 61–64; Vermes, *Jesus the Jew*, 25; and Sanders, *Jesus*, 264-67).

24. Though Luke's addition that it was his "right" hand, the more crucial hand for most activities, heightens the seriousness (6:6).

25. Nor is it helpful to pit morality against ritual as many do; for example, Johnson, *Gospel of Luke*, 102.

reveal a deeper-level debate in progress. If the Pharisees really believed the Sabbath was fundamentally for Israel's benefit, for the preservation of life and for the good of human beings, they would not resist Jesus' healing ministry, even on the Sabbath. In Jesus' view, their resistance points not merely to *halakhic* disagreement, but to "hardness of heart" (v. 5).[26] By applying this phrase to the Pharisees Jesus places them in the role of stubborn and rebellious Israel.[27]

We have noted above some slight differences in the parallel accounts of Matt 12:9-14 and Luke 6:6-11, but one addition in Matthew's version deserves particular comment. To the Pharisees' question—"Is it lawful to cure on the sabbath?" (12:10)—Jesus responds with a counter-question framed as a story.

> Suppose one of you has only one sheep and it falls into a pit on the sabbath; will you not lay hold of it and lift it out? How much more valuable is a human being than a sheep! (12:11-12a)

Without waiting for an answer, Jesus draws the conclusion, "So it is lawful to do good on the sabbath" (v. 12b). As seen in the CD quote above, the Qumran community would probably have rejected this conclusion. The Pharisees apparently disagree with the DSS on this point, but are unwilling to give a yes answer, since that would undercut their objection to Jesus healing on the Sabbath. At least it would undercut their position in the eyes of the Galilean synagogue crowd for whom such a story-question was less a matter of technical *halakhah*, and more a matter of rural commonsense.[28]

John, Mud in the Eye, and a Blind Beggar in the Temple

John's Gospel does not tell the Synoptic stories we have examined above, but it does include one Sabbath healing that the Synoptics don't (John 9:1-12). It takes place in the temple environs (8:59; 9:7) when Jesus uses mud on the eyes of a congenitally blind beggar to heal him (9:6-7). Unlike the Synoptic Sabbath-healing controversies, where the focus is on what

---

26. And in the parallel instance in Luke 13:10-16 to hypocrisy (v. 15).

27. The phrase stems from the OT prophets who accused Israel of such "hardness of heart" because they refused to listen to Yahweh (Jer 3:17; 7:24; 9:13; 11:18; 13:10; 16:12; Ps 81:13; Deut 29:18; also Isa 6:10), and is used in the NT elsewhere for Israel's refusal to acknowledge Jesus as Yahweh's messiah (Rom 11:7, 25; 2 Cor 3:14). In the current episode, Jesus views the Pharisees as refusing to recognize that Yahweh wishes Sabbath to be a gift of joy and life-giving goodness to Israel. Instead, they stubbornly insist on keeping their restrictive *halakhah*.

28. So Meier, *Marginal Jew*, 4:263.

is permitted on Sabbath, John focuses on Jesus' identity—is he from God or not? The healed man is brought to the Pharisees who interrogate him about the healing. This produces a division among the Pharisees, with some saying Jesus is not from God, he is a sinner, since he breaks the law (does not keep Sabbath), while others take Jesus' side since he healed the blind man (v. 16). Just as Luke differentiates (not all Pharisees are bad), so John confirms the Pharisees were divided over Jesus.[29]

Here is a great case-study in how John tells the same basic gospel, yet tells it so very differently from the Synoptics. Both the Synoptics and John know of conflict between Jesus and Pharisees over Sabbath healing. Like the Synoptics, John knows that the conflict had to do with Mosaic Sabbath law (9:16, 28), that some Pharisees thought Jesus' behavior constituted breaking this law (at least from their own perspective), and that not all Pharisees opposed Jesus in such matters. And, like the Synoptics, John sees this as one among many types of conflict that lead some of the Pharisees to mortal opposition. But we should note how differently John tells such a story. It takes place in Jerusalem, not Galilee; the conflict is not over Bible interpretation but messianic identity, which Jesus proclaims clearly to the blind man; and the narrative leads explicitly to either belief (the healed beggar) or unbelief (some Pharisees). In addition, the complete narrative is quite long (forty-one verses) compared to generally compact Synoptic accounts, and it is delightful in its use of irony and humor.[30] But in the end the point of it all is the same: Jesus is the authoritative interpreter of Moses.

What Sort of Sabbath Folks Are These Pharisees?

To those of us not familiar with a culture of Jewish Sabbath-keeping, these Pharisaic objections could easily seem like unnecessary nit-picking, like some sort of legalistic insistence on doing everything "just right" in order to please God. After trying to walk in their sandals a bit, however, we recognize they turn out to be fairly typical first century Jews serious about their faith who were trying to love and listen to their God. They challenge Jesus regarding Sabbath-healing and plucking grain, because they perceive such action as evidence of disloyalty to God's word. In their eyes

---

29. On the Pharisees in John as divided re. Jesus, see Poplutz, "Pharisees: A House Divided," 116–26.

30. One can almost hear the Pharisees sputtering in frustrated rage when the healed beggar says "Do you also want to become his disciples?" (John 9:27), and then proceeds to teach these supposed teachers of Israel (vv. 30–34).

Jesus is being a bad Jew and leading others astray. There is no reason for Christians to trash-talk them for this.

But they certainly do not come off scot-free in these episodes. Jesus accuses them of being hard-hearted and implicitly compares them with the worst of Israel's rebellious leadership in the past. In Jesus' eyes their hard-heartedness and rebellion rest essentially in their refusal to heed the announcement of the inbreaking kingdom of which he is the messenger. Just as Israel consistently refused the message of the prophets, so these Pharisees ignore the words of Jesus. An important element of this prophet's message concerns the mercy and forgiveness of the heavenly sovereign toward the poor and damaged among his people. Thus, he stresses the beneficent side of the Sabbath ("made for human beings") and finds Scripture examples in which human need (David's hunger) guides the application of Sabbath law. The Pharisees would not necessarily disagree as to the value of human beings and their needs in God's eyes, but they will not follow Jesus in giving these values such priority in interpretation.

CHAPTER 8

Eating with Sinners: Dinner with Levi the Toll-Collector

ALONGSIDE SABBATH ISSUES, JESUS' eating habits turn out to be one of the main sticking points with the Pharisees. They complain that he is "eating with tax collectors and sinners" (Mark 2:13–17; Matt 9:10–13; Luke 5:27–32). We will follow Mark's narrative but include comments on the parallels in Matthew and Luke, which vary in significant ways.

Meal Conflict (Mark 2:13–17)

We noted in the previous chapter that Mark collected five controversy stories between Jesus and scribes/Pharisees (2:1—3:6). The dinner dispute is the second of the five. This series of conflict stories in Mark is meant to show the rising opposition of the Pharisees, since it ends with, "The Pharisees went out and immediately conspired with the Herodians against him, how to destroy him" (Mark 3:6).[1] The alliance shows that the Pharisees were seeking some sort of official or public influence against Jesus.

Following the call of Levi the toll-collector near the sea of Capernaum (2:13–14), Jesus and his disciples dine in Levi's home with other toll-collectors and sinners.[2] In this first mention of Pharisees in Mark, he

---

1. The Herodians were probably "people associated with Herod's court, either as officials, partisans or men of standing and influence allied with him." Saldarini, *Pharisees, Scribes, and Sadducees,* 149n15. See also Rowley, "Herodians in the Gospels," 14–27.

2. Mark's Greek text is ambiguous as to whether "his home" refers to Levi's or Jesus' domicile. Both have been argued. Luke's version removes the ambiguity (5:29). For a convincing argument from social-scientific perspective that Mark intends Levi's house, see May, "Mark 2:15."

refers to scribes who were aligned with the Pharisees.³ These Pharisaic scribes were apparently not invited to the meal, and probably wouldn't have attended anyway, but they observe Jesus and his disciples attending ("saw that he was eating") and question the disciples about Jesus' praxis.⁴ Upon hearing them, Jesus himself responds on behalf of his disciples with an aphorism that focuses on his vocation: "Those who are well have no need of a physician, but those who are sick; I have come to call not the righteous but sinners" (Mark 2:17).⁵

But over what exactly was this disagreement? From Jesus' answer, one might get the impression that he wanted to "call sinners" and heal them, and the Pharisees did not; instead, they cared only about their own in-group, "the righteous," and ignored the rest. This interpretation fit well with the older view that Pharisees despised the common people, the *am ha'aretz*.⁶ Such Pharisaic disdain of other Jews has turned out, however, not to be the case historically, or at least has been much overblown. In fact, Jesus himself will castigate their evangelistic zeal (Matt 23:15, "cross sea and land to make a single convert"), and later Paul will be sent as a Pharisaic emissary to bring Jewish sinners to repentance (Acts 9:1–2).

Excursus: The Pharisees and the Common Folk, the *am ha'aretz*

Until fairly recently the Pharisees were thought to disdain the mass of non-Pharisaic Jews who did not observe Torah carefully or were not in accord with the right *halakhah*. This opinion was built largely upon John 7:49 ("this crowd, which does not know the law—they are accursed") and numerous

---

3. Luke has two groups, scribes and Pharisees (5:30), while Matthew has only Pharisees (9:11). See pp. 81–82 above on the identity of scribes.

4. Slightly different in Luke, where the Pharisees address the disciples *about their own behavior* ("why do you eat," 5:30).

5. Sanders notes that Mark's Jesus says simply "call sinners" without adding "to repentance" as in Luke. Such unconditional forgiveness with no required change of lifestyle is, he thinks, what particularly angered the Pharisees. Sanders, *Jesus and Judaism*, 206. This is unlikely to have been Mark's intent, however, since Jesus' initial message in Mark's Gospel is "repent and believe" (Mark 1:15).

6. Hebrew for "people of the land." In the OT it referred to the common people of Judah or Israel, esp. as distinguished from princes or priests (e.g., Ezek 45:22). At some point it took on a negative caste, such that the Talmud uses the phrase for uneducated rustics who are careless with respect to Torah. In modern Hebrew or Yiddish vernacular it refers to a boor or ignoramus.

later rabbinic passages that attested to an elitist and critical attitude. "The garments of the Am-haarez are unclean for the Perushim" (m. Ḥag. 2.7). "A Chaber does not go as a guest to an Am-haarez nor receive him as a guest within his walls" (m. Demai 2.3). This exclusivity was seen as the reason for their name, *perushim*, separatists (i.e., from unclean things and persons). Thus, as Schürer summarizes,

> In the eyes of Pharisaism however the former term [*chaber* = Pharisee] is restricted to the circle of those, who strictly observe the law together with the entire [tradition of the elders]. All besides are Am-haarez, and therefore do not belong to the true congregation of Israel.[7]

This near-consensus view is, however, almost certainly wrong. First, it cannot be squared with the popularity and respect for the Pharisees among the masses as seen in Josephus (pp. 43-46). Many of the non-priestly and non-scribal Pharisees lived and worked among the *am ha'aretz*. They were "one of them" and eager to influence them toward more careful and complete obedience. They probably viewed the practice and scriptural knowledge of the masses as inferior to their own, but such need not evoke disdain of one's neighbors.

Second, John 7:49 does testify to the authorities' disgust and anger in this heated instance, but not to a general Pharisaic disdain of the *am ha'aretz* ("crowd [*ochlos*]" in John). The stage is set when the chief priests and Pharisees seek to have Jesus arrested in the temple (7:32). The arresting officers back off when they see how impressed with Jesus' teaching many in the crowd are (7:40-44). The Pharisees are understandably enraged when they hear what has happened, and it is then that they say to the temple police, "Surely you have not been deceived too, have you? Has any one of the authorities or of the Pharisees believed in him? But this crowd, which does not know the law—they are accursed" (7:47-49). This is their frustrated and angry outburst that the officers were cowed by the opinions of people who were not sufficient experts in Bible interpretation. The common folk certainly "knew the law" in the general sense. The Pharisees were giving vent to their frustration, not making a careful observation. They did, of course, view themselves as having the correct

---

7. Schürer, *History of the Jewish People*, 2:23-28.

halakhah and opinion of Jesus, and were convinced that others, including Jesus, were failing to understand and practice Torah properly. However, the accusation of a sectarian and elitist attitude (only we are the true Israel) goes beyond the evidence. The same could have been said of Jesus himself, who considered only those who adhered to his new teaching to be part of the renewed Israel, yet we do not move on to accuse him of an attitude of disdain and elitism. Both he and the Pharisees viewed the masses as sheep without a shepherd, needing instruction.

Third, the supposedly strongest evidence for this Pharisaic disdain comes from the rabbinic literature. However, this literature actually evinces "radically differing opinions" toward the *am ha'aretz*.[8] Alongside the negative characterizations (noted above) are equally positive ones. Simeon, a respected disciple of Johanan ben Zakkai, was an *am ha'aretz* (t. 'Abod. Zar. 3:10). Eating together was fine (m. Ber. 7:1), as was intermarriage (t. 'Abod. Zar. 3:10; t. Demai 2:16–17). Although true that some Talmudic texts suggest such disdain, others paint the opposite picture. That Pharisees in general disdained the *am ha'aretz* cannot be sustained from a fair reading of rabbinic literature, nor the suggestion that such disdain accurately reflects first-century CE conditions.

Returning now to our examination of Mark 2, Johnson and others see separatism versus inclusion as the root of the controversy.[9] The Pharisees sought a pure society separate from the unclean, whereas Jesus pursued accessibility for all persons. This gets closer to the real issue (see below), but the Pharisees' interest in popular influence speaks against separatism as their main motivation in avoiding certain dinner companions. Others suggest the Pharisees thought Jesus was flagrantly violating Jewish common sense. "It was a commonplace of the wisdom tradition that the wise and the righteous should avoid association with the foolish and the wicked."[10]

---

8. For an excellent review of this evidence, see "Am Ha-Areẓ." *Encyclopaedia Judaica*. https://www.encyclopedia.com/religion/encyclopedias-almanacs-transcripts-and-maps/am-ha-arez. Also, Oppenheimer, *'am ha-aretz*.

9. Johnson, *Gospel of Luke*, 99.

10. Collins, *Mark*, 192. See Ps 1; Prov 1; etc.

Instead of, or in addition to such explanations, most interpreters rightly see in the passage a conflict over purity.[11] Because Pharisees were particularly stringent regarding ritual purity at table fellowship, some of them rejected not only eating with gentiles, but even eating with most other Jews, the less stringent (or even non-observant) *am ha'aretz*.[12] Eating with ritually unclean persons like toll-collectors, whose food was also probably unclean, could make the eater unclean as well, and this had to be avoided. Such impurity was contagious (see ch. 9).

Excursus: The Pharisees, ḥaberim, and Table-Fellowship with Non-Pharisees

But what exactly was the stance of Pharisees to having pure table fellowship? The reigning thesis has long been that the Pharisees, although themselves non-priests, sought to apply priestly purity to all Israel.[13] Even ordinary food not destined for sacrifice or priestly consumption was to be eaten in a state of ritual purity. Since the common people, the *am ha'aretz*, were not properly observant of this tradition, Pharisees organized *ḥaburoth*, members-only associations for meal fellowship, where the proper purity could be upheld. The members, the *ḥaberim*, would not eat with non-Pharisees. Rabbinic texts like m. Demai 2.2–3 seem to prove this point.

> He who undertakes to be trustworthy [one who is assumed to tithe all of his produce] tithes (1) what he eats, and (2) what he sells, and (3) what he purchases, and (4) does not accept the hospitality of an *am haares*. R[abbi] Judah says, "Also one who accepts the hospitality of an *am haares* is trustworthy." They said to him, "[If] he is not trustworthy concern hiself [viz., concerning food which he himself eats], how should he be trustworthy concerning that of others [viz., concerning food which he feeds or sells to others]?"

---

11. See Blomberg, *Contagious Holiness*.

12. This view can be found in many commentaries and studies. See, for example, Kilgallen, "Was Jesus Right," 590–600.

13. Schürer, *History of the Jewish People in the Time of Jesus Christ*, 2:22–25. See also works by Jeremias, Finkelstein and more recently, Waubke, "Die talmudische Haberim-Halacha und die Pharisäer," 108–32. A notable early critic of this view was Rivkin. For an overview of the academic debate, see Sanders, *Jewish Law*, 152–66.

He who undertakes to be a *haber* ... (1) does not sell to an *am haares* wet or dry [produce] and (2) does not purchase from him wet [produce], and (3) does not accept the hospitality of an *am haares*, and (4) does not receive [the *am haares*] as his guest while he is wearing his own clothes. (Neusner-Sarason translation)

Jacob Neusner strengthens the arguments for this Pharisaic concern for priestly purity. They were, he concludes, primarily concerned with maintaining the ritual purity of their table fellowship. "Of the 341 individual pericopae [dealing with pre-70 Pharisaic traditions] . . ., no fewer than 229 directly or indirectly pertain to table-fellowship, approximately 67% of the whole."[14] And he explicitly affirms the extension of priestly purity to non-temple settings, i.e., in homes. "Pharisaic table-fellowship required keeping everywhere the laws of ritual purity that normally applied only in the Jerusalem Temple, so Pharisees ate their private meals in the same condition of ritual purity as did the priests of the holy cult."[15] Neusner does not, however, affirm all aspects of the traditional interpretation. He concludes, for example, that the Mishnah text above could *not* be used to reconstruct first-century Pharisaism, and he is, in fact, quite skeptical that any of the Mishnaic passages tell us about the historical first-century Pharisees.[16] On the question of whether Pharisees ate only in their private members-only club settings, Neusner also dissents from the consensus: "The sect ordinarily did not gather as a group at all, but in the home."[17]

Ed Sanders takes exception to elements of Neusner's thesis and the traditional consensus, especially the idea that the Pharisees formed *ḥaburoth* and that they applied to themselves

---

14. Neusner, *Pharisees*, 313.

15. Neusner, *From Politics to Piety*, 67.

16. The cited authority in the Demai text, Rabbi Judah, was most likely Rabbi Judah ben Il'ai who flourished after the first century (c. 130 CE). Thus, the equation of this *ḥaver* with a Pharisee has to be assumed, it is not stated. Neusner himself, in fact, is quite skeptical about the historical value of these traditions, since even these demonstrably "early" traditions had probably already been shaped by later interests. "Even though we have been able to suggest reasons for thinking those disputes accurately convey relatively early traditions about the *themes* of Houses-disputes [Hillel vs Shammai], we cannot at this stage propose that either the form or the substance of the pericopae accurately represents the Houses-disputes of pre-70 times . . . ." Neusner, *Pharisees*, 254.

17. Neusner, "Pharisaic Law in New Testament Times," 340.

priestly purity regulations.[18] He agrees with Neusner and the consensus, however, that Pharisees felt the need to maintain a higher level of purity than other Jews and "would not eat with ordinary people . . . ."[19] Whether these Pharisees then ate in private association meals (consensus) or at home (Sanders), we can leave undecided, since our Gospel story deals only with eating in the home of a non-observant Jew.

Toll collectors like Levi were widely considered compromised Jews, quislings who cooperated with the Romans and their subsidiary rulers, like Herod Antipas in this case, to squeeze their countrymen for personal enrichment.[20] Their unrighteousness had become so proverbial that the Gospels often referred to them in the combination "tax collectors and sinners." "Sinners" refers here not only to the flagrantly wicked (i.e., gentiles, grossly sinful Jews, and apostates) as normally in the OT, but also to those whose behavior marked them as outside the boundaries of a particular faction. We saw this in the early history of the Pharisees during the days of the Maccabees when "renegade" Jews abandoned the covenant and circumcision and "sold themselves to do evil" (1 Macc 1). The Pharisees in Jesus' day considered Jews who consistently ignored purity and other regulations to be "sinners."[21] In the ever-present competition for social honor and standing, Jesus' practice of very liberal table fellowship was a direct challenge to the Pharisees' stricter teaching on the importance of purity and to their influence among the people.[22]

Why did Jesus seemingly flout this concern for purity? Not only the Pharisees, but the Qumran community, and probably only to a slightly lesser extent most serious Jews, were all agreed that Israel's purity according to the law was of great importance. We will deal with Jesus and purity

---

18. Sanders, *Jewish Law*, 131–254, esp. 166–84. For Neusner's response, see Neusner, "Mr Sanders's Pharisees and Mine," 73–95.

19. Sanders, *Jewish Law*, 248.

20. Levi was most likely a collector of duties on transported goods (toll-collector) rather than of direct taxes on income or land (tax-collector). Donahue, "Tax Collectors," 6.337–38. Matt's parallel names the toll collector "Matthew" (9:9). For differing resolutions of the discrepancy, see Porter, "Levi (Person)," 4:295.

21. Contra Sanders's attempt to restrict "sinners" here to disloyal Jews and apostates, Sanders, *Jesus and Judaism*, 174–211. For the view chosen above, see Dunn, *Jesus, Paul, and the Law*, 73–77.

22. On this agonistic competition for honor and status in the Gospels and elsewhere in the ancient world, see Gowler, *Host, Guest, Enemy, and Friend*.

in more detail in the next chapter, but we at least need to give a brief explanation here as to why Jesus contradicted the Pharisaic purity practice at meals so glaringly.

Not infrequently, one hears that Jesus swept away all such ritual concerns, either because he now saw ritual as inherently unimportant ("I desire mercy, not sacrifice"), or because the newly dawning kingdom made such "old" concerns passé. That Jesus sent a healed leper to the priests to "offer for your cleansing what Moses commanded" speaks strongly against this assumption (Mark 1:44). We have been arguing that a large part of Jesus' disagreement with Pharisees was *halakhic*. That is, he actually shared the same concerns—in this case to uphold Torah and its purity laws—but he disagreed on precisely what such laws demanded. The Pharisees interpreted "no work on Sabbath" to mean the disciples ought not to pick and eat grain, Jesus said this could be allowed (and he was claiming the authority to allow this).

In addition to this *halakhic* difference, however, I think there is one further reason for Jesus' disagreement with Pharisees over purity. They saw impurity as transmissible by contact, as contagious. Contact with a corpse made the clean person unclean. Likewise, for a number of reasons—Jewish wisdom, observing *kashrut*, communicable impurity—Pharisees probably generally avoided too much or too close intercourse with non-Pharisees. Jesus seemed supremely indifferent to all this; he ate with tax collectors and sinners at their table and in their home! He seemed to view holiness, or rather his holiness and the holiness of the inbreaking divine rule, as more powerful. Instead of impurity, it was the purity of the kingdom of God that was contagious. Hanna Stettler calls this the "infectious nature of holiness . . . It is in [Jesus] himself, the holy one of God, that God's holiness has arrived which overcomes impurity."[23]

Careful readers will have noted that we said nothing about what is more commonly thought to lie behind this and similar conflicts: the legalism of the Pharisees. And the reason should by this time be clear. Concerns about trying to earn God's favor through good works, through eating the right food with the right people, played no role in the Pharisees' thinking.[24] Their concern was to love the God of Israel by following in his ways. They gave much attention to spelling out these ways. These were their "traditions of the elders," their *halakhah*. Jesus was bringing a new "tradition," a new

---

23. Stettler, *Heiligung bei Paulus*, 164, author's translation. See also, Kazen, *Jesus and Purity Halakhah*, esp. ch. 7, "Impurity and Demonic Threat" (300–39).

24. They did use the language of "merit," but in the sense of a "worthy" person or deed, not in the legalistic sense normally imputed to them. See Egger, *Verdienste vor Gott?*

halakhah, a new spelling out of how one followed in the ways of Torah. His way revolved more fundamentally around mercy and the love of others. Again, this is not to accuse the Pharisees of ignoring that central element of the OT; rather, in Jesus' view they got the balance or the relationship between the letter and the spirit wrong.

And behind all this was the question of authority. Who was authorized to instruct Israel in the proper ways of following Yahweh? Who was authorized to determine how Israel should look? The Pharisees had been major players up to this point, with considerable popular influence. The newcomer was challenging not merely their *halakhah*, but more fundamentally their authority to lead and teach Israel.[25]

On these main lines of interpretation, Matthew (9:10–13) and Luke (5:27–32) agree. Luke, however, heightens the conflict by having the Pharisees "grumble,"[26] whereas in Mark it remains more of a disagreement. Matthew's account also heightens the conflict in two ways. First, this episode comes later in Jesus' Galilean ministry, so the Pharisees are already well-known as adversaries.[27] Second, in the midst of the sayings about healing and calling, Matthew adds: "Go and learn what this means, 'I desire mercy, not sacrifice.'" This is important for Matthew in explaining how Jesus differs from the Pharisees, since he also adds this same quotation from Hos 6:6 to another controversy story with the Pharisees (12:7; picking grain on Sabbath). Originally, in the face of Israel's cultic practice *without ḥesed* [= covenantal faithfulness] (6:4, "your *ḥesed* is like a morning cloud"), Yahweh had said through Hosea that his desire was not for such worship without *ḥesed*, but for *ḥesed* (with, of course, the cult now properly carried out).[28] Hosea promotes the "ideal of an

---

25. This is similar to N. T. Wright's position. Jesus' meal fellowship was anticipatory of the messianic banquet, and involved "open table-fellowship with anyone who shared his agenda, who wanted to be allied with his kingdom-movement." The Pharisees objected strongly to this redefinition of the people of God and of what the God of Israel was doing. Wright, *Jesus and the Victory of God*, 431, also 274.

26. BDAG defines this Greek word (*gogguzein*) "to express oneself in low tones of disapprobation." In a Jewish milieu this would probably evoke Israel's grumbling against Moses in the wilderness (Exod 15:24; 16:2; 17:3; Num 14:2, 29; 16:41). Luke tells another story about a tax-collector, Zacchaeus, against whom unidentified bystanders also "grumble [*diagogguzein*]" (19:1–10). The story does not revolve around a meal, but since it describes Jesus as an invited guest in Zacchaeus' house, a meal was probably involved. Since Pharisees are not explicitly involved, we will not give further attention to this parallel.

27. Matthew inserted Pharisees in the first conflict (3:7; Pharisees missing in Mark/Luke) and inserted an anti-Pharisee saying in 5:20.

28. This alleviates the problem of whether to read "but," "or," "more than" or "rather than" in the MT and LXX. Both the MT and the LXX (vll.) parallel these (MT: "*ḥesed* and not sacrifice, knowledge rather than burnt offerings"), indicating Hosea makes no

authentic cult imbued with *ḥesed*."²⁹ Jesus here follows the original meaning in Hosea, and it goes to the heart of Jesus' critique of the Pharisees in Matthew. As he repeats in ch. 5 and in 12:7, the Pharisees failed to exercise the divinely modeled *ḥesed* toward sinners and the "least of these." Like Hosea, Jesus was not driving a wedge between ritual and ethics, or between obedience to commandments and love for God. Rather, he was calling for the originally-intended way of Yahweh guided by *ḥesed*.³⁰

Rejoicing Over Finding Lost Sinners, Luke's Lost Sheep, Coin, and Son (15:1–32)

One further episode in Luke is important for this look at Jesus' conflict with Pharisees over his eating habits. No actual meal scene takes place, but in 15:1-2 Luke reports that "tax-collectors and sinners were coming near to listen to" Jesus, and "the Pharisees and the scribes were grumbling [*diagogguzein*] and saying, 'This fellow welcomes sinners and eats with them.'" Luke here presents Pharisees and scribes as two different, though closely related, groups.³¹ He expands considerably on what differentiated Jesus and the Pharisees in this meal praxis by appending two brief parables (the lost sheep [vv. 3–7] and a lost coin [vv. 8–10]) and one lengthy story usually referred to as the Prodigal Son (vv. 11–32). The concluding point of each is the joy over something found.

- "Rejoice with me, for I have found my sheep that was lost." (v. 6)
- "Rejoice with me, for I have found the coin that I had lost." (v. 9)
- "We had to celebrate and rejoice, because this brother of yours was dead and has come to life; he was lost and has been found." (v. 32)

Or as Jesus summarizes, "Just so, I tell you, there will be more joy in heaven over one sinner who repents than over ninety-nine righteous persons who need no repentance" (v. 7). Jesus himself had apparently shown such

---

great difference between them.

29. De Andrado, "Ḥesed and Sacrifice," 47–67, quotation from abstract. Similarly, the Israelites "keep to the letter of the law in observing sacrifice, but not to the heart of it, as they lack mercy and love"; Viljoen, "Hosea 6:6," 218.

30. Numerous commentators think this saying indicates Jesus' rejection of the temple sacrificial system ("I desire . . . not sacrifice"). However, this was not the meaning in Hosea, nor is there any indication in Matthew of Jesus' wholesale rejection of sacrifices (see 5:23–24).

31. The combination of the Greek particles *te . . . kai* means "both . . . and" (BDF §444.2). Some MSS omit *te*.

gladness in Zacchaeus's house since the Pharisees were upset that he "welcomes sinners." The contrast between Jesus' joy and welcome to the less observant, the toll-collectors, and sinners, and the grumbling of the Pharisees, could hardly be more jarring.

The appended story of the two sons reveals one further important element of Jesus and the Pharisees.

> The allegorical level of meaning is irresistible: they [the Pharisees], like the elder son, had stayed within covenant and had not wandered off; they had never broken any of the commandments. But . . . they resented others being allowed into the people without cost. The son refusing to come into the house of singing and rejoicing is exactly like those who stand outside the heavenly banquet while many others enter in (13:28–30).[32]

Pharisees are not portrayed in these parables and stories as negatively as those who are lost like toll-collectors and sinners. No, they are the elder brother who still lives in the father's house, who had stayed in the covenant and not wandered off. Their fault lies not in particular sinfulness like the younger brother or in self-righteousness, but in failure (refusal?) to welcome what God is doing through Jesus' proclamation and ministry for the outcasts in Israel. God is restoring his rule of joy and covenant faithfulness over his people, and the Pharisees are refusing.

Summary

The Pharisees are rightly concerned with purity; after all, God told Israel to be concerned with purity. They tangle with Jesus not over whether purity is a legitimate concern but over what exactly Mosaic purity requires. Had Jesus simply dismissed the OT purity concerns with something like "that doesn't matter any longer," he would have thoroughly disqualified himself as a Jewish teacher not only in the eyes of the Pharisees, but equally for the general Jewish populace for whom at least a minimal observance of purity was simply part of what it meant to be genuinely Jewish. This issue crops up in the Gospels when Jesus eats with Jews known to be careless regarding such purity issues (toll collectors). Jesus feels free to eat with these folks, eating their (unclean) food and dining in their (unclean) homes, apparently without concern for how this will affect his own purity. The Pharisees see a serious problem here. In their minds such eating habits make Jesus impure, not fit for contact with holy things (the temple) and

---

32. Johnson, *Gospel of Luke*, 242.

people (priests or others seeking to maintain their purity). Thus, their position is fully understandable. They do not have to be seen as particularly hard-hearted or as looking down their noses at the *am ha'aretz*. They are serious about doing what their God says regarding pure and impure. We will continue exploring this disagreement over purity in the next chapter dealing with touching impure persons.

CHAPTER 9

Don't Touch That! Eating with Unclean Hands and Other Disagreements over Purity Rules

Jewish Purity Concerns: Origin and Character

RELATED TO THE DINING restrictions we have just considered, purity also pertains to what and with whom one should come in contact. Most of us in the Western world have little personal experience with the kinds of purity concerns we read about in Leviticus and elsewhere in the Bible.

> When a woman has a discharge of blood . . . , she shall be in her impurity for seven days, and whoever touches her shall be unclean until the evening. Everything upon which she lies during her impurity shall be unclean; everything also upon which she sits shall be unclean. Whoever touches her bed shall wash his clothes, and bathe in water, and be unclean until the evening. Whoever touches anything upon which she sits shall wash his clothes, and bathe in water, and be unclean until the evening; whether it is the bed or anything upon which she sits, when he touches it he shall be unclean until the evening. (Lev 15:19–23)

Contact with a corpse had even more severe consequences, sometimes leading to being "cut off from Israel" (Num 19:11–13). These purity passages are not talking primarily about good hygiene, but about *ritual purity*, about acts or conditions that make a person temporarily unfit for contact with what is *holy*. A person who had become unclean could not enter the temple, present a sacrifice, or even touch the grain that had been set apart to be offered on the altar. All these were *holy* and the person had become *unclean*.[1] What is more, this ritual impurity could be passed via touch to other persons, it was contagious as it were.

Although there was some overlap between moral and ritual impurity, contracting ritual impurity was not sinful *per se*. Some impurity was natural and unavoidable (e.g., menstruation and burial). Ritual impurity was temporary, unlike the lasting guilt of sin, and could be removed via ritual means: time (waiting until sundown or a period of days), washing, and sacrifice.

A number of Jesus' behaviors raised purity concerns. He touched lepers and corpses, as well as women with discharges. Had he rejected such OT teaching? Did he think such purity concerns were no longer important? Or did he think the purity of the dawning kingdom of God overpowered all such impurity as we suggested above? And why then did he still uphold OT cleansing rituals for impurity ("go, show yourself to the priest, and offer for your cleansing what Moses commanded," Mark 1:44)? Although the Pharisees may well have had issues with Jesus on all these points, the Gospels make such a purity dispute between them explicit on only one behavior, eating with unclean or unwashed hands (Mark 7:1-23; Matt 15:1-20; Luke 11:37-41).[2]

The Key Dispute: Mark 7

Since the last encounter with Pharisees in Mark (3:1-6), Jesus has been teaching, healing and growing more in notoriety and popularity in Galilee (6:30-44, feeding of 5,000; 6:53-56, growing notoriety). Mark relates how a group of Pharisees and scribes from Jerusalem[3] observe and question the disciples' practice of "eating with defiled hands, that is, without washing them" (v. 2).

---

1. For an overview of purity-impurity in the OT, see Wright, "Unclean and Clean (OT)," 729-41.

2. Since this is Jesus' only recorded dispute focused explicitly on purity, the question of authenticity, of what the historical Jesus actually did and said, becomes important. Meier is representative of those who think that little of Mark 7:1-23 and parallels goes back to the historical Jesus, but was crafted by the early church to defend their non-observance of food and purity laws. "With the exception, then, of 7:10-12, nothing goes back to the historical Jesus." Meier, *Marginal Jew*, 4:413. This means "Jesus never made any significant pronouncements on purity rules" and "his silence is best interpreted as lack of concern or studied indifference" (411). We are not convinced one need be so skeptical. Supporting authenticity, see Booth, *Jesus and the Laws of Purity*.

3. The participial phrase ("coming from Jerusalem") could modify both the Pharisees and scribes, or only the scribes. Matthew has both groups coming from Jerusalem (15:1). Since Mark has depicted the scribes earlier as coming from Jerusalem (3:22), whereas Pharisees have always been local, the "from Jerusalem" comment applies most likely only to the scribes. So France, *Gospel of Mark*, 280.

Jesus responds by excoriating these "hypocrites" because they "abandon the commandment of God and hold to human tradition" (v. 8). He then gives a further example of their putting traditions above Torah when they use the law of *corban* to subvert honoring parents (vv. 9–13). Next he tells the crowds a saying about outside versus inside ("there is nothing outside a person that by going in can defile, but the things that come out are what defile," v. 15), and follows up with a private explanation to the disciples, "whatever goes into a person from outside cannot defile, since it enters, not the heart but the stomach, and goes out into the sewer" (vv. 18–19).

Taking these different segments of the story one by one, we begin with the Pharisees' question about hand-washing (vv. 1–2, 5):

> Now when the Pharisees and some of the scribes who had come from Jerusalem gathered around him, they noticed that some of his disciples were eating with defiled hands, that is, without washing them.... So the Pharisees and the scribes asked him, "Why do your disciples not live according to the tradition of the elders, but eat with defiled hands?"

Again, this was not primarily a matter of hygiene, but of ritual purity.[4] Such concern for ritual purity was apparently widespread by the first century as evidenced by the remains of a large number of stone vessels used for storing the water for ritual ablutions.[5] Although ritual purity was designed mainly for temple contact, interest in maintaining it more broadly was rooted not only among Pharisees but likewise in the general populace. As Mark inserts for his non-Jewish readers, "For the Pharisees, and all the Jews, do not eat unless they thoroughly wash their hands, thus observing the tradition of the elders" (v. 3).[6] Since impurity could be contracted via liquids and foodstuffs, some groups, among them at least some of the Pharisees, had developed washing procedures for removing this impurity prior to eating.[7] Jesus and his disciples stand out by their non-observance of this procedure.

---

4. So nearly all interpreters, contra Maccoby, *Ritual and Morality*, 157, who thinks it is merely a matter of "good manners and hygiene."

5. On this see esp. Deines, *Jüdische Steingefässe*. Also, Regev, "Pure Individualism," 176–202.

6. Numerous scholars view Mark's claim that "all the Jews" followed this practice as exaggerated or completely false. It is more likely, however, that Mark intends this as a general explanation for gentile readers about a point of Jewish praxis, and not an attempt at precise historical accuracy. See *Aristeas* 305 for a similar generalizing use of "all the Jews" to explain Jewish views to gentiles.

7. This paragraph summarizes a complex debate over Jewish purity laws. I rely here largely on the major studies by Booth, *Jesus and the Laws of Purity*, and Kazen, *Jesus and Purity Halakhah*. See also the helpful summary in Dunn, "Jesus and Purity," 449–67.

DON'T TOUCH THAT!

A clash over this issue should not be at all surprising. As Meier notes,

> around the turn of the era, there were probably contrasting and clashing tendencies within Palestinian Judaism in regard to purity. Some groups seemed to be pressing for more rigorous implementation of purity rules in daily life or the extension of purity rules to new areas of life, while other groups may have sought to modify or adapt purity laws to the practical demands of daily life . . . . Those advocating an expansive thrust . . . and those favoring a restrictive approach . . . may well have competed for adherents among ordinary Palestinian Jews, that is, Jews without any particular party adherence or any great education in Torah.[8]

The Pharisees would have viewed the lax purity practice of Jesus both as a danger to the nation (Israel polluting the land via impurity) as well as a competitive challenge to their own influence among the people, hence their questioning of Jesus' deviant praxis.[9]

Jesus does not, however, enter into *halakhic* debate. Instead, he applies a prophetic word of judgment to them because they prefer their "human tradition" to "the commandment of God" (vv. 6-8). In these verses he answers their question as to why he differs, why he does not follow their traditions. The quotation in v. 6 stems from Isa 29:13, where originally the prophet was crying out against the cultic officials in Jerusalem who ignored the words of true prophets, preferring instead their own conventional wisdom. This conflict of outer versus inner devotion ("draw near with their mouths and honor me with their lips, while their hearts are far from me") is what Jesus now summarizes as "hypocrisy" and applies to the Pharisees. He equates their "traditions of the elders" with Isaiah's "human tradition" and claims these traditions "abandon the commandment of God."

The previous segment (vv. 6-8) charged the Pharisees with abandoning the commandment of God via their traditions, but did not explain or justify that charge. The next segment (vv. 9-13) will do just that, but in regard to another of their traditions, the use of *corban*. Jesus first cites the fifth commandment, "honor your father and your mother" (Exod 20:12; Deut 5:16). In the ancient world such "honoring" included the obligation of providing for care and support in old age. It was possible, however, for an adult son to declare some items as dedicated to sacred use. Such items were considered *corban*, that is vowed for sacred use. If not yet transferred

---

8. Meier, *Marginal Jew*, 4:351.

9. In Matthew's version their questioning verges on accusation ("your disciples break the tradition of the elders," 15:2).

to the temple, a piece of farmland, for example, would still be available for the son's use, but not for use by others such as parents. Jesus poses the situation in which a son no longer honors (supports) parents because the support has been vowed to sacred use. In such a case, Jesus charges that the Pharisees would not even "permit" a son to obey the commandment and use the vowed items for the parents' support.

On the surface this looks like an open and shut case of greed and religious hypocrisy, using a legal loophole to avoid financial and moral obligations.[10] It is certainly possible that such cynical persons existed, even among Pharisees, but it is unlikely such behavior was typical among those like Pharisees who were highly regarded in society. So, if they weren't out-and-out cynical hypocrites, what was their motivation and why did Jesus accuse them this way? As to motivation, we should first remember that dedicating some of one's possessions for sacred use was not a bad thing. Christians should be able to understand this without difficulty, since they dedicate "tithes and offerings" regularly. The IRS even allows, and churches often encourage, a transfer of ownership of investments to a church or charity prior to death. In such a charitable gift, one continues living off the dividends, and then directs that the investment go to the charity when the donor passes on. In such a case, of course, the bulk or capital of this investment no longer benefits family and heirs. The motive for both good-hearted Pharisees and Christians is not greed or avoiding family responsibilities, but honoring God with one's possessions. Second, there was disagreement about the use of this *corban* material while the giver still had use of it. The issue revolved around the inviolability of an oath or vow. If one vows "I give this to God," can one later undo this vow? We know that some Jewish teachers allowed such vows to be annulled for legitimate reasons like support of family (which, by the way, would bring them close to Jesus' position), while others considered such vows inviolable as some OT passages indicate (Deut 23:21–23; for the rabbinic debate see m. Ned. 9.1 and t. Ned. 1.6.4). The latter found themselves caught between a true rock and a hard place, between the command to honor parents and the command to honor one's vows. And third, Jesus does not accuse the Pharisees themselves of making such hypocritical vows, but of permitting a legal loophole for such ("you say that if anyone tells father or mother").[11]

So, if the Pharisees were honestly attempting to navigate a difficult legal thicket, was Jesus being unfair in charging them with hypocrisy and

---

10. See the DSS criticism of Pharisaic "loopholes" earlier, pp. 51–52.

11. On Jewish vows, see Benovitz, *Kol Nidre: Studies*. Benovitz discusses Mark 7 (16–27). Similarly, Collins, *Mark*, 351–53.

preferring their traditions to God's commandment? As with the Sabbath work controversy, Jesus consistently interpreted God and Torah as being most fundamentally about the divine intent for human flourishing. Any interpretation that found its center somewhere else missed the point, and its claim to love and honor God amounted to hypocrisy. It was the Pharisees' stubborn focus on such legal details in the face of Jesus' God-sent hermeneutic that he branded as hypocrisy. He was not unfairly smearing all Pharisees as greedy loophole finders.

Following this sharp disagreement with some Pharisees, Mark appends two scenes that expand on Jesus' stance toward ritual purity, one with the crowd (7:14-15) and one privately with the disciples (7:17-23).[12] To the crowd Jesus gave a veiled saying (referred to as a "parable" in v 17) about what goes into a person from outside versus what comes out from the inside. Only the latter can "defile," i.e., make ritually unclean. Privately he explained this saying with a focus on how things entering and coming out affect one's "heart," the core of one's identity, one's true essence. "What goes in from outside" clearly referred to food, as in the opening scene in vv. 1-5. Such food entered the stomach and was then excreted, but did not affect the heart. What "is from within," however, referred to moral actions and intentions: fornication, avarice, pride, etc. Such actions came "from the human heart," and it was these rather than foods which actually made a person unclean, unfit for contact with what is sacred. To underline the point for his later non-Jewish audience, Mark inserts a small parenthetical remark: "Thus he declared all foods clean" (7:19; see below for additional details).[13]

Jesus, Food, and Ritual Purity Laws

On the face of it, Mark 7:1-23 certainly looks like far more than a *halakhic* dispute,[14] or even a disagreement about whether Jesus' more humane interpretations are correct. This looks like a straightforward rejection of all OT food laws and related purity regulations! "No food entering from outside can render a person impure." And that is, in fact, what many scholars and

---

12. Verse 16 ("If anyone has ears to hear, let them listen"), found in many MSS, is retained in some versions (KJV, NAS, NJB), but is lacking in numerous early MSS and omitted by nearly all recent translations.

13. Some MSS read this as a continuation of Jesus' statement rather than a Markan parenthesis (so the KJV).

14. For the view that this was, in fact, an *halakhic* dispute, see Furstenberg, "Defilement Penetrating the Body," 176-200.

Bible readers have concluded. However, for a number of reasons, this can hardly have been Jesus' intention.[15]

1. Since the food laws were so central to Jewish identity, their rejection by Jesus would certainly have called forth a staunch condemnation of this very point by his opponents, but a "rejection" played no role in their controversies or his arrest and trial.[16]
2. It is hard to imagine Jesus now doing what he had just condemned the Pharisees for doing, namely ignoring a commandment of God.
3. Elsewhere Jesus was portrayed as Torah-observant. For example he wore the "tassels" Jewish men wore on their robes in obedience to Num 15:38–39 (Mark 6:56; see also Matt 23:5).
4. Jesus' saying was not actually a rejection of ritual purity in favor of moral purity. This language of "not x . . . but y [Gk. *ou . . . alla*]" can point to an absolute contrast, but can also be used, esp. in Semitic contexts, for a relative contrast ("dynamic negation"). In such cases "not x . . . but y" means "not so much x . . . as much as y." This was clearly the case in Hos 6:6 ("I desire steadfast love and not sacrifice") quoted by Jesus in his conflicts over eating with sinners and Sabbath work (Matt 9:13; 12:7). Both the prophet and Jesus meant God desires mercy *more than* he desires sacrifice, not that he does not desire sacrifice at all.[17]
5. If Jesus had so clearly rejected OT food laws, one is hard-pressed to understand why Peter and other early Jewish church leaders still seemed to think they were in force after the resurrection (Acts 10; 15).

So, what does Mark 7 (and Matt 15:1–20, see below) say about Jesus' attitude toward Jewish purity and food laws? Some answer "not much," since they conclude the historical Jesus actually said little of what is recorded in this passage. For the less historically skeptical, and who agree that Jesus did not simply reject such OT laws, most end up with a Jesus who was "indifferent" or "careless" toward Jewish purity concerns.[18] The proposed rationale behind such indifference varies according to the interpreter. Perhaps the

---

15. These reasons are adapted from Rudolph, "Jesus and the Food Laws," 294–302.

16. This would have resulted in a "firestorm . . . with observant Palestinian Jews of any and every stripe." Meier, *Marginal Jew*, 4:393.

17. "There is nothing outside a man which *cultically* defiles him as much as the things coming from a man *ethically* defile him." Booth, *Jesus and the Laws of Purity*, 214, see also 69–71.

18. Esp. Kazen, *Jesus and Purity Halakhah*.

dawning kingdom of God rendered such laws moot or less important[19]; or perhaps Jesus had a different conception of purity in which the positive power of holiness was contagious and triumphed over the negative contagion of ritual impurity.[20] Whatever the ideological rationale, Jesus' more relaxed attitude toward purity restrictions put him more in line with the simple folk in rural Galilee who tended toward pragmatism in such technical disputes, and it puts him at odds with the Pharisees who were known for their exacting [*akribeia*] interpretations.[21]

Matthew's Version: Softer or Harsher?

Matthew's version of this hand-washing controversy is fairly close to Mark's, but there are several differences that have led interpreters to think Matthew "softened" or "minimized" the radical edge of Mark's account.[22] Most noticeably he lacked Mark's "declared all foods clean" (7:19). In addition, Mark's "*nothing* outside a person that by going in can defile" (7:15; also v 18) becomes "it is not *what goes into the mouth* that defiles a person" (Matt 15:11; also v 17). Since both authors thought Jesus had food in mind, this latter difference amounted at most to a slight difference in tone ("nothing" sounds more radical or unlimited) not in substance. The omission of "declared all foods clean" sounds more significant. Did Matthew disagree with Mark's seeming dismissal of OT food laws? Did he worry that his more Jewish audience might misunderstand it in that dismissive direction?

Several things lead me to think Matthew's differences were not as theologically loaded as many have supposed. It is commonly, and rightly, thought that Matthew wrote to a more Jewish audience. We noted how

---

19. "the purity to which Torah pointed would be achieved by the prophets' dream of a cleansed heart; and that, as a result, the traditions which attempted to bolster Israel's national identity were out of date and out of line," Wright, *Jesus and the Victory of God*, 398.

20. See esp. the nuanced treatment of Thiessen, *Jesus and the Forces of Death*, who argues that Jesus remained convinced of the reality of ritual impurity but that he could deal with its source. Also, Blomberg, *Contagious Holiness*, and earlier, Berger, "Jesus als Pharisäer," 240.

21. "Jesus' attitude made it possible [for Galileans] to regard oneself as remaining faithful to ancestral religion without compromising table fellowship or other types of social interaction, especially important at the village level. His attitude was more in line with the pragmatism of little tradition, and did not entail economic losses for the poor. His authority as a charismatic religious leader and 'man of deed' was more readily recognized and accepted in a Galilean context, than that of the halakhic teachers and scribal retainers of Jerusalem tradition." Kazen, *Jesus and Purity Halakhah*, 299.

22. See, for example, Hagner, *Matthew 14–28*, 429, 433.

Mark explained these purity issues to his more gentile audience (Mark 7:2–4), an explanation not necessary for Matthew's audience. The same applies to Matthew's lack of "declared all foods clean." We noted above that Mark intended this for his gentile audience. The sense was not "all foods are clean for everybody" (which would, indeed, abolish the OT foods laws), but "all foods are clean *for gentiles.*" That is, the point for Mark was that *gentile followers* of Jesus were not obligated to observe Jewish food laws. (Although not stated, the assumption could well be that Jewish followers of Jesus still observed Torah and ate kosher.) This was an important point to make in the early church of the 60s–70s of the first century, when there was ongoing debate about how gentiles would fit into the still quite-Jewish Jesus movement (see Acts). Mark's explanation echoed Paul's position (Rom 14). It may also be the case that Matthew did not really "omit" the Markan saying at all. The concept of "omission" implies that Matthew had the version with the saying, and chose to "omit" it. This is the standard Synoptic literary hypothesis, where Matthew had Mark's text in front of him, and redacted (edited) that written text. If Dunn and others are correct that this conceives of the process in too literary a fashion, and that oral tradition and memories played a greater role, it may be that Matthew did not "omit" anything, but reproduced the Jesus tradition as his more Jewish community was telling the story. It would never have included Mark's editorial insertion.[23] "Never included" is not the same as "omitted."

Finally, what of the Pharisees in Matthew's version? Several differences are of note here. First, Matthew's Pharisees accused Jesus and the disciples of "breaking" or "transgressing" [*parabainō*] the traditions rather than simply "not walking" according to them as in Mark. Matthew's wording is harsher and sets up Jesus' counter-charge that the Pharisees "transgress" the Torah-commandment. Matthew also added the following to Jesus' words to the disciples.

> Then the disciples approached and said to him, "Do you know that the Pharisees took offense when they heard what you said?" He answered, "Every plant that my heavenly Father has not planted will be uprooted. Let them alone; they are blind guides of the blind. And if one blind person guides another, both will fall into a pit." (Matt 15:12–14)

Matthew's disciples almost sound like they were coming to the defense of the poor Pharisees. Jesus will have none of this. The clear opposition between Jesus and the Pharisees signaled by the language of "breaking" is reinforced by the implied denial that the Pharisees have been "planted" by God

---

23. Dunn, "Altering the Default Setting," 139–75; also Dunn, *Jesus Remembered.*

the father. Repeatedly in Jewish tradition Israel is God's "planting": "They are the shoot that I planted, the work of my hands" (Isa 60:21; also 61:3; 1 En 10:16; 84:6; Jub 1:16; 7:34; 1QS 8:5; 11:8; etc.). But Jesus denies this to the Pharisees. Rather than being planted by God, they will be uprooted. They are "blind guides" rather than teachers of God's will. As typical for Matthew, the opposition between Jesus and the Pharisees is extreme.

Luke: Cleaning Cups in a Pharisee's Home

Luke's Gospel lacks the episode we have been looking at in Mark and Matthew, but it does include a brief encounter in a Pharisee's home over purity at meals that has some similarities.

> While he was speaking, a Pharisee invited him to dine with him; so he went in and took his place at the table. The Pharisee was amazed to see that he did not first wash before dinner. Then the Lord said to him, "Now you Pharisees clean the outside of the cup and of the dish, but inside you are full of greed and wickedness. You fools! Did not the one who made the outside make the inside also? So give for alms those things that are within; and see, everything will be clean for you. (Luke 11:37–41)

Here is the same inside-versus-outside contrast we saw Jesus make in Mark. Inside, in the hidden realm of the heart, reside "greed [lit. robbery] and wickedness," whereas externally, where all can see, everything looks clean. Jesus' solution was repentance, "give for alms those things that are within." That is, the proceeds of their hidden thievery should be given to help the poor, then "everything will be clean."[24]

Other Contact-Impurity Scenes in the Gospels

Although Mark 7 narrates the only explicit conflict between Jesus and the Pharisees over purity, there are several non-conflict episodes that confirm the more relaxed attitude of Jesus toward purity we have discerned above.[25] Skin outbreaks ("leprosy") were a very serious source of ritual impurity (Lev 13–14).[26] Lepers and leprous items were to be quarantined,

---

24. On this connection with almsgiving, see Reardon, "Cleansing Through Almsgiving in Luke-Acts," 477–82.

25. On Jesus and purity in these non-conflict passages, see esp. Kazen, *Jesus and Purity Halakhah*, 89–198.

26. It is now generally agreed that the "leprosy" mentioned in the Bible was most

and sometimes lepers were required to cry out "unclean" to warn people of the purity danger they posed. Thus, it is truly striking to read early in Mark's Gospel of Jesus "touching" a leper in the process of healing him (1:40–45; par. Matt 8:1–4; Luke 5:12–16), something that a Pharisee or anyone concerned to preserve stringent ritual purity would have avoided. Jesus appears to have been careless or indifferent toward this impurity. He even dined in a leper's home (Mark 14:3; Matt 26:6).

However, it can hardly be called careless or indifferent when Jesus instructed the healed leper to "go, show yourself to the priest, and offer for your cleansing what Moses commanded, as a testimony to them" (Mark 1:44). The weeklong process Jesus refers to is described in Lev 14 and involved washing and the offering of sacrifices, after which the priest would pronounce the leper cleansed. This official pronouncement was important, since otherwise a leper would be shunned as still unclean in his/her community. It seems clear from this episode that Jesus was not indifferent but committed to the observance of Torah's purity laws and the associated cleansing rituals.[27] Compared with the Pharisees, Jesus could, especially by touching the leper, appear as "indifferent" or "careless." But in light of his honoring of the OT cleansing ritual, it would be more accurate to say he practiced purity in a more relaxed or humane, less strict, manner.

Another group of non-conflictual purity scenes revolved around various kinds of bodily discharges that rendered one unclean. These included giving birth, menstruation, and vaginal bleeding (Lev 12 and 15). The Synoptics tell of one such episode involving a woman who had suffered for years from such bleeding and associated impurity (Mark 5:25–34; Matt 19:20–22; Luke 8:43–48). Rather than Jesus touching her, in this case the woman "came up behind him in the crowd and touched his cloak" (Mark 5:27). It appears that in general at this time such touching would have been viewed as resulting in Jesus being made ritually impure.[28] Nothing is made in this case of the purity issue by Mark or the other Gospel writers, but Jesus does appear as relatively indifferent or relaxed regarding such consequences; he is more interested in the healing and faith of the woman.

Corpse-impurity was a third type of contact issue (Num 5:1–4; 19:11–22; 31:19–24), and again Jesus appeared relaxed or seemingly indifferent toward it. As we mentioned earlier, corpse impurity was often unavoidable and not sinful *per se* (since honoring deceased loved ones was a duty), but

---

often not the specific medical condition known today as Hansen's disease, but referred to a variety of skin diseases or outbreaks. Wright and Jones, "Leprosy," 277–82.

27. So the majority of interpreters (e.g., Guelich, France). For various interpretations, see Broadhead, "Mk 1,44: The Witness of the Leper," 258–60.

28. Kazen, *Jesus and Purity Halakhah*, 161–64.

it was a very serious matter. Ignoring it was a sin and could result in expulsion (Num 19:13, 20). On at least two occasions Jesus came into contact with a corpse: the raising of Jairus's daughter (Mark 5:21–24, 35–43 par.) and of a widow's deceased son (Luke 7:11–17). In both cases "touching" was mentioned, which would have resulted in Jesus being rendered ritually unclean. As in other purity episodes we noted above, the issue of purity was incidental to the Gospel writers and not the central concern in their stories. Nevertheless, here again Jesus acted with seeming indifference to what was widely considered appropriate purity praxis.

Summary: The Pharisees, Jesus, and Ritual Purity

It is a near consensus that Pharisees were centrally concerned with maintaining ritual purity as commanded in Torah and worked out in their *halakhah*. This was not a uniquely Pharisaic concern, but is shared by most serious Jews of the period, though the latter would have probably been more willing to "fudge" in certain cases. Jesus' more relaxed purity praxis in table fellowship struck many Pharisees as a violation of Torah's purity concerns, at least as the Pharisees spelled this out in their traditions. We have suggested Jesus may not have been indifferent to such concerns, but was willing to practice them in a more relaxed or humane manner, much like most non-Pharisaic, especially rural, Jews.

CHAPTER 10

Who Are You? Core Disagreements over Kingdom, Authority, and Identity

AT NUMEROUS POINTS IN our investigation we have noted various motivations for the opposition of the Pharisees to Jesus. They didn't like his distinctive *halakhah*; in fact, they sometimes questioned his authorization to teach at all. He challenged their authority with the common people. Of course, he called them names, which would probably make anyone mad. Perhaps, most importantly, he claimed that the crucial climax of Yahweh's work in and for Israel and the world was taking place now, and was taking place in his ministry and teaching. The kingdom of God was at hand, evil was being expunged (e.g., exorcisms), and Israel was being gathered and renewed. Along with the official leaders (scribes, elders, chief priests), many of the Pharisees, whose influence and authority were unofficial but widespread, disagreed with all this and opposed Jesus. As we will see, while deeply theological, this was not simply a theological or *halakhic* disagreement, but social and personal. Jesus' teachings and actions challenged their leadership of the people. This chapter will look at numerous interactions with Pharisees that give us entrée to these core disagreements over Jesus' message and identity.

Pharisees at the Jordan River, John the Baptist Preaches the Kingdom

The first appearance of the Pharisees in Matthew's Gospel comes not in a conflict with Jesus, but with his forerunner, John the Baptist (3:7–10). John's eschatological preaching was nearly identical to that of Jesus ("Repent, for the kingdom of heaven has come near" Matt 3:2; see 4:17 for Jesus' message) and was welcomed by common folk (Matt 3:5–6). As will Jesus, John announced the inbreaking of the long-awaited rule of God and cited Isaiah to this end ("Prepare the way of the Lord, make his paths straight" Matt 3:3; citing Isa 40:3). For the wicked this presaged "the wrath to come" when the chaff would be burned with unquenchable fire (Matt 3:7–12).

Matthew alone has the Pharisees, accompanied by the Sadducees, come out to John the Baptist. But why did they come?[1] Did they, like the crowds, come to confess their sins and receive John's baptism of repentance? This is not impossible since some Pharisees were sympathetic; it is suggested by the NRSV translation ("coming for baptism"). However, John's response doesn't paint them as honest seekers ("You brood of vipers"), and his further word ("Do not presume to say to yourselves, 'We have Abraham as our ancestor'") indicates they rejected his judgment preaching (confirmed by Luke 7:29–30). Thus, the text should be translated "coming *to* his baptism" (so NAB, ESV, NKJV).[2] As they will do once again with Jesus (16:1–12), here the Pharisees and Sadducees joined forces to investigate John, not to be baptized (as similarly in John 1:19–28). The Pharisees disagreed that the situation was as dire as John and Jesus proclaimed ("Even now the ax is lying at the root of the trees," Matt 3:10).

Jesus Preaches the Inbreaking Kingdom

When we turn to interactions with Jesus, we see the same disagreement over the message of God's inbreaking rule. From the very beginning of his public ministry, Jesus had made the announcement of God's impending kingdom central (Mark 1:14–15).[3] Yet, even as late as Luke 17:20–21, when Jesus was heading to Jerusalem, the Pharisees were still questioning him on precisely this point.

> Once Jesus was asked by the Pharisees when the kingdom of God was coming, and he answered, "The kingdom of God is not coming with things that can be observed; nor will they say, 'Look, here it is!' or 'There it is!' For, in fact, the kingdom of God is among you."

---

1. Luke has the same scene, but only the crowds are present (3:7–9). Matthew's combining of Pharisees and Sadducees is unique in the Gospels (see also 16:1–12). Some view this as "unhistorical," but there is no compelling reason to doubt that they were able to put aside differences on occasion. See France, *Gospel of Matthew*, ad loc.

2. The Greek preposition *epi* + accusative can occasionally indicate purpose ("coming for"), but its most common use is to mark location ("coming to," so BDAG).

3. Among the many excellent treatments of this central kingdom message, see Wright, *Jesus and the Victory of God*, 198–243.

Standard Jewish expectation was that Israel's God, or his anointed emissary ("messiah"), would enter the fray and crush Israel's enemies, exalt the chosen nation, and bring to pass the Edenic conditions promised in the prophets. It was obvious to all that none of this had happened, yet Jesus continued to preach and act out a present and coming rule of God. Quite naturally, the question of "when" arose. Jesus' answer in Luke 17 cut right across these standard Jewish scenarios. The expected cataclysmic events, in particular military-political events, were no longer the indubitable signs of the coming of God to rescue his people. This is why he never actually gave a precise guideline for determining "when" (see Mark 13), even in this instance where he has been asked pointedly "when?" Instead, without such expected and noticeable sign-events, Jesus claimed "the kingdom of God is *entos hymōn*," it is "among you," "in your midst" (not "within you").[4]

Many of Jesus' parables pointed to the same key disagreement. For example, after arriving in Jerusalem, Jesus told a parable to the Jewish leadership in the temple about a vineyard (Mark 12:1–12 par.). This story evoked the well-known image of God and his vineyard, Israel.[5] A series of tenants in the parable shockingly refused to share the vineyard's profits with the owner. He even sent servants one after the other to collect his rent, but these were insulted, beaten, or even killed. This evoked the story of rebellious Israel, consistently rejecting God's entreaties, including those of his servants, the prophets. Finally, he sent "a beloved son," whom the wicked tenants likewise killed. The expected result was that the owner (God) will destroy these tenants (Israel's current leaders), and find better ones (Jesus and his people?). The Jewish leaders, including the Pharisees,[6] recognize that this story was about themselves (v. 12). They were the ones who rejected the prophets and now God's beloved son. As Jesus and John the Baptist have announced, now is the time when God will destroy the wicked and renew faithful Israel. And this, the Pharisees reject.

---

4. BDAG, s.v. *entos*. On this majority interpretation of *entos* in this verse, and the long-lasting debate over its meaning, see Fitzmyer, *Gospel According to Luke (X-XXIV)*, 1160–62, and Holmén, "Alternatives of the Kingdom," 204–5 and notes (although Holmen prefers a different sense).

5. See, for example, "For the vineyard of the LORD of hosts is the house of Israel, and the people of Judah are his pleasant planting" (Isa 5:7).

6. Only Matt says explicitly that the "chief priests and Pharisees" were listening and knew this applied to them (21:45), but Luke probably includes Pharisees in his "scribes and chief priests" (20:19), and Mark closely associates Pharisees with these leaders and the parable (12:13).

Jesus Enacts The Inbreaking Kingdom

We see this core conflict over the dawning kingdom of God not only in Jesus' preaching, but equally in his healings and exorcisms. We often read these stories as demonstrations of his power and authority, and that element is certainly present. However, if we stop there, we will miss the more crucial point ... the healings and exorcisms are key signs that God's rule is arriving. Or to put it more pointedly, *in these events God's rule is actually taking place.* "But if it is by the Spirit of God that I cast out demons, then the kingdom of God has come to you [lit. has arrived upon you]" (Matt 12:28/Luke 11:20). This was Jesus' point in quoting Isa 61 in his first recorded sermon in Luke.

> The Spirit of the Lord is upon me, because he has anointed me to bring good news to the poor. He has sent me to proclaim release to the captives and recovery of sight to the blind, to let the oppressed go free, to proclaim the year of the Lord's favor. (Luke 4:18–19)

And he concluded that reading with, "Today this scripture has been fulfilled in your hearing" (Luke 4:21). The promised age to come, when Israel's sins would be forgiven, when disease and evil would reign no more, this was being experienced in the ministry of Jesus.[7] We see this same connection between the kingdom and Jesus' healings and exorcisms in the Gospel of Mark. Immediately after announcing the kingdom (1:14–15) and beginning to gather the renewed Israel (1:16–20), Mark narrates an exorcism (1:23–28) and healings (1:29–34). What Jesus announced is taking place.

For some of the Pharisees, his actions were neither signs of the coming kingdom of God nor instances of it. Instead of the saving action of their covenant God, they saw the work of the adversary. "By the ruler of the demons he casts out the demons" (Matt 9:34; also 12:24).

Who Authorized You?

At first it might not appear that the Pharisees wrangled much with Jesus over the issue of his authority (Gk. *exousia*). Only one passage specifically associated this term with such Pharisee disputes (Luke 5:21–26). The parallels in Matt 9:6 and Mark 2:10–11 have only the scribes present (although scribes often overlap with Pharisees as we have seen). It would, however,

---

7. See the helpful explanation of this in Wright, *Jesus and the Victory of God*, 191–96.

be a mistake to conclude that the issue of authority was not an element of Jesus' disagreements with Pharisees.[8]

The Greek term *exousia* encompasses the power to do something as well as the authority or right to do it.[9] Thus, the crowds marveled at the authority seen in his teaching (Mark 1:22) and at his ability to cast out demons (Mark 1:27). Jesus granted his disciples this same *exousia* to teach, heal, and cast out demons (Mark 3:15; 6:7; Luke 10:19; Matt 28:18). Matthew's Pharisees accused Jesus of deriving such power and authority not from God, but from Beelzebul (Matt 9:34; 12:24).[10] The chief priests, scribes and elders challenged Jesus regarding his *exousia* and its source: "By what authority are you doing these things? Who gave you this authority to do them?" (Mark 11:27-33, par.) In Mark 2:10-11 mentioned above, Jesus referred to the son of man's *exousia* to forgive sins on earth in response to the opponents' accusation of blasphemy when he pronounced a healed man's sins forgiven. Thus, such disputes over Jesus' power and authority followed him wherever he went and were commented on by all parties, both favorably and unfavorably.

The Beelzebul controversy points to fundamental disagreement as to the source of Jesus' power and authority (Mark 3:22; Matt 12:24, 27; Luke 11:15-19). Jesus claimed he cast out demons by the Spirit of God (Matt 12:28), whereas his opponents attributed this to the power of Beelzebul. This was a core disagreement over who Jesus is (see below).

A similar issue arose when Jesus said to a man he had healed, "your sins are forgiven" (Mark 2:5, par.). The scribes ("scribes and Pharisees" in Luke 5:24) countered with, "Why does this fellow speak in this way? It is blasphemy! Who can forgive sins but God alone?" Technically in the OT, blasphemy referred to some abuse of the name of the Lord (Lev 24:10-11, 14-16, 23). However, by the time of the NT this had been expanded to include any "violation of the power and majesty of God."[11] Since God alone can forgive sins, the scribes and Pharisees apparently saw Jesus' pronouncement of forgiveness as an encroachment on divine prerogatives.

Jesus' response has proven difficult to understand. "'But so that you may know that the Son of Man has authority on earth to forgive sins'—he said to the one who was paralyzed—'I say to you, stand up and take your

---

8. The paucity of *exousia*-disputes involving Pharisees (only Luke 5:24) can be explained in various ways: 1) coincidence, 2) some *exousia*-disputes with "scribes" may have been with Pharisaic scribes, or 3) since Pharisees, like Jesus, had no official authority, this would not be a major point of contention.

9. Foerster, "*exousia*," 2:562-74.

10. Beelzebul = Satan or the "ruler of demons" (Mark 3:22).

11. Beyer, "*blasphēmia*," 1:622.

bed and go to your home'" (Luke 5:24). Some think he was, in fact, claiming the divine prerogative of which the Pharisees accused him. This reading assumes Jesus wished to identity himself as the son of man and meant, "I have authority on earth to forgive sins." While possible, this understanding faces two difficulties: 1) it does not really answer the charge, but plays right into its hands, and 2) some early hearers understood it as a reference not to Jesus' authority, but to that of *human beings*.[12] Thus, some think that Jesus was simply claiming the authority to *pronounce* forgiveness, like a priest in the temple, while the forgiveness itself belonged to God. Thus, he does not say, "I forgive you your sins," but uses the passive, "your sins are forgiven" (i.e., by God). According to the Gospel traditions, Jesus spoke of forgiveness of sins as a result of his ministry and message, and this seemed to be without the normal priestly and sacrificial requirements in the temple.[13] But this interpretation faces the problem of the wording of Jesus' rationale. He does not say, "the son of man has authority on earth to *pronounce* forgiveness," but "to forgive sins." Of course, into the middle of this comes the vexed question of the meaning of "son of man," whether a messianic title ala Dan 7, a reference to a human being or an oblique way of saying "I." For our purposes, whichever solution we prefer, a core disagreement over Jesus' identity and related authority remains.[14]

One thing particularly noticed by people listening to Jesus teach was this matter of authority or *exousia*. Jesus and his disciples "went to Capernaum; and when the sabbath came, he entered the synagogue and taught. They [the onlookers] were astounded at his teaching, for he taught them as one having authority, and not as the scribes" (Mark 1:21–22). But what was it about his teaching that struck the onlookers as particularly authoritative? Some think it was the *manner* of his teaching—his powerful prophet-like delivery, or perhaps his sense of personal authority ("but I say") versus the scribes' appeal to a chain of tradition ("rabbi X reports that rabbi Y said"). Others think it was the *content* of his teaching—the announcement of an imminent inbreaking kingdom or a teaching more focused on mercy than on *halakhic* accuracy. There is good evidence for both suggestions and it may well be that both impressions were found among differing onlookers.[15] Although these authority passages contrast

12. Matt 9:8b says the crowds "glorified God, who had given such authority *to human beings*." In this case, son of man is not a messianic title, but a general reference to human beings.

13. Besides the passage under consideration, cf. Luke 7:47–8; Matt 26:28.

14. On the interpretation of this passage, see Bock, "Son of Man in Luke 5:24," 109–21, who argues for the first-mentioned view above.

15. For the *manner* of his teaching, one might appeal to Mark's connection of this

directly only Jesus and the scribes, it is not much of a reach to extend the comparison also to Pharisees, at least to Pharisees who were scribes. When the crowds remark "not as the scribes," this need not mean their teaching was weak or ineffectual in content and delivery. Rather, it lacked the eschatological urgency and prophetic character of Jesus' kingdom message. They did not join it to miracles, focusing instead on spelling out in rather detailed manner the implications of biblical commands and prohibitions. Another possibility has been suggested by Chris Keith.

> The scribal authorities likely disagreed with what he taught and how he taught it, but a central part of the problem was that, from their perspectives, Jesus did not have the right to be teaching in the first place. . . . Jesus was not a member of the authoritative scribal elite class, but acted in some ways as though he were, and managed to convince some of his audiences that he was.[16]

He was not qualified in terms of literacy and training. Today such scribal opponents might say, "Who does he think he is?"

Who Are You? (John 7:31–32, 47–48; 9:16; 11:45–48; 12:42–43)

Another common Christian perception of why Pharisees opposed Jesus is their disbelief that he was the son of God, the messiah of Israel. As the Pharisees themselves admitted in a rhetorical question, "Has any one of the authorities or of the Pharisees believed in him?" (John 7:48) This common conception contains a good basic instinct—many Pharisees did disagree with Jesus (and with other Pharisees it turns out) as to who he was. As we have seen in the other chapters, many Pharisees rejected Jesus as a teacher . . . his relaxed practice of Torah (his *halakhah*) was not careful like theirs. They rejected him as the herald of the inbreaking kingdom of God, just as they had also rejected John the Baptist. And they rejected him as a prophet to lead and

---

impression with power to cast out demons (1:27) or to Luke's wording ("his word was *en exousia*," i.e., delivered with authority; see also John 7:46 (NIV), "No one ever spoke the way this man does"). For the *content*, we note that this impression comes after Jesus' kingdom message in Mark (1:14–15) which the crowds refer to as "a new teaching—with authority" (1:27) and after the sermon on the mount in Matt (7:28). Less likely is Daube's suggestion that it referred to the binding *halakhic* authority (= ordination) of the later rabbi's (Daube, "ἐξουσία in Mark 1, 22 and 27," 45–59). On the whole, see Dawsey, "Jesus and the Language of Authority," 14–18.

16. Keith, *Jesus against the Scribal Elite*, 6.

renew Israel. Thus, Christian perceptions that many Pharisees rejected Jesus over questions of identity, who he was, are on target.

However, whether their rejection, their unbelief, was specifically over a claim by Jesus to be the "son of God" and "messiah" turns out to be a bit more complex. First, let's be clear, strictly speaking the Gospels do not present the Pharisees as a whole as unbelieving. Some do, of course, oppose aspects of his teaching and praxis as we have seen in other chapters. But it is equally clear that some (how many?) are open to his teaching, or are even inclined to believe in and follow him.

Excursus: Friendly Pharisees

Nicodemus, identified as a Pharisee and a "leader of the Jews," is a prime example of a friendly Pharisee. At first he was merely curious (John 3:1–15). Then he defended Jesus against other hostile Pharisees (John 7:45–52). And finally, after the crucifixion, he joined another Jewish leader, a disciple, to see that Jesus' body was properly buried (John 19:38–42). In addition, the Gospels regularly portray the Pharisees as divided over Jesus. "Some of the Pharisees said, 'This man is not from God, for he does not observe the sabbath.' But others said, 'How can a man who is a sinner perform such signs?' And they were divided" (John 9:16; also 10:19). Some Pharisees invited Jesus into their homes (Luke 7:36; 11:37; 14:1), and others warned him of danger (Luke 13:31). Acts reported that after the resurrection there was a substantial wing in the earliest church composed of Pharisees who had become active followers of Jesus (Acts 15:5; see below ch. 15). Of course, in some ways the chief friendly Pharisee would have to be the apostle Paul, but that depends on whether we consider him still a Pharisee after becoming a Jesus-follower (see ch. 15 below for details). Thus, while true that "the Pharisees" are the main opponents of Jesus, it is not true that such opposition or unbelief was somehow inherent to Pharisaism or true for all Pharisees.

Second, the impression that the Pharisees primarily rejected Jesus' claim to be "son of God" and "messiah" stems largely from the Gospel of John. In the Synoptic Gospels Jesus actually refrains from identifying himself this way. Without question, the Synoptic authors writing for their later Christian audiences do view Jesus as the messiah of Israel, the Christ or anointed one, and the son of God (Matt 1:1; Mark 1:1; Luke 1:32; 2:11). But they portray Jesus himself as ambivalent regarding these titles. When Peter openly confesses him as messiah, Jesus' response is "don't tell anyone" (Mark 8:30), and he immediately begins to explain to them the suffering that will be required not of the messiah, but of the son of man (Mark 8:31). Matthew shows Jesus with the same ambivalence at the very end when the high priest asks him directly, "tell us if you are the Messiah, the Son of God" (26:63). Jesus' response is hardly a ringing affirmative— "You have said so" (26:64).[17] As at Peter's earlier confession, he then immediately speaks about the son of man, not about messiah or son of God. The most likely explanation for this ambivalence, this seeming secrecy, is that these titles, as popularly understood, failed to communicate Jesus' self-understanding. Both messiah and son of God evoked the image of a conquering king, an heir of King David, who would bring to Israel victory over the gentile rulers. This was clearly how the crowds interpreted Jesus' arrival in Jerusalem when they cried "Hosanna . . . Blessed is the coming kingdom of our ancestor David!" (Mark 11:1–10 par.) But this messiah-as-conqueror portrait was just as clearly *not* how Jesus understood his own mission. He had come not to conquer but to suffer. This explains his hesitance regarding the titles messiah and son of God,[18] and his preference for the mysterious and little-understood suffering son of man.[19]

However, refusal to believe that Jesus was the one sent from God, the messiah and son of God, did constitute the central motive in the Pharisees' opposition *in the Gospel of John*. In chapter 7 the crowds believed that Jesus was the messiah (v. 31), but this provoked opposition by the chief priests and Pharisees (v. 32). Soon thereafter at a festival in Jerusalem, the crowds were divided, some believing Jesus was messiah, others not (vv. 37–44). This prompted the Jewish authorities to say "Has any one of the authorities or of the Pharisees believed in him?" (v. 48) Unlike the Synoptic Jesus, the Jesus of John's Gospel showed little ambivalence or hesitation in proclaiming openly his identity. When a Samaritan woman wondered about the messiah,

---

17. Luke has Jesus respond in different words with the same ambivalence ("If I tell you, you will not believe," 22:67) while Mark has Jesus finally affirm openly "I am" (14:62). But each of the Synoptics has Jesus move immediately in this instance to speak not of messiah but of the son of man. Besides, we must remember the Pharisees in the Synoptics are no longer present for the trial scenes.

18. Prior to the trinitarian controversies of the second to fourth centuries, "son of God" was understood to refer especially to Israel and the Davidic king, not to the second person of the trinity. See Collins and Collins, *King and Messiah as Son of God*.

19. For a helpful overview of Jesus and messianic identity in the Gospels, see Bird, "Christ," 115–25.

Jesus said clearly, "I am he, the one who is speaking to you" (4:26). In the prayer recorded in John 17, Jesus spoke plainly.

> Father, the hour has come; glorify your Son so that the Son may glorify you, since you have given him authority over all people, to give eternal life to all whom you have given him. And this is eternal life, that they may know you, the only true God, and Jesus Christ [i.e., messiah Jesus] whom you have sent. (17:1-3)

As to why John's portrait differs so noticeably from the Synoptics, the simplest solution, shared by the vast majority of serious students of the NT, is as follows.[20] John's Gospel was put together near the end of the first century, when tensions were high between Jewish followers of Jesus and the leadership of Jewish synagogue life. The divide between the two was more clear-cut than in earlier decades. Some synagogues expelled Jesus' followers and declared belief in his messianic identity out-of-bounds. John's Gospel sought to speak into this situation, and thus portrayed "the Jews" (= the current Jewish synagogue leadership) as a single entity opposed to Jesus as Israel's messiah. Since Sadducees, Essenes and others were no longer active subgroups, the Pharisees were the main named Jewish sub-group in John's Gospel and largely overlapped with "the Jews" as well as being central players in the Sanhedrin. John's Gospel contains a great deal that reliably portrays the historical Jesus, but its portrayals of opposition and conflict tend to owe more to the later situation.

So, to summarize: the Pharisees in Jesus' day were divided as to his identity. Some were impressed by his teaching and power and were open to accepting his message. Others, perhaps a majority, opposed his teaching, saw his miracles as satanically inspired, and viewed him as a dangerous misleader of the nation. Although most were in disagreement with the popular acclamation of him as messiah and Davidic son of God, this was not a frequent point of debate, since Jesus did not openly make such claims.

---

20. See esp. a number of the essays in Anderson et al., *John, Jesus, and History*.

CHAPTER 11

Political Dynamite: Pharisees, Politics, and Power

AT QUITE A NUMBER of points the Pharisees interacted with Jesus over what could be called political or power issues. The crucifixion, since it involved the Roman authorities, was an inherently political event. In addition, there were questions about taxes and Zealot resistance. And, of course, Jesus' message of a new power center, a new kingdom, was bound to be politically explosive.

From our study of Josephus we learned that the Pharisees possessed official political power at only one point in their development. During the reign of Queen Salome Alexandra (mid-first-century BCE) Josephus claimed they "became . . . the real administrators of the state" (*J.W.* 1.111). A few decades later, during Herod's reign, they appear as still influential in religion and politics, but without official political status.

Pharisees and Jesus' New Kingdom Announcement

In the Synoptic tradition the Pharisees' rejection of Jesus' kingdom message is clear, but usually through more indirect means rather than as the subject of a direct controversy (see ch. 10 on the nature of this kingdom message). Luke is explicit as narrator that the Pharisees and lawyers have rejected both John's and Jesus' kingdom message by rejecting John's baptism (Luke 7:24-30). When the Pharisees accused Jesus of casting out demons by the power of Beelzebul rather than God, Jesus tied this to his kingdom message (Matt 12:22-32; also 9:34-35; Mark 3:22-27). In numerous parables Jesus portrayed Pharisees and other Jewish leaders as rejecting God's messengers generally, and Jesus specifically (Matt 21:33-46), and he accused the Pharisees directly of rejecting the kingdom for themselves and hindering others from entering (Matt 23:13). When Jesus entered Jerusalem to the messianic acclamation of the crowds ("blessed is the king"), the Pharisees were incensed (Luke 19:28-40).

The one direct interaction over the kingdom message occurs in Luke 17:20-21, when the Pharisees questioned Jesus as to "when" the kingdom was coming (cf. also Mark 13:3-4).[1] Standard Jewish expectation was that Israel's God, or his anointed emissary, would enter the fray and crush Israel's enemies, exalt the chosen nation, and bring to pass the Edenic conditions promised in the prophets. That is, there would be quite obvious observable events. It was equally obvious to all that none of this had happened, yet Jesus continued to preach and act out a present and coming rule of God. Quite naturally, the question of "when" arose regarding this observable event.

Jesus' answer cut right across these standard Jewish expectations of cataclysmic events, in particular military-political events as signals of that day. This event "is not coming with things that can be observed" (v. 20). Instead, without such expected and noticeable sign-events, Jesus claimed "the kingdom of God is *entos hymōn*," it is "among you," "in your midst" (not "within you").[2] Thus, as we have seen a number of times elsewhere, it was this disagreement regarding the kingdom of God that separated Jesus from the Pharisees and which lay at the root of his critique of them. Of course, this did not mean all Pharisees rejected Jesus' message. We hear of Nicodemus in John's Gospel, and Mark tells of a scribe (= a lawyer/Pharisee in Matt 22:34-40/Luke 10:25-28) who responded positively to Jesus' teaching about the greatest commandment and was told he is "not far from the kingdom" (12:28-34).

Pharisees and Herodians

On two occasions Pharisees made common cause with supporters of Herod Antipas against Jesus. After a Sabbath healing in a Galilean synagogue, the two groups conspired to get rid of Jesus (Mark 3:6). Later in Jerusalem, members of the same two groups were sent by the temple leadership to trap Jesus in a question about paying taxes (Mark 12:13/Matt 22:16). Other than these two instances, these Herodians do not appear in the Gospels.[3]

---

1. Even here, however, Luke presents this not as a conflict but merely a question. Luke seems to have placed this question from Pharisees here in order to introduce the private teaching to the disciples about the "when" of the kingdom (17:22-37).

2. See above, p. 125 and n. 4.

3. A third instance occurs in a vl. of Mark 8:15. Some MSS read "leaven *of the*

"Herodians" probably referred not to a well-organized movement or party, but to anyone who was a supporter of the current Herodian ruler.[4] The two groups were not regularly in partnership, but when someone became politically risky, like the too-popular Jesus, they could join forces.

Pharisees, Jesus, and Revolt Against Rome

The first half of the first century CE was filled with outbreaks of revolutionary fervor and repeated (failed) attempts to get rid of the iron fist of Rome.[5] At times, scholars have sought to bring Jesus as well as the Pharisees into partnership with such revolutionary sentiment.[6] Jesus did, after all, follow the prophets in predicting a future violent military conflict between the forces of good and evil and said he had come to bring a sword rather than peace (Matt 10:34; also Luke 22:36–38). But overall the Gospel tradition presents Jesus committed to the path of nonviolence. Instead of a sword-bearing warrior against injustice, he goes as a lamb to the cross.[7]

When we speak of revolutionary movements in the Gospels, most think of the Zealots, a group of Jews committed to the violent overthrow of Roman and Herodian political power. After all, one of Jesus' disciples was "Simon *the Zealot*" (Luke 6:15; also Acts 1:13). Two considerations should cause us to rethink this common perception of Simon. First, a group bearing this moniker, a clearly delineated Zealot party, probably did not appear until shortly before the Jewish revolt of 66–70 CE as seen in Josephus. Second, Simon's Zealot connection may not refer to a party affiliation at all, but to his religious zeal or his patriotism.[8] Whichever the case, the Gospels do not indicate much connection between the Pharisees (or Jesus) and what later became known as the Zealot party. If anything, the tax-trap episode (see below) as well as the reaction of both to public messianic acclamation of Jesus argue for an avoidance of Zealot identity.

Herodians" rather than "of Herod."

4. Bond, "Herodian Dynasty," 382.

5. For a helpful overview, see Heard and Yamazaki-Ransom, "Revolutionary Movements," 789–99.

6. Arguing for a Zealot Jesus, see Brandon, *Jesus and the Zealots*.

7. See, for example, Bryan, *Render to Caesar*, esp. ch. 3 ("Jesus and Empire"), 39–54.

8. Heard and Yamazaki-Ransom, "Revolutionary Movements," 796. In the parallel accounts, instead of *zēlotēs* (zealot) he is called "Simon *ton Kananaion*" (Mark 3:18/ Matt 10:4), which stems from Aramaic *qan'ānā'* (enthusiast, zealot) and could indicate he was zealous toward God (piety) or toward Israel (patriotism).

Joining a Tax Revolt?

In one well-known instance, the Pharisees along with the politically-connected Herodians sought to set a political trap for Jesus (Mark 12:13–17; par. Matt 22:15–22; see also Luke 20:20–26).

> Then they sent to him some Pharisees and some Herodians to trap him in what he said. And they came and said to him, "Teacher, we know that you are sincere, and show deference to no one; for you do not regard people with partiality, but teach the way of God in accordance with truth. Is it lawful to pay taxes to the emperor, or not? Should we pay them, or should we not?" But knowing their hypocrisy, he said to them, "Why are you putting me to the test? Bring me a denarius and let me see it." And they brought one. Then he said to them, "Whose head is this, and whose title?" They answered, "The emperor's." Jesus said to them, "Give to the emperor the things that are the emperor's, and to God the things that are God's." And they were utterly amazed at him. (Mark 12:13–17)

The political trap was fairly obvious. If Jesus answered, "yes, pay the tax," he would lose favor among the populace who hated the Romans and their taxes and who hoped he would set them free from such foreign oppression. But, if he answered, "no, don't pay the tax," he sided clearly with the revolutionary elements in Jewish society and brought himself into danger with the authorities, like the circle of Herod who were watching carefully.[9]

We can assume the Herodians as friends of Rome expected a "yes" answer. Whether the Pharisees personally favored one answer over the other is not clear. They faced the same dilemma as Jesus. Josephus relates the opposition of Judas the Galilean to a poll tax imposed in 6 CE (*J.W.* 2.118). Some thought Torah forbad paying such taxes; Moses, after all, warned against using one's wealth to serve other gods (Deut 8:17–19). Elsewhere in Scripture, however, passages could be found which seemed to make such accommodations possible (e.g., Eccl 8:2; Jer 29:1–9).

Jesus' response did not appear to answer the question of whether to pay the tax or not. He first asked to see a Roman coin, a denarius, and pointed specifically to the image and inscription on the coin. It would have borne the stamped image of the emperor Tiberius and the inscription "son of the divine Augustus," both of which were deeply offensive to Jewish sensibilities. Following this came a two-part retort which has caused "disagreement

---

9. This is true whether the particular tax (Mark/Matt: *kēnson*; Luke: *phoron*) is a poll tax or a Roman tribute. On the Roman taxation system in Judea, see Udoh, *To Caesar What Is Caesar's*.

... so widespread as to defy categorization."[10] The first half—Give to the emperor the things that are the emperor's—appeared to endorse paying the tax. If Jesus had stopped there, everyone would have taken it as a clear "yes," and reacted accordingly. The second half, however—and to God the things that are God's—qualified a simple "yes" answer, but could be taken in widely varying ways. Perhaps this was a "two kingdoms" perspective, well-known from Lutheran tradition, in which the secular and spiritual kingdoms have somewhat different rules. Thus, it is allowable as a participant in the secular kingdom to pay taxes, even though God alone is ruler in the spiritual realm. Or, was it actually a nod to the Zealot position, since in reality everything, even the coins and the taxes, belonged to God, not to Caesar? I will not pretend to have the final word on this one. The questioners clearly did not take it as either a "yes" or a "no," since they were not able to spring their trap. Christian tradition, not unlike Jewish tradition, has generally taken what we might call a "relativized civil obedience" position. That is, one should be an upstanding citizen, but only to the extent that does not bring one into conflict with one's obligation to obey God.[11]

Pharisees and Galilean Synagogues

The field of synagogue research has exploded in the past few decades. New ruins have been discovered and explored, and previous "knowledge" revised or discarded. For instance, a synagogue should not be viewed as the Jewish form of a church. "Contrary to popular belief, 'synagogues' . . . served a variety of functions that contemporary western culture would regard as properly belonging to municipal institutions. These included council halls, law courts, schools, treasuries, and public archives."[12] And more germane to the topic of this subsection, "Recent research has convincingly argued that Pharisees did not have more influence in synagogues than any other group."[13] This is a particularly important point to stress since nearly all earlier treatments, as well as some more recent authors (and nearly all preachers I have ever heard), make quite an issue of the Pharisees being in charge of synagogue life, especially its liturgy, its beliefs, etc. But as Levine

---

10. Owen-Ball, "Rabbinic Rhetoric and the Tribute Passage," 1.

11. On the debate over Christian relations to the secular state, Kemeny, *Church, State, and Public Justice*.

12. Runesson et al., *Ancient Synagogue*, 8. On this "all-encompassing centrality" of the synagogue to most aspects of Jewish life, see esp. Levine, *Ancient Synagogue*, ch. 10 ("The Communal Dimension") 381–411.

13. Runesson et al., *Ancient Synagogue*, 9.

emphasizes, "the truth of the matter is, the Pharisees had little or nothing to do with the early synagogue."[14] Although perhaps slightly overstated, his point stands that the Pharisees were not in charge.[15]

Thus, when we encounter Gospel stories about Jesus in a synagogue, we need first to envision this as a gathering of the village or town populace. Those in charge would have been the town dignitaries, elders and other respected individuals. If a local Pharisee or priest was such a person, they could conceivably have had a leading role. Otherwise, they were just another of the synagogue crowd, though, in the case of a lay Pharisee or Pharisaic scribe, someone with a reputation for greater Bible knowledge.

Of prime importance, however, when these two parties—Jesus and Pharisees—appear in a synagogue encounter is the matter of influence, or power and honor. Both had a vision for Israel and firm ideas about what that meant for the national life. For the Pharisees that revolved around more careful adherence to Israel's God and his instructions in Torah. For Jesus, while Torah remained at the core, the interpretation and praxis of Torah must now be viewed through the lens of the advancing rule of God (e.g., Matt 5–7). The teaching of Jesus, the newcomer, clearly presented a challenge not only to the teaching of the Pharisees, but equally to their position of honor and theological respect among the people. They were competitors, both with plenty to lose as far as popular influence; this explains the seriousness, even the feistiness, with which both approached their encounters.

Excursus: Pharisees in Galilee?

We have assumed thus far that the Synoptic presentation of Jesus tangling with Pharisees mostly in Galilee was largely accurate. This confidence is not universally shared and a number of scholars have argued there was little Pharisaic presence in Galilee at this time (e.g., R. Bultmann, M. Smith). They note that Josephus, John, and rabbinic literature all place Pharisees mainly in Jerusalem and rarely in Galilee, and suggest that Mark was responsible for the insertion of Pharisees into the Galilean conflict scenes. This skepticism is unwarranted. Josephus, John and the rabbinic literature focused intentionally more on Jerusalem and were not interested in giving a thorough geographic presentation. Further, as Saldarini notes, the argument that Mark's early oral tradition had already *inserted* Pharisees in Galilee and *removed* them from Jerusalem is hardly cogent.[16] Thus, as Freyne concludes, "Pharisaism had made certain inroads into [Galilee] prior to 70 C.E. and . . .

---

14. Levine, *Ancient Synagogue*, 41.

15. Synagogue encounters between Jesus and Pharisees in the Gospels suggest that Pharisees were at least as involved as was Jesus (e.g., Luke 6:6–7; cf. also 11:43).

16. Saldarini, *Pharisees, Scribes, and Sadducees*, 291–93.

its greatest successes were in the settlements along the lake front–Tiberias, Tarichaeae, Caesarea Philippi, and probably Caphernaum, Corozain and Bethsaida also." While some Pharisees were scattered throughout Galilee, he finds no traces of organized *haburoth*.[17]

A Seat in the Sanhedrin

During the period of Jesus' ministry the Sanhedrin was "the supreme Jewish religious, political and legal council in Jerusalem."[18] This group had more the nature of an ad hoc advisory board to the high priest than a permanent decision-making body.[19] It was, of course, subject to the limits placed on it by the Roman procurators such as the power to execute those convicted of capital crimes. And its continuance in power hinged upon how well the high priest and this council kept the populace in line so taxes could be collected. Too much unrest or tax evasion could lead to Roman suppression of the Sanhedrin's power or even a change in its membership, which explains their eye on the Romans during Jesus' time in Jerusalem and at his trial (Mark 14:2; John 11:48).

This advisory board to the ruling high priest in important decisions was typically made up of the current high priest, other leading priestly families ("chief priests"), lay aristocracy ("elders") and scribes. Many of these would probably have been Saducean in sympathy. The Pharisees appear to have had a place as well according to Josephus (*Life* 189–94; *J.W.* 2.411) and the NT (John 11:47; Acts 5:34; 23:6). Older depictions of the role of Pharisees in the council relied heavily on rabbinic literature to argue for their dominance.[20] Such dominance may have occurred during their political heyday during Alexandra's reign (*A.J.* 13.408–9), but was not the case in the early first century CE.[21] Some of the evidence for this overlaps with the question of Jewish responsibility for the crucifixion which is our next issue.

Pharisees and the Passion Events

We noted earlier that the Gospels differ somewhat from one another regarding the involvement of Pharisees in the arrest, trial, and crucifixion

---

17. Freyne, *Galilee, from Alexander the Great to Hadrian*, 322.
18. Twelftree, "Sanhedrin," 836–40, quotation p. 836.
19. See esp. McLaren, *Power and Politics in Palestine*.
20. The Talmud spoke mainly of "sages" as making up the council, not priests. See Grabbe, "Synagogue and Sanhedrin in the First Century," 1730–44.
21. They were "not prominent" according to McLaren, *Power and Politics in Palestine*, 221, see esp. 213–17.

of Jesus. In Mark's Gospel the Pharisees last appear shortly after Jesus' entry to Jerusalem when they were part of a delegation (with Herodians) sent by the chief priests, scribes and elders to trap Jesus in a trick question about taxes (Mark 12:13). Luke recorded this same incident but called the questioners "spies" rather than Pharisees (Luke 19:20). Instead, he last had Pharisees present in the Gospel when they objected to the crowd's messianic acclamation at the triumphal entry (19:39). In neither of these Gospels are the Pharisees named as taking any part in the passion events themselves. Matthew also included Pharisees in the tax controversy (22:15-16) but replaced them with chief priests and scribes at the triumphal entry (21:15). Although they did not appear during the arrest, trial or crucifixion, Matthew does have them show up afterward when they joined with chief priests to ask Pilate for a guard at the tomb (27:62). John, like Mark and Luke, included the irritated Pharisees at the triumphal entry (12:19). John alone, however, named the Pharisees along with chief priests as those who sent soldiers and temple police to arrest Jesus (18:3; see also 11:57), but they were missing from the subsequent passion events.

Thus, apart from John's inclusion of them in the arrest and Matthew's inclusion in requesting a tomb guard, all the Gospels agree in removing the Pharisees from the events resulting in Jesus' crucifixion. Yet, this seems a strange conclusion to draw in light of the fact that Pharisees have been portrayed elsewhere as wanting to kill or destroy Jesus, as present in Jerusalem and opposed to the popular messianic acclamation, and as involved in the Sanhedrin. Some think the trial and condemnation took place in a smaller gathering, not the larger Sanhedrin group, and that Pharisees were not invited. This is possible but must remain speculative. Even less likely is that the Pharisees were, in fact, involved and (partly) responsible for the crucifixion, but the Gospel authors wished for some reason to cover this up. One wonders why they would go soft on them at this point when they had been so hard on them previously. My own sense is that Pharisees were involved in the passion events and were in agreement with the priestly leadership that something had to be done (see above on the triumphal entry, arresting party and tomb guard request). However, as we have noted at numerous points they were a divided group regarding Jesus. In addition, they did not hold decisive power in the Sanhedrin nor was their major focus on politics and relations with the Romans. Thus, they may well have played a less important role in the proceedings against Jesus which had to focus on politically relevant crimes and not simply on *halakhic* disagreements.

CHAPTER 12

Why Do You Eat So Much? Jesus, Fasting, and the Pharisees

Background to the Disagreement

IN MARK'S GOSPEL CERTAIN unnamed persons asked Jesus, "Why do John's disciples and the disciples of the Pharisees fast, but your disciples do not fast?" (2:18) In Luke's account the questioners were "the scribes and the Pharisees" themselves (5:30, 33), while Matthew had the "disciples of John [the Baptist]" pose the question (9:14). Whoever posed this question, all are agreed that the issue revolved around the differing fasting praxis of Jesus (doesn't fast) and the Pharisees (do fast often).[1]

Fasting in the ancient world referred to voluntarily abstaining from food for a period of time for religious reasons, and had been part of Jewish piety for some time. The OT mentioned occasional public fasts (e.g., Jer 36:6), sometimes for the purpose of penance (e.g., 1 Sam 7:6) or to reinforce prayer (Ps 35:13). The practice of fasting with prayer grew significantly during the intertestamental period. "Prayer with fasting is good" (Tob 12:8). "The Lord heard their prayers and had regard for their distress; for the people fasted many days" (Jdt 4:13). By the first century, "fasting like a Jew" had become proverbial among Romans.[2]

Mark's story does not portray an actual fasting conflict between Jesus and the Pharisees, but this difference in their fasting piety apparently stood out to onlookers. If anything, Jesus was accused of the opposite ("Look, a glutton and a drunkard," Luke 7:34/Matt 11:19). We get the impression

---

1. Mark only says the Pharisees fast, while Luke and Matthew (vl.) add that they do this "often."

2. Seutonius, *Aug.* 76. On fasting in Jewish tradition, see Muddiman, "Fast, Fasting," 773–74.

that the Pharisees' practice was viewed as normal, as characteristic of good piety, while Jesus and the disciples were deviating from that norm. Thus, "Why do . . . your disciples . . . not fast?" (Matt 9:14) We will look in a moment at the rationale for the Jewish/Pharisaic praxis, but will first note Jesus' threefold rationale for his own non-fasting which is the focus of this pericope (Mark 2:18-22 par.).

Three Reasons Jesus Does Not Fast Now

He first answered with a saying about a wedding.

> The wedding guests cannot fast while the bridegroom is with them, can they? As long as they have the bridegroom with them, they cannot fast. The days will come when the bridegroom is taken away from them, and then they will fast on that day. (Mark 2:19-20)

Jesus refrained from fasting because he thought now was the time of the bridegroom's presence. The Pharisees apparently disagreed. For this rationale to make sense, Jesus must be thinking of himself as the present bridegroom, and the future "taking away" as his coming crucifixion. Interestingly, Jesus' disciples will return to the Jewish norm ("they will fast") at this future point after the bridegroom "is taken away." Thus, Jesus' praxis differed from the Pharisees because he thought the eschatological clock had struck a different hour. Now is the dawning of the kingdom of God, the moment of the bridegroom's appearing and presence and of the eschatological wedding banquet.[3]

The next two points of Jesus' non-fasting rationale revolved around "new" versus "old" in two brief sayings.

> No one sews a piece of unshrunk cloth on an old cloak; otherwise, the patch pulls away from it, the new from the old, and a worse tear is made.
> And no one puts new wine into old wineskins; otherwise, the wine will burst the skins, and the wine is lost, and so are the skins; but one puts new wine into fresh wineskins. (Mark 2:21-22)

---

3. The image of God as Israel's bridegroom was common in the OT and Second Temple Jewish literature (e.g., Hos 2:18,21; Ezek 16; Isa 54:5-8; 62:5; Jer 2:2), but was not common for messianic figures (possibly in the DSS, see Brownlee, "Messianic Motifs of Qumran and the New Testament," 195-210).

When patching an old garment, the use of new (unshrunk) cloth for the patch would result in the ruin of the valuable old garment. Likewise, new wine which is still fermenting and expanding should not be poured into old wineskins, since the expansion would burst the skins and ruin both the wine and the skins. As often in Jesus' brief sayings or parables, he doesn't make the point explicit, but in relation to fasting praxis, his must be the *new* praxis and the Pharisees' the *old*. Perhaps he simply meant the two cannot be mixed or combined, but more likely is a continuation of the eschatological point from the bridegroom saying. Now is the time of the new.

Christian interpreters will want to be cautious here. Jesus was not saying this is the time when Christianity (the new) replaces Judaism (the old). He was not rejecting Judaism, Torah, Moses, Israel's covenant, the importance of commandments, etc. After all, the time will come, he says, when his disciples *will* fast like the Pharisees. The old is not "Judaism," but the fasting praxis of the Pharisees (and probably of most pious Jews) *at this time*. And it was not rejected as inherently wrong, but only as not appropriate for the current eschatological moment. Readers should not miss this; it is quite different from what we commonly hear.

> It is precisely because Jesus in his coming brought with him the kingdom of God that the practice of fasting, washing pots and pans (7:2–4), food regulations (7:14–22), and ultimately circumcision (Acts 10:1–11:18) were understood by the early church as having been superseded. . . . with the coming of Jesus and the kingdom, it is impossible to maintain the old practices . . . .[4]

We stated above this was not really a conflict or controversy story in Mark. That is also true for Matthew (9:14–17), but Luke portrays the scene as a direct question from the Pharisees to Jesus himself (5:33–39). The sense of an underlying disagreement is heightened in Luke when the Pharisees contrast their fasting with the "eating and drinking" of Jesus' disciples. This may be related to their charges elsewhere that Jesus is "a glutton and a drunkard" (Luke 7:34), but it is more likely prompted by the immediately preceding scene in which Jesus was castigated by the Pharisees for eating and drinking with tax collectors and sinners (Luke 5:29–32).[5]

---

4. Stein, *Mark*, 134–5. Rice misses the mark when calling this a general "release from cultic tradition"; Rice, "Luke 5:33–6:1," 127–32.

5. Luke's account also adds a difficult closing saying about the old wine being "good" or "better" (missing in some MSS). The simplest explanation may be to read the Greek text as does the NLT, "no one who drinks the old wine seems to want the new wine. 'The old is just fine,' they say." Thus, it is a reproach to the Pharisees who content themselves with their (old) point of view, and hence reject Jesus' (new) claims.

Why Did the Pharisees Fast?

In order to explore further the rationale for the Pharisees' fasting practice, we will need to include some additional Gospel passages. A Pharisee in one of Jesus' parables claimed to "fast twice a week" (Luke 18:12),[6] and Jesus criticized "hypocrites" (probably Pharisees) for trying to "look dismal" when they fast (Matt 6:16). This last text (Matt 6:16–18) provides a window into what exactly separated Jesus and the Pharisees in areas of piety such as fasting, prayer and almsgiving.

> And whenever you fast, do not look dismal, like the hypocrites, for they disfigure their faces so as to show others that they are fasting. Truly I tell you, they have received their reward. But when you fast, put oil on your head and wash your face, so that your fasting may be seen not by others but by your Father who is in secret; and your Father who sees in secret will reward you. (Matt 6:16–18)

The Pharisees are not named directly here, but most commentators agree they are in view.[7] As with almsgiving and prayer shortly before (Matt 6:1–6), Jesus here charged the Pharisees with fasting ostentatiously, to be seen by others, whereas the fasting (and almsgiving and prayer) he recommends was to be in secret and known only to God. Apparently, an element of Pharisaic ostentation in fasting was changing their appearance to look sad or sorrowful. As the NLT translates, "they try to look miserable and disheveled."[8] This may well be nothing other than following biblical guidelines, since the OT spoke of fasting with the term "afflict oneself," and biblical fasting was often accompanied by rending garments, wearing sackcloth and putting ashes on one's head (e.g., 1 Kgs 21:27; Neh 9:1; Isa 58:5; Esth 4:3). The Pharisees were not doing anything out of the ordinary. Whether they actually tried to put on a sad face and act particularly downcast we cannot know, but Jesus' charge that they were "play-actors" (*hypocritēs*) suggests it. In quite the contrast, Jesus directed his disciples to act naturally, to "put oil on your head and wash your face."[9]

---

6. There is limited evidence of regular fasts by Jews (e.g., b. Ta'an 24b), and later by Christian churches, probably in imitation of Jewish practice (Did. 8:1, "Wednesdays and Fridays").

7. Since 5:20 the focus has been on the righteousness that "exceeds that of the scribes and Pharisees," and in ch. 23 the repeated use of "hypocrites" in the woes against the Pharisees further reinforces our impression that these hypocrites in 6:16–18 are Pharisees. Also, the Pharisees in 23:5 do their works "to be seen by others" just as the fasting hypocrites do in 6:16. Hagner, *Matthew 1–13*, 138–39.

8. This communicates the sense more clearly than "they disfigure their faces."

9. Since anointing one's head with oil could be a sign of rejoicing (Ps 23:5; 104:15), some think Jesus is telling those fasting to act happy; but this would seem to replace

So what was going on here? Were Pharisees as a group particularly prone to showing off their piety? Is this ostentatious fasting like their wearing of long tassels? Was Jesus revealing a flaw inherent to the very nature of Pharisaism? This has been the traditional way Christians have understood these charges. Pharisees were hypocrites, self-righteous, ostentatious, etc. This infected the whole movement. This was their nature.

The problem, of course, is that this doesn't seem to match the historical reality. We noted earlier that Josephus portrayed them as generally popular and influential with the masses, as upright and virtuous. We suggested there it is highly unlikely the masses would grant popular trust and adulation to a group known for hypocrisy. We also noted that Josephus himself was more dubious about their uprightness than the masses and he hinted at pride and haughtiness among Pharisees who he says "pretend" (*A.J.* 17.41). We concluded there, "the Pharisees end up looking like we might expect of a serious religious movement, deeply and authentically committed to their principles, to their God and heritage, yet quite humanly capable of pettiness and occasional hypocrisy."[10] The Talmud confirmed this picture for a later period. Even though the Pharisees were valorized in some traditions, others were highly critical of them and, in fact, explicitly accused them of hypocrisy. And finally, even the Gospels knew of good, non-hypocritical Pharisees like Nicodemus (John 3:1–2). As Liebowitz argues convincingly, the picture of Pharisees is remarkably consistent across Second Temple literature, the NT, and the Talmud.[11] The Pharisees were by-and-large upright, serious practitioners of Torah. However, as with any movement there were instances of hypocrisy. In the midst of sectarian controversy, such instances could be used to define the whole. One who was already opposed on other grounds could take such instances and charge, "See, they are (all) hypocrites." Later readers, like ourselves, must be careful to hear these charges appropriately, not as historical description, but as powerful words of opposition, as invective. This same thing happens all the time in our own day and age. "Liberals are soft on crime" or "Evangelicals are pushy and judgmental." Any careful observer knows not *all* evangelicals are pushy nor are *all* liberals soft on crime, but such language certainly gets the speaker's point across with desired emphasis.

Thus, when Jesus cried out against the Pharisee-hypocrites who paraded their piety while fasting, he was almost surely correct that there were some Pharisees who succumbed to this temptation. All our sources agree, as does

---

one hypocrisy with another. Much simpler is to recognize the everyday nature of using oil and washing one's face, so Jesus is simply saying, act naturally. Davies and Allison, *Gospel according to Saint Matthew*, 1:619.

10. See p. 46 above.

11. Liebowitz, "Hypocrites or Pious Scholars?" 53–67.

common sense, that some Pharisees fell short of the ideal, sometimes in very noticeable ways. When making this seemingly blanket charge, Jesus meant to strongly oppose them in this area of disagreement. In their fasting praxis, they ignored and rejected the change demanded by the dawning kingdom of God. They had tasted the good old wine and still preferred it to the new. He did not, however, mean that all Pharisees were hypocrites, or put on sad faces when they fasted. Nor was he generalizing that Pharisees as a group were inherently hypocritical. If we tried to phrase Jesus' charge in more objective language, it might sound like this. "Some of you Pharisees still fast like nothing has changed, like our God's rule is not arriving! You are still putting ashes on your head, rending your garments and putting on sad faces mourning your sins. Wake up you play-actors!"[12] But you have to admit, this doesn't have near the rhetorical punch of the simple "you hypocrites."

Conclusion

The actual practice of fasting turns out not to have been a major point of disagreement between Jesus and the Pharisees. True, during the period of his earthly ministry, he and his disciples did not fast, while most Pharisees did. The disagreement was not, however, over fasting itself; Jesus says at a later point his disciples will fast. The disagreement was over whether the current moment is the time for fasting or for feasting. Jesus preaches "the time is near," the eschatological banquet is opening its doors; most Pharisees reject this.

But there was one additional point of tension. Since biblical fasting was often meant to accompany mourning or repentance, and could include signs of sorrow such as rending garments or putting ashes on the head, it appears some Pharisees may have over-acted. Jesus calls them out for this hypocritical play-acting. Instead, when his disciples fast in the future, they should act naturally rather than putting on a sad face. Most Pharisees probably agreed.

---

12. The English word "hypocrite" leads us automatically to assume something is being said about the person's intent. They think one thing, but do another; the outside does not match the inside. It might help to follow the lead of several versions which use "play-actor" rather than "hypocrite" (Phillips, The Message, New Testament for Everyone). This more accurately conveys the sense of the original.

Part 4

New Testament Portrait: Attitudes toward Pharisees

CHAPTER 13

Were the Pharisees Legalists?

If there is one trait of the Pharisees that up until fairly recently would command nearly universal assent, it is their self-righteous legalism. And if there is one Gospel passage that proves this trait, it is the parable of the Pharisee and the tax-collector (Luke 18:9–14).

> He also told this parable to some who trusted in themselves that they were righteous and regarded others with contempt: "Two men went up to the temple to pray, one a Pharisee and the other a tax collector. The Pharisee, standing by himself, was praying thus, 'God, I thank you that I am not like other people: thieves, rogues, adulterers, or even like this tax collector. I fast twice a week; I give a tenth of all my income.' But the tax collector, standing far off, would not even look up to heaven, but was beating his breast and saying, 'God, be merciful to me, a sinner!' I tell you, this man went down to his home justified rather than the other; for all who exalt themselves will be humbled, but all who humble themselves will be exalted."

The comments of Charles Childers on the Pharisee in this parable can stand in for a whole cloud of witnesses.

> [The Pharisees] did not trust in the grace of God for their righteousness, but relied on their own good works. They considered themselves to be justified by good deeds.... The Pharisees were the strictest, narrowest, most legalistic of the Jewish sects.... This is the prime example of the prayer of a self-righteous man. It really does not deserve to be called a prayer. It is scarcely more than a recitation of the Pharisee's supposed good qualities and deeds, an attempt to demonstrate to God that he deserved

divine consideration. . . . [The Pharisee's] sin was that of self-righteous egotism.[1]

Our review of the Pharisees in Jewish literature did not support this legalistic portrait and modern scholars generally avoid using this term to describe their soteriology.[2] True, they were known for their exceeding *akribeia*, their commitment to the precise interpretation of the law's commands and prohibitions, but this was not typically viewed as their gateway to grace. Nor do the rabbinic writings yield a self-righteous theology of earning one's way into the God of Israel's good favor. Although previous generations of Christian interpreters culled the Talmud to prove Jewish legalism, this error has been laid to rest. Instead, the intense focus on detailed performance of God's will in Torah was built on a foundation of God's electing grace to Israel and was seen as the way to walk in faithfulness to this God, not the way to earn his love.[3]

So, what was going on in this parable? Was this an atypical Pharisee? Was Jesus exaggerating or caricaturing?[4] Our problem is that centuries of Christian tradition have made it difficult for us to hear this story the way a first-century Palestinian Jew would have heard it. We have seen evidence that the Pharisees were generally popular and influential among the Jewish crowds and were considered godly. The opposite was true of tax-collectors whose reputation was closer to that of traitors and quislings. Thus, the initial presumption of a hearer would have been that the Pharisee was the good guy, the tax-collector the bad guy. And this presumption is confirmed by the story; though, we twentieth-century non-Jews must listen carefully.

The opening detail ("Two men went up to the temple to pray") pictures a typical godly act of prayer in the temple. That a Pharisee does this would be positive and fully expected, wholly in line with biblical instructions ("shall be called a house of prayer for all people," Isa 56:7). Such a pious act by a despised tax-collector would be more surprising, but understandable in light of his ensuing prayer of confession. Crossan suggests as a modern analogy, "A pope and a pimp went into St. Peter's to pray."[5]

The contrast continues with the descriptions of their physical stances. Both are standing, which was the normal posture for Jewish prayers (e.g.,

---

1. Childers, "Gospel According to St. Luke," 577–8. For a classic presentation of legalistic Pharisees, see Robertson, *Pharisees and Jesus*.

2. For example, the new Schürer (2014) has eliminated such language in its description of the Pharisees.

3. See esp. Sanders, *Paul and Palestinian Judaism*, 33–428.

4. So Holmgren, "Pharisee and the Tax Collector," 252–61.

5. Crossan, *Raid on the Articulate*, 108.

Tob 6:18; Matt 6:5), and both are engaged in private, not corporate, prayer. However, the Pharisee gets only the brief note that he stood "by himself,"[6] while the tax-collector's stance receives a detailed description. He stood "far off, would not even look up to heaven" and was "beating his breast" as a symbol of contrition and sorrow. This all suggests that the Pharisee's stance was unremarkable,[7] while the tax-collector's was surprising. Here was a sinner acting like a truly repentant son of Abraham.

Contrary to the understanding of generations of Christian interpreters, the Pharisee's prayer (vv. 11–12) would sound not self-righteous, but biblical and godly. Many have thought he was proudly pointing to his own self-generated good works, much like we might say "thank God I'm better than those so and so's." But comparison with similar-sounding ancient Jewish prayers suggests otherwise. Rather than praising himself, he was giving thanks to God for keeping him on the path of righteousness, for aiding him to avoid the path of evildoers such as thieves, adulterers or tax-collectors. By God's helping guidance, he did "not follow the advice of the wicked, or take the path that sinners tread, or sit in the seat of scoffers" but his "delight is in the law of the Lord" (Ps 1:1–2). His fasting and tithing showed the depth of his delight in the law, even going beyond the minimum requirements laid out in Torah. His righteousness was not merely in word but also in deed. Such recounting of one's loyal faithfulness to God's ways, such confession of righteousness in prayer, was modeled in the Psalms and not thought of as self-righteous boasting.

> Hear a just cause, O LORD; attend to my cry; give ear to my prayer from lips free of deceit. From you let my vindication come; let your eyes see the right. If you try my heart, if you visit me by night, if you test me, you will find no wickedness in me; my mouth does not transgress. As for what others do, by the word of your lips I have avoided the ways of the violent. My steps have held fast to your paths; my feet have not slipped. I call upon you, for you will answer me, O God; incline your ear to me, hear my words. (Ps 17:1–6; similar Ps 26)

---

6. Difficult text-critical, grammatical and translation issues lie behind this seemingly simple phrase. Does "by himself [*pros heauton*]" go with the verb "standing" (NRSV: standing by himself) or should it be taken with "praying" (NIV: prayed about himself; NASB: spoke this prayer to himself), with most scholars favoring the former. For thorough discussion of the issues reaching the conclusion taken in my comments above, see Friedrichsen, "Temple, a Pharisee, a Tax Collector," 95–97, and Snodgrass, *Stories with Intent*, 399 and nn.

7. Some speculate that the Pharisee's standing "by himself" hints at a haughty stand-offishness.

> I have chosen the way of faithfulness; I set your ordinances before me. I cling to your decrees, O LORD; let me not be put to shame. I run the way of your commandments, for you enlarge my understanding. (Ps 119:30–32)

The Pharisee's prayer sounds not unlike prayers we hear from Qumran or later prayers in rabbinic sources.

> I give you thanks, Lord,
> because you did not make my lot fall in the congregation of falsehood,
> nor have you placed my regulation in the counsel of hypocrites. (1QH[a] XV.34)

> I thank you, O Lord, my God, that you have assigned my portion with those who sit in the house of learning, and not with those who sit at street corners; for I am early to work on the words of the Torah, and they are early to work on things of no importance. I weary myself, and they weary themselves; I weary myself and profit from it, while they weary themselves to no profit. I run and they run. I run towards the life of the Age to Come, and they run towards the pit of destruction. (b. Ber. 28b)[8]

Though it is debated, the Pharisee's prayer, including the element of tithing, may echo Deut 26:12–15.[9]

> When you have finished paying all the tithe of your produce in the third year . . . then you shall say before the LORD your God: "I have removed the sacred portion from the house, and I have given it to the Levites, the resident aliens, the orphans, and the widows, in accordance with your entire commandment that you commanded me; I have neither transgressed nor forgotten any of your commandments . . . . I have obeyed the LORD my God, doing just as you commanded me."

The tax-collector's prayer of penitence was short and sweet: "God, be merciful to me, a sinner!" It would remind Jewish hearers of David's prayer of penitence in Ps 51:1 ("Have mercy on me, O God.").

Most parables have some sort of surprise or reversal that shocks the hearer into reflecting more deeply on the story. This is certainly the case with this story: the good guy, the righteous Pharisee, is humbled, while

---

8. Cited in Evans, "Pharisee and the Publican," 348–49.

9. So Evans, "Pharisee and the Publican," 342–55. Disputed by Blomberg, "Midrash, Chiasmus," 217–61.

the traitor and godless person finds justification and exaltation. But why? For this we need to return to Luke's introduction to the parable which we skipped over previously.

> He also told this parable to some who trusted in themselves that they were righteous and regarded others with contempt. (v. 9)

Traditionally, this phrase ("trusted in themselves that they were righteous") has been understood to mean they were *self*-righteous, their confidence was in themselves and their own deeds, not in God. But this doesn't line up with what we know about the theology of the Pharisees as participants in "common Judaism." To belong to the righteous, the elect, the people of God's good favor, was a central element of the entire OT tradition. And identifying those who were the righteous was not all that difficult . . . they were those who walked in God's ways, according to God's direction or Torah. Those walking on this path rejoiced to be on it and gave thanks to God for his kindness in calling and empowering them toward this end. They were "confident about themselves that they were [among the] righteous." This is a better translation of Luke 18:9a. Such confidence was to characterize the righteous, and was contrasted with the uncertainty of the wicked. "The wicked are overthrown by their evildoing, but the righteous find a refuge in their integrity" (Prov 14:32). This is even clearer when comparing the Greek text of Luke 18:9a with the LXX version of this Proverb.

| Prov 14:32 LXX | but the one who is confident in their own holiness is righteous. | ὁ δὲ πεποιθὼς τῇ ἑαυτοῦ ὁσιότητι δίκαιος |
| Luke 18:9 (author's translation) | some who were confident about themselves that they were righteous | τινας τοὺς πεποιθότας ἐφ' ἑαυτοῖς ὅτι εἰσὶν δίκαιοι |

The linguistic parallels, although not exact, are striking. Both use a participial form of the verb *peithō*, use the reflexive pronoun (*heautos*) to describe the personal referent of this trust or confidence, and describe the outcome of the confidence with *dikaios*. Note also how this phrase is used to describe the genuinely upright *over against the wicked*, just as in the Pharisee's prayer in Luke 18. Thus, the Pharisee does not trust in arrogant self-righteousness, but is confident that his life has been lived in accordance with the ways of God's covenant, and that he belongs to the righteous, and not to the wicked.[10]

10. So Wilk: "The parable is aimed at Jews . . . who are rightfully confident in their

This leaves us with only vv. 9 and 14 to explain, and they turn out to be the key to the whole. Notice how these opening and closing verses form bookends.

> He also told this parable to some who trusted in themselves that they were righteous and regarded others with contempt (v. 9b).

> . . . for all who exalt themselves will be humbled, but all who humble themselves will be exalted (v. 14b).

The Pharisee "regarded others with contempt," or as the closing puts it, they "exalted" themselves and "humbled" or put others lower. As Snodgrass notes, "What may have started as legitimate affirmation that he has kept the covenant has detoured into disdain and self-congratulation."[11] It was the Pharisee's attitude that was the target of the parable . . . not an attitude of legalism or self-righteousness, but an attitude of disdain for those who did not follow his standards.

Jesus, on the other hand, preached the advent of a kingdom that seemed to turn the normal covenantal expectation on its head. Sinners were welcomed and justified, and those normally thought to be the righteous ones and heirs were turned out. But here we must be careful to follow Jesus' reasoning. This reversal of expectations was not due to a rejection of the former standard, of Torah. He was not implying that loyalty to God's ways, to commandments such as Sabbath rest, tithing, circumcision, avoidance of sin, etc., were overturned or unimportant. No, they still marked out the way of the righteous in Israel. But the final page in God's eschatological playbook had now been turned. Something that "exceeds [the righteousness] of the scribes and Pharisees" (Matt 5:20) had arrived on the scene.

What Was Inadequate About the "Righteousness of the Pharisees" (Matt 5:20)?

After the Beatitudes and sayings about salt and light (5:1–16), Jesus turned in the Sermon on the Mount to the question of Torah, prophets, and commandments.

> Do not think that I have come to abolish the law or the prophets; I have come not to abolish but to fulfill. For truly I tell you, until heaven and earth pass away, not one letter, not one stroke of a

---

way of life oriented around God's commands." Wilk, "(Selbst-)Erhöhung und (Selbst-)Erniedrigung," 118 (author's translation).

11. Snodgrass, *Stories with Intent*, 401.

letter, will pass from the law until all is accomplished. Therefore, whoever breaks one of the least of these commandments, and teaches others to do the same, will be called least in the kingdom of heaven; but whoever does them and teaches them will be called great in the kingdom of heaven. For I tell you, unless your righteousness exceeds that of the scribes and Pharisees, you will never enter the kingdom of heaven. (Matt 5:17-20)

This is undoubtedly Jesus' most Torah-affirming statement in the Gospels. And it is precisely as the one who upholds Torah to the uttermost ("not one letter, not one stroke of a letter") that he contrasts the righteousness of his disciples with that of the scribes and Pharisees. In this context "righteousness" is clearly a term referring to behavior, to how one lives, and especially how one lives vis-à-vis the will of God expressed in Torah.[12] This was laid down in vv. 17-19. It has to do with "breaking" and "doing" the "commandments." This is also how righteousness was most commonly understood in Jewish circles.[13]

As we have seen, the righteousness taught by the Pharisees revolved around careful obedience to the will of God in Torah. It was scrupulous and detailed in the desire to fully conform to the commandments. Yet, Jesus claimed that the righteousness he taught *in some way* far exceeded that promoted by the Pharisees. Perhaps, like the DSS, Jesus thought the Pharisees relaxed the commandments too much, making them too "smooth."[14] His sermon has sometimes been read this way as pushing the commandments to the nth degree of difficulty.[15] Not merely murder is prohibited, but even an angry, judgmental word (vv. 21-22). Not merely adultery is forbidden, but even lustful looks and thoughts (vv. 27-28). However, elsewhere his teaching and praxis, especially in regard to Sabbath and purity, appear to relax the commands, to make them easier. Eating with unwashed hands, or plucking grain on the Sabbath, helping an animal out of a pit, or healing a diseased person—these are all allowable. The righteousness he teaches certainly does not exceed *in difficulty* that promoted by the Pharisees on these points, and he castigates those who make keeping Torah a "burden" (23:4).

Exactly how the righteousness he proposed exceeded that of the Pharisees is laid out in the antitheses which follow (vv. 21-48). Only by

12. This must be insisted upon against interpreters who see this "exceeding righteousness" as primarily the imputed righteousness of Christ himself, rather than the behavior of the believer.

13. On this see, for example, Przybylski, *Righteousness in Matthew*.

14. See pp. 51-53 above.

15. "Jesus' words . . . require even more than the Torah itself requires." Davies and Allison, *Gospel According to Saint Matthew*, 1:501.

following this path of righteousness could one enter the kingdom of heaven (5:20) and be complete (5:48). The difference revolved around letting love, mercy and kindness be the guiding light in understanding how to keep the commands (see esp. vv. 43–48). Thus, not only literal murder was out-of-bounds, but any expression violating love and mercy towards others (vv. 21–22). Not only literal adultery was forbidden, but equally more hidden acts of merciless and loveless violence toward women (vv. 27–28). The contrast was not with a supposed legalism, externalism, or ritualism of the Pharisees. Nor should we mistakenly think that they allowed loving-kindness no place in their own Torah-interpretation, for evidence is abundant that they surely did make allowance for human need. *The difference is the radical way Yahweh's lovingkindness functions as the hermeneutical key for all the commandments in the new era of God's dawning reign.* In one way this was not really "new," since Torah itself placed divine mercy at the heart of Israel's relationship to her God, and first-century Jews, including the Pharisees (and later the rabbis), were quite aware of its centrality. Its "newness" was not that Jesus was the first to discover it, but that he placed it more consistently and more radically at the heart of his Torah-interpretation. The Pharisees rejected this hermeneutical move, just as they rejected his authority to teach the way of God, and as they rejected his announcement of the dawning of God's new era for the nation and the world.

CHAPTER 14

Woe to You Hypocrites

NINETEEN TIMES IN THE Synoptic Gospels Jesus charged the Pharisees with hypocrisy. He warned the disciples about the "yeast of the Pharisees, that is, their hypocrisy" (Luke 12:1). And in the memorable series of woes in Matt 23, Jesus thundered over and over, "Woe to you, scribes and Pharisees, hypocrites!"[1] We have touched on this hypocrisy elsewhere, but now it is time to focus in on a central question of this book: Were the Pharisees hypocrites?

Here we face a seeming historical paradox. Fact #1: Jesus called Pharisees hypocrites. Fact #2: Pharisees were not typically hypocrites, at least as far as the evidence we have in Jewish and Christian sources is concerned. Although the first point might seem self-evident, some scholars do argue that Jesus never called Pharisees hypocrites or other insulting names. They contend these conflict stories arose in the church of the latter part of the first century when Christians were in conflict with Jews who rejected Jesus' claims. Jesus did not say these things; later Christians did.[2] We have argued earlier that such a skeptical view regarding the authenticity of the Gospels is unwarranted.[3] One argument against authenticity is that the criticisms miss the mark historically (#2 above). "The reforms already existed in Pharisaic thinking, and Jesus is advocating measures which had already been enacted in the Pharisaic movement."[4] We have indicated elsewhere our agreement that Jesus was not the first or only Jewish teacher to advocate a more lenient, human-friendly, *halakhah*, but Maccoby has overstated the *halakhic* harmony at this point. Disputes over

---

1. Matt 23:13, 15, 23, 25, 27, 29.
2. Maccoby, *Jesus the Pharisee*.
3. See pp. 87–89 above.
4. Maccoby, *Jesus the Pharisee*, 119.

halakhah, including some of the issues recorded in the Gospels, are historically realistic as the DSS have demonstrated.

So, if Jesus did call Pharisees hypocrites, what did he mean? At first glance, the repeated charge seems pretty straightforward. They are one thing on the outside while being the opposite on the inside. Or as Jesus phrased with a quote from Isaiah, "This people honors me [outwardly] with their lips, but [inwardly] their hearts are far from me" (Matt 15:8).

What Exactly Was a "Hypocrite"?

This outside/inside contrast, or contrast between appearance and reality, reflects the original setting of the Greek term, *hypokritēs*, which spoke of stage-actors who wore masks.[5] They appeared to be a character other than their own identity. To call someone *hypokritēs*, a "role-player" or "mask-wearer," was not meant negatively. In Greek culture of the first century to call someone a hypocrite did not generally imply the pretense and deceit that is typically meant with the English word.[6]

However, by the first century in Hellenistic Jewish circles, this same Greek term had taken on inherently negative implications. In fact, *hypokritēs* and cognates had become the unanimous choice of later Greek translators of the OT (Aquila, Symmachus, Theodotion) for Hebrew *ḥanēf*, which referred in the Hebrew OT to one who was godless, profane, or impious (Job 8:13; 17:8; etc.), and was translated in the LXX by words such as *asebēs* (ungodly), *anomos* (lawless), and *paranomos* (lawbreaker), but not *hypokritēs*. Barr is probably correct that this linguistic development was decisively influenced by events in the Maccabean era, when deceitful villains like Apollonius outwardly "pretended to be peaceably disposed [*ton eirēnikon hypokritheis*]," when they inwardly intended to put everyone to the sword (2 Macc 5:25). Conversely, righteous Jews like Eleazar refused to save themselves "by pretending [*hypokrinomenos*] to eat pork" (4 Macc 6:15), while wicked Jews were hypocrites by doing the opposite (2 Macc 6:25).[7]

Although we do not have Jesus' original Hebrew/Aramaic words, it is most likely he called the Pharisees *ḥanēf*, which had come to mean an impious

---

5. Wilckens, "*hypokrinomai*, etc.," 8:559–63.

6. English "hypocrite" = "One who falsely professes to be virtuously or religiously inclined; one who pretends to have feelings or beliefs of a higher order than his real ones; hence generally, a dissembler, pretender." *Oxford English Dictionary*.

7. On this linguistic development of *hypokritēs*, see Barr, "Hebrew/Aramaic Background of 'Hypocrisy,'" 309–17.

pretender to godliness, a fake, a religious imposter.[8] Thus, Jesus could say of a wicked slave, God "will cut him in pieces and put him with the hypocrites [the wicked, the imposters], where there will be weeping and gnashing of teeth" (Matt 24:51). Ironically, the very group who arose from the Maccabean struggle against godless hypocrisy are now charged with being fakes, imposters, and pretenders themselves. That must have stung!

The Nature of Insulting Speech ("Invective")

Before exploring Jesus' charge more deeply, we need to say a word about the use of insulting, abusive or highly critical speech in the ancient world, what is often termed invective. Whether "hypocrites," "fools," "whitewashed tombs," "blind leaders of the blind" or "brood of vipers," Jesus seemed ready with an insult toward Pharisees and other opponents. This, of course, poses a problem, since Jesus elsewhere said his followers should not speak this way. They should turn the other cheek instead of retaliating against opposition (Matt 5:39) and should not call others names like "fools" (Matt 5:22).

A variety of solutions have been proposed for this seeming discrepancy. A popular approach among scholars is to simply deny that Jesus said such things.[9] The opposite tendency is to affirm not only that Jesus did say these harsh things but also that these were objectively true and accurate descriptions of the Pharisees, at least for many if not all.[10] According to these interpreters, many Pharisees did rob widows and load burdens on poor peasants without lifting a finger to help them. They did measure out precise tithe amounts of garden herbs but couldn't care less about justice and mercy. Neither of these positions has a strong claim in my opinion. As we have mentioned before, the latter has to explain how a revolting group of uncaring hypocrites could be popular and influential among those very people they mistreated. And the former relies upon form-critical theories under increasing attack by Gospel scholars.

---

8. "It is widely accepted that, if there is a particular Hebrew term that 'lies behind' the Greek terms of the NT, that term is *hanēf*." Barr, "Hebrew/Aramaic Background of 'hypocrisy,'" 309. This strongly negative intent of Jesus' charge is confirmed by the substitution of "evil" (Matt 22:18), "trickery" (Luke 20:23) and "unbelievers" (Matt 24:51) for "hypocrite" in Synoptic parallels.

9. Matthew's "exaggerated and vindictive polemic has its origin in his community's conflict with these more powerful opponents," i.e., at the time and social location of Matthew's writing (not that of the historical Jesus). Sim, "Polemical Strategies," 498. Similar, Saldarini, "Delegitimation," 659–80.

10. "Ostentatious pride was one of the besetting sins of the Pharisees. . . . Of course, not all Pharisees were like that, but too many were." Earle, "Matthew," 207.

A large number of scholars and serious Bible students fall somewhere in between these two extremes. Jesus was not trying to give a detached, objective description, he was thundering as a prophet ("woe to you"). Yet, his critique had to connect with reality to some degree unless we think he was simply "letting off steam." It turns out Jesus was speaking just like we might expect a first-century Jewish teacher to speak. As Johnson summarizes, this is simply "the way all opponents talked about each other back then."[11] To give the readers a flavor of this, here is Josephus on Egyptians: "these frivolous and utterly senseless specimens of humanity . . . filled with envy . . . folly and narrowmindedness" (*Ag. Ap.* 1.225–226). Philo also caricatures them, "the Egyptian disposition is by nature a most jealous and envious one" (*Flacc.* 5.29), as well as the Alexandrians who behaved "with greater brutality and ferocity than even the most savage beasts" (*Legat.* 19.131). Of Jewish zealots and Sicarii Josephus says "every dictate of religion is ridiculed by these men who scoffed at the prophets' oracles as imposter's fables" (*J. W.* 4.385). They are "imposters and brigands" (2.264), "slaves, the dregs of society, and the bastard scum of the nation" (5.443–444). Not to be outdone, the Qumran community described all outsiders, including other (non-sectarian) Jews, as characterized by

> greed, frailty of hands in the service of justice, irreverence, deceit, pride and haughtiness of heart, dishonesty, trickery, cruelty, much insincerity, impatience, much insanity, impudent enthusiasm, appalling acts performed in a lustful passion, filthy paths for indecent purposes, blasphemous tongue, blindness of eyes, hardness of hearing, stiffness of neck, hardness of heart in order to walk in all the paths of darkness and evil cunning. (1QS IV.9–11)

As should be obvious these are hardly accurate historical descriptions of all Egyptians, Alexandrians or non-Essene Jews. *Some* of the charges may be true for *some* of the intended target, *but even to focus on this question of historical accuracy is to miss the point of invective.* It is not trying to convey detailed historical information, it is trying to discredit, warn and persuade. The Qumran covenanters knew theirs was the true way and other Jews were on the path of error and evil. The invective makes this point in the strongest and most unforgettable way through generalization (the entire group is by nature characterized by these vices), exaggeration (they are not just bad but "walk in all the paths of darkness and evil") and stereotyped language (see list below). The bad apples that exist in every group or movement simply prove the point: "See, didn't we warn you."

11. Johnson, "Anti-Jewish Slander," 429.

Stereotypical Jewish Language of Invective[12]

- Hypocrites
- Good in appearance only
- Misleaders
- Blind
- Foolish or ignorant
- Teachers of wrong *halakhah*
- Guilty of economic sins
- Guilty of sexual sins
- Unclean
- Persecutors/murderers of the righteous
- Likened to sinful generations of the past
- Compared to snakes
- Destined for eschatological judgment
- The cause of God forsaking his temple

Jesus grew up in a culture accustomed to the use of such invective. The charges he made in the Gospels against the Pharisees overlap remarkably with the above list of stereotypical charges against opponents.

So, Jesus was employing stereotyped invective speech rather than careful historical description, but he still must have meant something. Howard Marshall notes there are two distinct nuances of "hypocrisy" in English: 1) pretense, dissimulation (intentionally behave other than one professes), and 2) inconsistency (also to act differently than professed, but out of "ignorance, thoughtlessness, or self-deception" rather than intentional deceit).[13] Both senses can be seen in the Gospels. Judas appeared outwardly to care for Jesus when he greeted him with a kiss in the garden of Gethsemane, but inwardly his intent was to betray him to the authorities in exchange for money (Mark 14:43-46). This was clearly *intentional* hypocrisy. On another occasion, however, Jesus called people hypocrites when they failed to apply their weather forecasting skills to the observation of heavenly signs (Luke 12:54-56). This was *inconsistency* through laziness or carelessness, not intentional deception. For this reason, as we suggested above, it might be

---

12. For this list with full references to Jewish literature, see Davies and Allison, *Gospel according to Saint Matthew*, 3:259-60.

13. Marshall, "Who Is a Hypocrite?" 133.

better to translate these occurrences with something like "you play-actors," "you imposters." And this was, indeed, at the heart of Jesus' invective against the Pharisees. Although they enjoyed a popular reputation as godly and wise, Jesus called them fakes. Just as many of them rejected his ministry and message, so he rejected their claims to teach Israel the will of God.

Jesus Hurls Seven "Woes" Against the Pharisees (Matt 23:13–36)

Armed now with a better understanding of hypocrisy and ancient invective, let's probe Jesus' specific hypocrisy charges against the Pharisees. The heaviest concentration occurs in Matt 23:13–36 where Jesus uttered a series of seven "woes" against the scribes and Pharisees.[14] With the exception of the third woe, all begin "Woe to you, scribes and Pharisees, hypocrites." Such cries of "woe to you" were expressions of judgment as in Isa 5:8–22 (six woes) and Hab 2:6–20 (five woes). The word used (*ouai*) "connotes a powerful and denunciatory judgment akin to a curse."[15]

Woe #1

> But woe to you, scribes and Pharisees, hypocrites! For you lock people out of the kingdom of heaven. For you do not go in yourselves, and when others are going in, you stop them. (Matt 23:13; par. Luke 11:52)

Jesus pictured the kingdom of God (heaven) as a room whose door of entry had been locked to others by the scribes and Pharisees. He did not give further explanation here, but we have plenty of clues elsewhere to his meaning. "The kingdom of God (or heaven) has drawn near" was the heart of Jesus' message (Matt 4:17; Mark 1:15). The disciples, who were loyal to Jesus and accepted his teaching, have "the keys of the kingdom of heaven" (Matt 16:19). The scribes and Pharisees for the most part rejected Jesus' authority and teaching. They "lock people out" by their public rejection of Jesus and his teaching. In Luke's words, "you have taken away the key of knowledge; you did not enter yourselves, and you hindered those who were entering"

---

14. An additional "woe" included in numerous Greek MSS (23:14) and some translations (KJV) is a later interpolation. See Metzger, *Textual Commentary*, ad loc. Luke has a somewhat similar series of woes addressed first to Pharisees, then lawyers (11:42–52).

15. Garland, *Intention of Matthew 23*, 87, further 64–90 on meaning of "woe."

(11:52).¹⁶ It is this conflict—who is authorized to teach and lead Israel?—that characterized nearly all of Jesus' rivalry with Pharisees.¹⁷ And it is this which underlay Jesus' charge of hypocrisy against them. Those who claimed to serve, love and obey the God of Israel, rejected the truth from the teacher-emissary he had sent . . . this was the pinnacle of hypocrisy.

Woe #2

> Woe to you, scribes and Pharisees, hypocrites! For you cross sea and land to make a single convert, and you make the new convert twice as much a child of hell as yourselves. (Matt 23:15)

Most discussions of this woe center on whether "crossing land and sea to make a single convert" referred to Jewish missionary activity among diaspora gentiles or to something else. Although such Jewish missionary activity to make proselytes of gentiles used to be assumed based on this verse, this view has been largely abandoned.¹⁸ Instead, this woe may refer to Jewish efforts at informing and educating gentiles about Jewish faith,¹⁹ or may refer to "proselyting" other Jews to Pharisaic *halakhah*.²⁰

Whatever the precise historical referent of this proselytizing activity, the point is nearly identical to the charge of hypocrisy in the first woe. They appeared to expend great effort toward greater obedience to the God of Israel. Yet, in reality, they were leading people in the opposite direction.

Woe #3

> Woe to you, blind guides, who say, "Whoever swears by the sanctuary is bound by nothing, but whoever swears by the gold of the sanctuary is bound by the oath." (Matt 23:16)

---

16. Similar, Gos. Thom. 39, they "have received the keys of knowledge and have hidden them."

17. Pickup sees this as a central difference in Matt between Jesus and his opponents. "Throughout Matthew, the differences between Jesus and the Pharisees consistently center around the matter of whose explication of the Torah is correct. The thrust of Matthew's gospel is this: Jesus properly teaches and exemplifies the Torah, while the scribes and Pharisees do not." Pickup, "Matthew's and Mark's Pharisees," 102.

18. See esp. McKnight, *Light Among the Gentiles*, and Goodman, *Mission and Conversion*.

19. So Paget, "Jewish Proselytism," 65–103.

20. So Goodman, *Mission and Conversion*, 70.

Although the term "Pharisee" does not occur, this was clearly addressed to them as were the rest of the woes. Instead of "hypocrites," Jesus here called them "blind guides," and will continue to accuse them of blindness in other woes (vv. 17, 19, 24, 26; cf. 15:1–20). The issue concerned binding vs. non-binding oaths. The Pharisees, according to Jesus, taught that oaths sworn "by the sanctuary" and "by the altar" were non-binding, but oaths sworn by the "gold of the sanctuary" or the "gift on the altar" were binding. Our evidence of Second Temple praxis regarding oaths is very limited, but different groups apparently held differing positions.[21] In one instance the later rabbis opposed the position held by the Pharisees in our text. Both the houses of Shammai and Hillel ruled that a declaration that figs were *corban* (i.e., dedicated to the temple) did *not* apply to members of one's own family. I.e., one could not evade obligations to parents by this means.[22]

Whatever the historical tradition of the Pharisees on such points, Jesus employed what we might today call a common sense argument to point out the Pharisees' blindness regarding oaths: "Which is greater, the gold or the sanctuary that has made the gold sacred?" (23:17) The Pharisees were "blind fools" for giving the lesser (gold) more importance than the greater (sanctuary).[23] Again, those who claimed to honor God ended up minimizing him by their traditions. Thus, one was not bound even by an oath sworn "by the one who dwells in" the sanctuary, "by the one who is seated upon" the throne of God (vv. 21–22).[24]

Woe #4

> Woe to you, scribes and Pharisees, hypocrites! For you tithe mint, dill, and cummin, and have neglected the weightier matters of the law: justice and mercy and faith. It is these you ought to have practiced without neglecting the others. (Matt 23:23; par. Luke 11:42)

---

21. See on this Davies and Allison, *Gospel according to Saint Matthew*, 3:290–91.

22. As so often, there may be evidence that some allowed such use of *corban* (cf. Philo, *Hypothetica*, 7.3, 5), but the intent of this text is unclear. Arguing *for* such precedent in Philo, Sanders, *Jewish Law*, 54, 57.

23. Calling them "fools [*mōroi*]" seems to contradict Matt 5:22 ("if you say, 'You fool,' you will be liable to the hell of fire"). The prohibition in Matt 5:22, however, speaks of excluding a brother or sister from salvation, whereas Matt 23:17 applies the well-known OT trope of the "fool" to non-disciples who are actively rejecting Jesus. See Garlington, "'You Fool!': Matthew 5:22," 61–83.

24. In Matt 5:33–37 Jesus prefers a simple "yes" or "no" to all such reinforced oaths (swear by God, temple, gold, etc.).

Tithing was a common practice among Jews, whether Pharisees or not.[25] In passing, Jesus here noted his agreement with this practice ("these [weightier matters] you ought to have practiced *without neglecting the others* [tithing]"). The pharisaic concern for accuracy apparently led them to tithe even produce not specifically mandated in Scripture. Nowhere in the OT were tithes on mint, dill, or cummin required, but the Pharisees wanted to make sure they covered all the bases. The Pharisee in one of Jesus' parables pointed specifically to his tithe on "everything" he brought in (Luke 18:12). For the later rabbis, "The general principle obviously was that foodstuff should be tithed, but there is room for disagreement about what counts as 'food.' According to the House of Hillel, black cummin is susceptible to impurity and also should be tithed, while the House of Shammai disagreed (Uktzin 3.6). The seeds of black cummin . . . could be used in very small quantities as a spice. Apparently the Shammaites did not consider it to be a food."[26]

Jesus' critique was not that they focused on minor issues,[27] but that they did so to the "neglect" of important matters: justice, mercy, and faith (or faithfulness). As he will quip, they "strain out a gnat but swallow a camel!" (v. 24) The three "weighty" virtues formed central pillars of Torah piety.[28] Their importance was recognized by all branches of Judaism, including the Pharisees. The Pharisees' "neglect" of central Torah virtues was, as we have seen regularly in Jesus' critique, not overt. They did not preach abandonment of the just duty to parents, but by their *corban* policy they effectively broke with this duty (Mark 7:9-13). They did not teach against giving merciful aid to the ill and injured, but their concern to keep the letter of the Sabbath law sometimes resulted in unmerciful behavior (Mark 3:1-6). There is certainly no need to deny that some Pharisees may well have been hypocrites of the intentional sort, never really intending to love and obey God in spite of what they said. But one of the main points of this book is that this cannot have been true of Pharisees in general. Instead, much of their hypocrisy was the unintended result of their focus on careful obedience to the letter of Torah. Their blindness (v. 24a) lay at the root.

---

25. See above, pp. 66-67.

26. Sanders, *Jewish Law*, 48.

27. In fact, as Hagner recognizes, Jesus "sanctions . . . even the Pharisees' extension" of the tithing requirements, as long as they give proper attention to the weightier matters. Hagner, *Matthew 14-28*, 670.

28. Justice: Isa 1:17; Jer 22:3; Mercy: Hos 6:6; Zech 7:9-10; Faithfulness: Hab 2:4. Luke's version has two virtues, "justice and the love of God" (11:42).

Woe #5

> Woe to you, scribes and Pharisees, hypocrites! For you clean the outside of the cup and of the plate, but inside they are full of greed and self-indulgence. (Matt 23:25; par. Luke 11:39-41)

Jesus' rebuke dealt with a distinction between purity inside and outside, first in relation to vessels used in meals, then to humans. The OT spoke of cleansing or destroying vessels rendered unclean by an unclean animal (Lev 11:33) or a discharge (Lev 15:12), but there was no differentiation between purity of the inside or outside of the vessel. Neusner argued that such distinctions between purity of vessels inside versus outside were known pre-70, but that the purity of one did not necessarily affect the other.[29] "The outer part of the cup may be clean *even* while the inner part is unclean."[30] Neusner sees evidence after 70 CE that the house of Hillel came to "*regard the state of the inner part as decisive*," similar to Jesus' stance (at least in Matthew's version, "cleans the inside *first*," 23:26). Whatever the precise *halakhic* background, it would appear that disputes over inside versus outside were not strange or unknown.

Jesus, however, moved beyond such an *halakhic* dispute and connected it with a moral issue. This is explicit in Luke's version: "Your inside," in the heart, inner person, "is full of greed and wickedness." Matthew retained the ritual purity context ("inside *they* [i.e., the cups and dishes] *are full*"), yet also clearly had the metaphorical meaning equally in mind. In what sense can cups and plates be "full of greed and self-indulgence"?

Traditionally, Jesus' rebuke has been taken to mean "take care of the inner wickedness, and you do not need to worry so much about the external purity."[31] However, his statement about God creating both inside and outside and his call to "first clean the inside of the cup" does not privilege one over the other. Instead, as he will make clear regularly elsewhere, he was charging them with hypocrisy, of giving proper attention to external purity commanded in Torah while failing in weightier matters.[32]

Again, there may well have been some Pharisees who demonstrated greed and self-indulgence, but this was not their general reputation.[33] Jesus was engaged in invective speech, not historical description.

---

29. See also Derrett, "Receptacles and Tombs (Mt 23:24–30)," 257.

30. Neusner, "First Cleanse the Inside," 486–95.

31. So Marshall: then "ritual washing will presumably not be necessary." Marshall, *Gospel of Luke*, 495.

32. Luke's version calls them "fools" rather than "hypocrites" (11:40), but we have argued these terms make a similar point (see above).

33. See above pp. 45–48.

Woe #6

> Woe to you, scribes and Pharisees, hypocrites! For you are like whitewashed tombs, which on the outside look beautiful, but inside they are full of the bones of the dead and of all kinds of filth. So you also on the outside look righteous to others, but inside you are full of hypocrisy and lawlessness. (Matt 23:27-28; par. Luke 11:44)

Here is the same inside versus outside contrast central to the charge of hypocrisy.[34] The precise referent of "whitewashed graves" has been much disputed. Often reference is made to the pre-Passover practice of marking graves around Jerusalem with lime-chalk so as to warn pilgrims not to inadvertently make themselves unclean. However, such chalk markings, esp. if on grave plots in the ground (i.e,. just a white mark on the ground), could hardly be called beautiful. A variety of attempts to get around this have been proposed, but the easiest in my view is that of Lau, who documents the presence of beautiful white-washed tomb-monuments around Jerusalem in the time of Herod, which, of course, contained the bones of the dead.[35]

Woe #7

> Woe to you, scribes and Pharisees, hypocrites! For you build the tombs of the prophets and decorate the graves of the righteous. (Matt 23:29; par. Luke 11:47)

This woe may seem puzzling at first. Jesus initially pointed out the Pharisees' involvement in building tombs and decorating graves, but these were actions normally done to honor a deceased person, and thus were positive actions rather than blameworthy. He then quoted them as asserting, "If we had lived in the days of our ancestors, we would not have taken part with them in shedding the blood of the prophets" (Matt 23:30). Again, a seemingly praiseworthy attitude. Jesus, however, concluded from this, "Thus you testify against yourselves that you are descendants of those who murdered the prophets" (v. 31). It is this conclusion that is at first puzzling. How exactly does building tombs and disavowing the bad deeds of ancestors implicate them in hypocrisy?

---

34. Although the Lukan verse (11:44) has similarities, it is quite different. The problem there is that the graves are unmarked, not whitewashed and clearly marked, and thus people walk over them unknowingly.

35. Lau, "Geweißte Grabmäler," 463-80.

The missing logical link, as noted by most commentators, is probably that the coming crucifixion of the prophet Jesus ("some you kill and crucify," v. 34) and the persecution of his righteous disciples ("some you will flog in your synagogues and pursue from town to town," v. 34) will prove that the Pharisees are "children of their ancestors."[36] That is, they are just like them in spite of their disclaimers. Just as Yahweh had repeatedly sent prophets, sages and scribes whom Israel has rejected, so "this generation" will do the same. As Jesus will note shortly, Jerusalem is the city that "kills the prophets" (v. 37). Here again, as throughout these woes, the heart of their hypocrisy lay in their rejection of God's prophet and anointed one, while simultaneously proclaiming adherence to Yahweh.

It is this fundamental resistance to their God and what he is currently doing alongside their claim to love him and teach his ways that calls forth not only the repeated charge of "hypocrites," but now the fiercest condemnation.

> You snakes, you brood of vipers! How can you escape being sentenced to hell? (Matt 23:33)

And Jesus saw this most fundamental sort of hypocrisy foretold in the words of the prophet Isaiah.

> You hypocrites! Isaiah prophesied rightly about you when he said: "This people honors me with their lips, but their hearts are far from me; in vain do they worship me, teaching human precepts as doctrines." (Matt 15:7–9)

Show-offs Who Love to Parade Their Piety?

One of the common perceptions of the hypocritical Pharisees in the Gospels is that they were show-offs, that they claimed to seek after God's approval and glory, but in reality sought human honor and praise. They loved the places of honor in synagogues and at dinners, desired to be called rabbi, wore long tassels to advertise their piety, made sure others noticed they were fasting. Since we deal with the fasting issue elsewhere, this chapter will take up the first three matters.

---

36. "For the sons, by their hostile rejection of Jesus and his disciples, are repeating what their fathers had done in rejecting the prophets. . . . And no rejection of God's messengers is more grievous than the Pharisees' rejection of God's supreme messenger, Jesus." Hagner, *Matthew 14–28*, 672.

> They do all their deeds to be seen by others; for they make their phylacteries broad and their fringes long. They love to have the place of honor at banquets and the best seats in the synagogues, and to be greeted with respect in the marketplaces, and to have people call them rabbi. But you are not to be called rabbi, for you have one teacher, and you are all students. And call no one your father on earth, for you have one Father—the one in heaven. Nor are you to be called instructors, for you have one instructor, the Messiah. The greatest among you will be your servant. All who exalt themselves will be humbled, and all who humble themselves will be exalted. (Matt 23:5–12)

Jesus here criticized the "scribes and the Pharisees" (Matt 23:2) for their attention-seeking ("to be seen by others"), and then illustrated this with a number of specific behaviors.[37] To some extent, each of the behaviors noted by Jesus had its roots in Scripture and could have characterized Jesus and his disciples. Let me illustrate. Having one's good works "seen by others" was encouraged by Jesus in Matt 5:16 ("so that they may see your good works"). Of course, Jesus added the goal as "that they may . . . give glory to your Father in heaven," whereas he accused the Pharisees of doing this to receive glory from the people who observe them. The behavior itself, however, was commendable and identical; it was the unseen motivation that differentiated. The same was true of the wearing of phylacteries and tassels. Phylacteries were the small black leather boxes containing a bit of Scripture strapped by Jewish males to the forehead and left arm in obedience to Deut 11:18 ("You shall put these words of mine in your heart and soul, and you shall bind them as a sign on your hand, and fix them as an emblem on your forehead"). Jesus probably wore phylacteries.[38] In this case, along with the unseen bad motivation ("to be seen by others"), Jesus pointed to visible differences. A "broad" or "large" phylactery could refer to a lengthier strap holding the leather box, or to a larger box itself, or could even mean they "enlarge" the time period for wearing them.[39] The charge of loving long fringes or tassels referred to the blue or white threads sown to the four corners of a garment as commanded in Num

---

37. In the main Synoptic parallels (Mark 12:37–39; Luke 20:45–46) only the scribes are mentioned.

38. Though we have no specific evidence regarding his phylacteries, he likely did wear them, since the practice was viewed as biblically commanded, was widespread not just for scribes and Pharisees, and continued among Christians even into the fourth century. Davies and Allison, *Gospel According to Saint Matthew*, 3:274n56.

39. On these possibilities, see Davies and Allison, *Gospel According to Saint Matthew*, 3:273.

15:38–39 and Deut 22:12. Jesus himself wore tassels (Matt 9:20; 14:36), but claimed those of the Pharisees were "longer" and indicated their desire to be noticed for piety. But the question remains regarding both larger phylacteries and longer tassels... larger or longer than what? Scripture did not dictate a particular size to these items, and we hear that at some point (first century?) the schools of Hillel and Shammai debated tassel length and number.[40] That is, there was legitimate diversity among Jewish teachers on this matter. Possibly, Jesus' standard as a simple Galilean was for simpler and shorter, while the "Pharisee style," if such existed uniformly, was larger and longer. We noted in Josephus that Pharisees were known for simplicity of lifestyle in contrast to Sadducees, so it is unlikely they went over the top on this matter. Nevertheless, Jesus pointed to this difference as indicative of their inner attitude of self-seeking.

The next three behaviors involved symbols of honor in social situations. The closer one sat to the host at a dinner party, the higher one's status in the group. Likewise, there were apparently better seats in synagogues, presumably located in more prominent or desirable parts of the room. According to one of Jesus' parables, seat selection at a dinner party was up to the host (Luke 14:7–11), so it is unlikely they simply grabbed the best seat.[41] As respected and popular members of Jewish society, it is more likely Pharisees were not infrequently given such positions of honor than that they actually had to angle for the good seats. Again, however, Jesus imputed an unseen evil motive to their seating. They did not so much "try to obtain" such seats, but they "loved" them. As with the phylacteries and tassels, the seating itself turns out to be neutral and not bad *per se*. One can easily imagine Jesus being offered the seat of honor at dinners and synagogues.[42] The real issue in all of these charges is where one's deepest sense of honor lay. Jesus charged the Pharisees with loving human honor above divine, while his disciples were to reverse this, preferring heavenly exaltation and embracing earthly humility (Matt 23:12). The same applies to the last of the three social behaviors, loving titles of respect like "rabbi." Later on, rabbi would become a more official title for a properly trained and recognized teacher-leader in the Jewish community and in modern times involves professional ordination. However, in the early and mid-first century CE it did not carry such official overtones. It was a general term of respect, meaning

---

40. *Sipre* on Num 15:37–41.

41. Against Wilckens and others who think the Pharisees "claim for themselves" such symbols of honor. Wilckens, "*stolē*," 7:690.

42. Not to mention being "seated at the right hand" of God himself as the son of man (Mark 14:62 par.).

literally "my master" as in a master-disciple relationship.[43] This sense of "master-teacher" is confirmed when Jesus follows up the prohibition of being addressed as rabbi with "for you have one teacher" and should not to be called "instructors."[44] As with the other criticisms, this one is accusing the Pharisees of being motivated by human glory-seeking. It is not the use of the titles *per se* that is being criticized—since Jesus and his disciples will use them[45]—but the unseen motive imputed to the Pharisaic use.[46]

So, back to the original issue . . . Were the Pharisees show-offs, glory-seekers? As with all invective, Jesus was not seeking primarily to paint an accurate historical description of all Pharisees. He was warning disciples and others against the Pharisaic movement, and the warning-invective was made particularly memorable by

1. generalization: as though "all Pharisees" were characterized by such glory-seeking
2. exaggeration: they do "all their deeds" to be noticed by others
3. stereotyped language: "to be seen by others" ("to impress people," PssSol 4:7, 19)

As to the behaviors cited, it is likely that many Pharisees did wear phylacteries and tassels, and sat in honored places and were addressed with respect ("rabbi," "father," "teacher"). But as we noted none of these were evil *per se*, and probably applied to Jesus, as well. The evil behavior in each case was an invisible motive, to be exalted by others rather than by God. But how did Jesus know this invisible evil motivation? He knew it because the Pharisaic movement as a whole (with exceptions, of course) was setting itself against the God of Israel, against Jesus and his kingdom message. Yahweh was inaugurating his rule and his prophet-agent was announcing it, but the Pharisees were rejecting what their God was doing. They were on the wrong side, and those on the wrong side of God's will were *ipso facto* hypocrites, self-seeking, blind, arrogant, etc.

43. On the term and office, see Schwarzfuchs, *Concise History of the Rabbinate*.

44. "Father" in "call no one your father on earth" may be a similar term of respectful address for one's teacher-master or other respected members of the religious community (e.g., Acts 22:1). See, Davies and Allison, *Gospel according to Saint Matthew*, 3:276–77.

45. Jesus is called "rabbi" by disciples, opponents and onlookers: (by disciples) Mark 9:5; 11:21; John 1:38, 49; 4:31; 9:2; 11:8); (by Judas) Matt 26:25, 49; Mark 14:45; (by opponents) John 3:2; (by onlookers) John 3:26; 6:25.

46. This should also warn against making this prohibition of titles like "father" into a new law as in Protestant aversion to Catholics referring to priests as "father." The title itself is not problematic, but the potential underlying motivation in its use.

We have concentrated on Matt's account since he gathers these behaviors most conveniently.

Behavior/Sayings	Matthew	Mark	Luke
"do all their deeds to be seen by others"	23:5		
"make phylacteries broad"	23:5		
"fringes long"	23:5	12:38 "long robes"	20:46 "long robes"
"place of honor at banquets"	23:6	12:39	20:46
"best seats in synagogues"	23:6	12:39	20:46; also 11:43
"greeted with respect in the marketplaces"	23:7	12:38	20:46; also 11:43
"be called rabbi"	23:7		
"be called father"	23:9		
"be called instructor"	23:10		
"greatest will be servant"	23:11	9:35; 10:43–44	9:48; 22:26
"exalted ... humbled"	23:12		14:11; 18:14

Both Mark and Luke include some of this critique, but omit elements that would be less meaningful to a non-Jewish audience (phylacteries, fringes, rabbi, father). Instead of the specifically Jewish "fringes," they add the more general "like to walk around in long robes [*stolais*]," referring probably to white outer garments, widely seen as marking higher status in contrast to simple clothing [*himatia*].[47] As noted above, Mark and Luke have Jesus speaking of scribes in the main parallels, but Luke's duplicate of the "best seats" and "greetings in the marketplace" (11:43) makes clear that Pharisees are equally in view.[48]

Matthew has one additional collection of hypocrisy charges unique to his Gospel and tied to such ostentatious behaviors (6:1–18). He does not explicitly say these hypocrites are Pharisees, but they are most likely in view.[49] Matthew, who loves numerical groupings, gathers three instances of Pharisaic piety in which Jesus perceived hypocrisy.

---

47. Fleddermann, "Warning about the Scribes," 54–57.
48. On the overlap between scribes and Pharisees, see pp. 12–14, 81–82.
49. Hypocrites are explicitly identified as Pharisees in Matt 15:7 and 22:18, and, of

- So whenever you give alms, do not sound a trumpet before you, as the hypocrites do in the synagogues and in the streets, so that they may be praised by others. (6:2)
- And whenever you pray, do not be like the hypocrites; for they love to stand and pray in the synagogues and at the street corners, so that they may be seen by others. (6:5)
- And whenever you fast, do not look dismal, like the hypocrites, for they disfigure their faces so as to show others that they are fasting. (6:16)

These are classic examples of religious hypocrisy. We comment on two of these items elsewhere, so can now be brief.[50] Here are religious folk parading their superior religiosity in public so others will see them and praise their piety. Yet, it is all "so that they may be seen by others" (v. 5; also vv. 1, 2, 16). Self-glorification was their true inner intention, not the selfless pursuit of God and his righteousness. To assure the latter, Jesus teaches that such acts of piety should be done in secret, where only God will see and reward.

This has led to the traditional view of the historical Pharisees (and of Judaism) as intentional religious hypocrites. They were really only after human applause, and did not truly care for God's approval. But keep in mind this is not a differentiated characterization ("some are like this, others not"). No, it is invective, which by its very nature generalizes, exaggerates, and stereotypes. And for that reason we ought not to draw the traditional historical conclusion. The fact is, Jews themselves had long recognized the danger of such ostentatious religious hypocrisy and recommended against it. Thus, they noted Job who avoided public display before those seeking alms from him (T. Job 9:7–8), and the later rabbis said "A man who gives charity in secret is greater than Moses our teacher" (b. B. Bat. 9b) and warned against similar failings among Pharisees. The Babylonian Talmud (b. Soṭah 22b) warned, for example, against the following:

- the "shoulder" Pharisee, who wears his good deeds on his shoulder like a badge
- the "wait a little" Pharisee, who wants more time to perform a meritorious action

---

course, in the seven woes in ch. 23. The only exceptions to this consistent matthean pattern are 7:5 (general accusation) and 24:51 (in a parable).

50. On almsgiving, see ch. 9; on fasting, see ch. 12.

- the "bleeding nose" Pharisee, who shut his eyes to avoid looking lustfully at a woman and ran into a wall
- the "hump-backed" Pharisee, who walked around slumped over lest anyone touch and defile him
- the "accounting" Pharisee, who kept track of every little good deed[51]

So, at the end of it all, were the Pharisees hypocrites? Our answer is yes and no. Yes, some Pharisees may well have been hypocrites, as is usually the case with any religious group. Yes, from Jesus' perspective and that of the early church, the Pharisees were hypocrites by claiming to love and listen to God, yet they refused to listen to the one whom God had sent. No, as a group Pharisees were not characterized by hypocrisy. And most importantly, Jesus' accusations need to be understood as invective, as a form of generalized and exaggerated speech to warn against someone or something.

---

51. Pratheron, "Reclaiming the Reputation."

CHAPTER 15

A More Positive Spin on the Pharisees in Acts and Paul?

OUTSIDE THE GOSPELS, THE Pharisees are mentioned in the NT only in Acts (9x) and once in Paul's letters (Phil 3:5).[1] We can focus our examination with three questions.

1. Why does a leading rabbi, Gamaliel, protect the Jesus-movement? (5:33–39)
2. Was there a "Pharisee wing" in the earliest church? (Acts 15:1–5; 23:6–10)
3. Was the apostle Paul a Christian Pharisee? (Acts 26:5; Phil 3:5)

A Leading Pharisee Protects Peter and the Other Apostles

Peter and the Jerusalem apostles had been arrested for preaching about Jesus in the temple environs, but an angel had engineered their release and they continued preaching (Acts 5:12–20). The authorities brought them before the council (Gk. *synedrion*) and ordered them to stop. Peter's response that he must obey God and will continue to preach in Jesus' name didn't go over well. The Sanhedrin authorities, which included the high priest, other Sadducees and leading citizens, were enraged and "wanted to kill them" (5:33).

At this explosive point a Pharisee named Gamaliel, who also belonged to the Sanhedrin, spoke out against this murderous intent. His speech cited two recent instances where messianic pretenders (Theudas and Judas) had also gathered followers, but were eventually killed and their movements

---

1. In the majority of the NT documents the Pharisees no longer play any role. This is probably due to the Diaspora situation in which Pharisees were less influential.

dispersed. Since Jesus had already been eliminated the same dispersal of his movement would likely also come to pass. No murderous action need be taken. Then for good measure he added, "if [this movement] is of God, you will not be able to overthrow them—in that case you may even be found fighting against God!" (Acts 5:39)

This respected Pharisee is given a positive portrayal by Luke in his first mention of Pharisees in Acts. Although his speech suggested Jesus was probably another pretender like Theudas and Judas, it also left open the possibility that Jesus was "of God" (v. 39). This points to the same question of Jesus' authorization that we have seen throughout the Gospels. Although Gamaliel could hardly be called a believer or disciple or even a supporter of Jesus, he is portrayed as rescuing the apostles from the deadly crowd.

Excursus: The Historical Gamaliel[2]

Many Lukan scholars have doubts regarding the historical accuracy of this reference to Gamaliel, particularly since his tolerance here seems to conflict with the intolerance of one famous pupil, Paul of Tarsus.[3] While the arguments against authenticity are serious, I find them unconvincing.[4] If a Pharisaic "teacher of the law" named Gamaliel did, indeed, come to the rescue at this point, who was he? Most take Acts 5 to be referring to Gamaliel I (the Elder), mentioned also by Josephus as the father of Simon (*Life* 189-94).[5] The impression gained from some rabbinic sayings agrees with the portrait in Acts 5 that Gamaliel was well respected and generally lenient in rulings.[6] He probably belonged to a wealthy and influential family in Jerusalem whose familial traditions aligned with those of the Pharisees.[7] Acceptance of rabbinic legends about him led earlier scholars to see him as the grandson of the great Hillel, but there is cause for skepticism.

---

2. For this brief sketch, see Keener, *Acts,* 2:1222-23, and the important correctives of Bauckham, "Gamaliel and Paul," 87-106.
3. See, for example, Chilton, "Gamaliel," 2:904-6.
4. See the defense of historicity in Keener, *Acts,* 2:1222-39.
5. On the rabbinic Gamaliel traditions, see Neusner, *Pharisees,* ch. 3, 23-58.
6. m. Soṭah 9:15; b. Pesaḥ. 88b; m. Giṭ. 4:2-3.
7. See esp. Bauckham, "Gamaliel and Paul," 87-106.

Was There a "Pharisee Wing" in the Earliest Church?

The Pharisees crop up a number of times in the story of the earliest church in the book of Acts, but unlike in the Gospels where they are opponents, here they are insiders. So, what exactly was the relationship of this Pharisee movement to the early Jesus movement and was there a wing of "Pharisees for Jesus" within the Christian community?

First, we should be clear, the Pharisees had by no means converted *en masse* to Jesus as messiah. Acts makes this clear when Saul/Paul, at the behest of the Jewish authorities, persecuted the fledgling Jesus movement.[8] Nor is there any indication that a significant portion of the Pharisees had become followers of Jesus. However, some Pharisees had joined the new movement and, not surprisingly, were influential there just as they had been in other Jewish circles before.

Early in the church's development from a largely Jewish sub-group to a mixed community of Jews and non-Jews, Luke narrates in Acts 15 the story of a crucial fork in the road. Paul and Barnabas had been successfully evangelizing in cities of Asia Minor and had seen both Jews and gentiles become Jesus adherents (Acts 13–14). At this point "certain individuals came down from Judea and were teaching the brothers, 'Unless you are circumcised according to the custom of Moses, you cannot be saved.'" (Acts 15:1) We are not told exactly who these people were, but they appear to have been Jewish believers in Jesus as messiah.[9] It was decided that Paul, Barnabas, and some others would need to consult with the apostles and other leaders in Jerusalem about this question of gentile circumcision. That is, do non-Jewish followers of Jesus need to become Jewish, to bear the sign of Jewishness in their flesh (circumcision), in order to be messianic children of Abraham? Or, as was becoming common in a number of mixed Jesus congregations, could they be full members *as non-Jews*?

The consultation occurred in Acts 15 where the issue was framed once again ("It is necessary for them to be circumcised and ordered to keep the law of Moses"), but this time explicitly by "some believers who belonged to the sect of the Pharisees" (Acts 15:5). Those of us reading this today as gentile Christians can easily miss the serious "fork-in-the-road" nature of this

---

8. Acts 23:6–10 tells of Paul appearing before the Sanhedrin in Jerusalem where both Pharisees and Sadducees are present. These Pharisees do not appear to be Jesus-followers, yet they are still willing to side with Paul ("we find nothing wrong with this man") over a theological matter.

9. Reference to "teaching the brothers" implies a teaching role *within* the Jesus community, and their insistence that converted gentiles be "circumcised according to the custom of Moses" points to Jewish concerns.

meeting. For us the answer is a foregone conclusion. But at this stage (c. 50 CE) the early movement could truly have gone either way. These Pharisees insisting on circumcision were not unbelievers or heretics, they were zealous for divine truth as revealed in Torah. According to Moses, circumcision was an eternal commandment that applied not only to natural-born Jews, but also to outsiders such as slaves who would be part of the elect people (Gen 17:9–14). And Jesus had not given specific guidance on this question. In the end, the Pharisee believers lost the argument (Acts 15:7–21), but as this episode makes clear, they were a potent force in the early church.

Were the Opposing "Teachers" in Galatians and Other Pauline Letters Pharisees?

In Paul's letters we also encounter Jesus-followers who insisted on gentile circumcision, but they are never explicitly identified as Pharisees. The clearest example comes in the letter to the Galatians. Unnamed teachers were propagating "another gospel" (Gal 1:7) which sought to "to compel [the Galatians] to be circumcised" (6:12; also 2:3–4). This sounds suspiciously like the Pharisee wing in Acts 15. In a number of Paul's other letters, pro-circumcision Jewish missionaries crop up causing problems for Paul and his gentile communities. We do not have sufficient clear evidence to identify some of these opponents as Pharisees, but it is a reasonable supposition.[10]

Was the Apostle Paul a Christian Pharisee? (Acts 26:5; Phil 3:5)

Those looking to prove that Pharisaism was the antithesis of Christianity have sometimes turned to the apostle Paul himself. He was at one time the epitome of the fully committed Pharisee. In his "earlier life in Judaism" he was "far more zealous for the traditions of [his] ancestors" (Gal 1:13–14). This last phrase evoked one of the main characteristics of the Pharisees seen in Josephus and the Gospels. But on the road to Damascus he had a startling about-face. "But when God, who had set me apart before I was born and called me through his grace, was pleased to reveal his Son to me . . . ." (Gal 1:15–16) And the result was "The one who formerly was persecuting us is now proclaiming the faith he once tried to destroy" (Gal 1:23). Saul the Jewish Pharisee turned from that identity and became Paul the Christian apostle.

---

10. On opponents in Paul's letters, see Sumney, *'Servants of Satan.'*

Or did he? That is, would Paul himself have described this revolution in his perspective as a change in his religious identification, from Jew to Jesus-follower (Christian), or more pertinently for our investigation, from Pharisee to non-Pharisee?[11] Most will agree that something momentous happened to Paul's sense of personal identity after Damascus, that he now found his most central identity "in Christ" (Phil 3:7–11). But, does this mean that he abandoned his self-identification as a Pharisee? Two passages should give us pause. The first comes from Luke's pen and reports Paul's words before the Sanhedrin. "Brothers, I am a Pharisee, a son of Pharisees. I am on trial concerning the hope of the resurrection of the dead" (Acts 23:6). It is possible that this is merely a tactic on Paul's part to get out of a jam. Seeing Sadducees who do not believe in the resurrection, and Pharisees who do, Paul tossed a smoke-bomb as it were into the room, saying in effect, "I believe in the resurrection like the Pharisees." But Paul didn't say "I believe in the resurrection *like a Pharisee*." Nor did he say "I *used to be* a Pharisee and, thus, a believer in resurrection," although either of these would have worked. No, he said "Brothers, *I am a Pharisee* [*egō pharisaios eimi*], a son of Pharisees."[12] At least in this instance, Paul seems willing to currently identify himself as a Pharisee.

If some object that is Luke's wording not Paul's, we can turn to the second passage. In recounting his seven Jewish "badges of honor" in Phil 3:5–6 Paul claimed to have been "as to the law, a Pharisee." His seven reasons for "confidence in the flesh" were: 1) circumcised, 2) Israelite, 3) Benjamite, 4) Hebrew of Hebrews, 5) Pharisee, 6) zealous (persecutor of church), 7) blameless. The first four were Paul's by birth; the next three by choice. The apostle was comparing himself with (Jewish?) opponents who placed confidence in visible marks like circumcision (vv. 2–3).[13] He was even richer in such badges of honor. The point of this boasting contest for Paul was, "we . . . have no confidence in the flesh" (v. 3). That is, Paul no longer pointed to these observable badges of honor as the marks of his righteous standing.

---

11. The question as to Paul's own identity vis-à-vis Judaism is hotly debated at present. According to Michael Bird some of the positions are: 1) a former Jew (F. Watson, L. Sechrest), 2) a transformed Jew (N. T. Wright, T. Donaldson), 3) a faithful Jew (M. Barth, M. Nanos), 4) a radical Jew (D. Boyarin), 5) an anomalous Jew (J. Barclay, M. Bird). Bird, *Anomalous Jew*, 6–16. The modern debate as to whether Paul was "converted" (changed religions) or "called" was kicked off by Stendahl, "Introspective Conscience," 78–96.

12. The phrase "son of Pharisees" may mean his father had been a Pharisee or that Paul was a disciple of the Pharisees.

13. "confidence in the flesh [*sarx*]" refers here not to "sinful nature" as sometimes in Paul, but to "physical qualifications" (NJB) or "human [i.e., outward, visible] credentials" (NET).

"I regard everything [these seven marks] as loss because of the surpassing value of knowing Christ Jesus my Lord. For his sake I have suffered the loss of all things, and I regard them as rubbish, in order that I may gain Christ and be found in him, not having a righteousness of my own that comes from the law, but one that comes through faith in Christ, the righteousness from God based on faith" (vv. 8–9).[14]

But does his rejection of these *as marks of righteous standing* also mean that he rejected their application to himself *per se*? This was clearly not the case with the first four. He was still a circumcised Israelite of the tribe of Benjamin. But how about the last group of three? Zeal was still something Paul treasured, but, of course, no longer focused on persecuting the church but on serving Christ and one another (1 Cor 12:31; 14:12; 2 Cor 7:7; 9:2; Col 4:13; Titus 2:14). Likewise, blamelessness (*teleios* = completeness, wholeness, integrity) remained the Christian goal and standard (Phil 3:15; Col 1:28; 4:12).[15] But how about "as to the law, a Pharisee"? I would suggest this had not been reversed either. Paul was still concerned to be a "separated one" from sin and impurity and to interpret and obey Torah carefully. He was still a Pharisee. However, that was no longer what he pointed to as marking out his righteousness.

---

14. For the interpretation of this passage, see Dunn, "Philippians 3.2–14," 469–90.
15. On this blameless wholeness, see Yinger, *God and Human Wholeness*.

Taking Stock of the Pharisees: Conclusions and Suggestions

IN SPITE OF HOW thin our ancient sources are for reconstructing the historical Pharisees, they have still yielded a fairly full picture of this brief movement (c. 165 BCE–90 CE). The following list gives many of the important points discovered about them along with cross-reference to the detailed discussion and notes in some cases as to how this differs from what we have often thought previously.

Pharisees probably got their start in connection with the Maccabean rebellion in the mid-second century BCE (ch. 1) as those faithful to Israel's heritage sought to protect her ancient identity from Hellenistic corruption. They likely arose from the ranks of the scribes and *hasidim* at that time, but there is no evidence they were widely known as Pharisees that early. Although later rabbinic legend traces them clear back to the time of Ezra, this is incorrect. The name Pharisee (from *perushim*, the separated ones) was probably adopted at first by opponents who saw them as overly separatistic. Not long after, however, it was accepted as a badge of honor by the group itself, highlighting their separation from impurity and sinners (pp. 14–15, and n. 21).

The Pharisees persisted as a group committed to Israel's spiritual reform into the first century CE alongside other varieties of Judaism such as Sadducees, Essenes, Zealots, etc. They did not exercise official political power except for one brief period under Queen Salome Alexandra (mid-first century BCE; pp. 17–20). They were, however, held in high regard by many of the general Jewish population and thereby exercised significant informal influence.

Under the Herods and the Roman procurators (37 BCE–66 CE) the Pharisees continued to be a force to be reckoned with, though again mostly due to informal popular influence. Although concentrated in and around Jerusalem, Pharisees could also be found widely throughout Israel, including Galilee. Only a few of them, due to wealth, social status or priestly descent (not because seats were allotted to Pharisees), probably held positions on leading Jewish councils (e.g., Sanhedrin). Most Pharisees were not members of the small Israelite upper class, but respected tradesmen, retainers in governmental service, scribes and even priests. Relations with the Herods and other political leaders varied due to circumstances. Most of the time they appear to have "kept their heads down" so to speak, some even urging accommodation to Rome prior to the revolt of 66–70 CE. However, if the political powers threatened their way of life, they could join the resistance, as seen numerous times during Herod's reign (pp. 20–22).

Thus, in the time of Jesus, Pharisees were viewed by most other Jews as upright individuals known particularly for their precise interpretation and practice (*akribeia*) of the Mosaic commands. They were not widely considered hypocrites or insincere show-offs, although cases of such were known and were condemned by the Pharisees themselves. Their precision led to spelling out the implications of the commandments which themselves remained fairly general. This was termed *halakhah* (the way one should walk) which formed a body of "traditions of the fathers" passed down through generations and families (pp. 53–56). Rather than being known as overly strict, the Pharisees were, in fact, criticized by some (e.g., DSS) as making obedience too easy or "smooth." It would appear they sought to promulgate a path of obedience that was both carefully accurate and practicable for Israel.

They were a relatively small group, yet influential due to the widespread respect of the populace for their careful commitment to Israel's ways. This influence was not of a formal nature; they did not control the Jerusalem Sanhedrin or synagogue life nationwide. Rather, common Jews listened to Pharisees when they spoke about how Jews should live under God's Torah. For this reason, other teachers, like Jesus of Nazareth, giving different advice as to how authentic Judaism was to be lived posed a challenge, and especially so if they were able to gather a noticeable following.

Pharisees shared with most other Jews the common beliefs in the identity of their God, his election of Abraham and the patriarchs, the Mosaic Torah as their divinely given foundational constitution, the necessity of walking in obedience, etc. On the perennial issue of theodicy (who controls events, God or humans?), like most Jews they took a "both/and" position. They were distinctive in their willingness to "separate" from those living in what the Pharisees deemed disobedience. The bulk of Jews probably took more of a "live and let live" approach, within limits, of course. Although their origins lay in the anti-Hellenistic spirit of the Maccabean era, by the first century CE they had adopted hellenistically-influenced positions such as resurrection and the accompanying belief in a post-mortem life with rewards and punishments (both of which appear to have been rejected by Sadducees).

Those familiar with comments on Pharisees derived from older studies will see quite a few differences (see elements of this older view, pp. 57–58). For example, it used to be asserted that Pharisees were obsessed with minor details of purity. Hopefully, readers can now perceive that one person's "obsession" is another's "careful obedience," and that Christians and Jews might reasonably differ over what is minor and major. In any case, it is unlikely that most first-century Jews would have accused them of being "obsessed." Another pillar of the older view is that Pharisees were legalists. Actually, this used to be the view of Jewish soteriology in general, with the Pharisees taken as a particularly egregious example. This view of Jewish soteriology has been effectively dismantled by others, and we have found no evidence that Pharisees viewed their acts of obedience as earning them salvation, righteousness or turning God from being angry with them to favorable (pp. 63–64, 149–50).

If all this is true, and we Christians have largely misunderstood and consistently misrepresented the Pharisees, what might we do about it? My comments will address primarily those who preach and teach, whether from a pulpit or in a living room or classroom as Bible discussion leader. Those of us without such responsibilities are not left entirely off the hook, of course. When we read Scripture or discuss the Bible with others, we can remind ourselves that Pharisees were in many ways "just like us," though with a Jewish twist that we non-Jews don't normally think about. They were not the bad, hypocritical Jewish "other," but the serious pursuers of God and holiness. If we could transport them to our situation, they were the "committed" of our day.

For those who preach and teach, let me make a few practical suggestions. Whenever speaking about Pharisees in NT passages, pause a moment and reflect on whether you are "bearing false witness" with your portrayal. Are you generalizing ("*The Pharisees* were thus and so")? Would you be fairer and more accurate to say, "*Some Pharisees* were probably thus and so"?[1] Do your words about the Pharisees take on an emotional edge

---

1. See the similar heart-felt plea of Rabbi David Rosen in dialog with a Christian pastor. "[A]ll I ask . . . is that you might consider referring . . . to *those* Pharisees or *some* Pharisees whom Jesus criticized. . . . Because when all Pharisees are presented as sinners, you bear false witness against me." Kendall and Rosen, *Christian and the Pharisee*, 10.

that is neither true nor necessary? "They were haughty know-it-alls who couldn't care less about the poor publican."

The real nub of the issue arises, of course, when we teach on a passage where a "bad" Pharisee actually seems to appear. What are we to say when Jesus accuses them of rank hypocrisy, of straining at gnats while ignoring justice and mercy, of preferring their traditions to God's own words? I have provided details in various chapters to help sort out these matters, and to do that in a way that is faithful both to the historical record concerning the Pharisees and to the conviction of many of us that the Gospel writers faithfully recorded the memories that Jesus actually did confront Pharisees this way. Key interpretive elements that surfaced repeatedly were,

1. Jesus' intention was to describe *some* Pharisees, those who acted in such blameworthy fashion, not to paint a clearly unjustified caricature of all Pharisees. In fact, the Gospels portray the Pharisees' attitudes toward Jesus on a spectrum from accepting, to curious, to skeptical to deadly opposition.

2. He employed *invective*, a form of insulting speech common at the time which utilized generalization ("you Pharisees"), exaggeration ("strain out gnats") and stereotyped language ("blind leaders of the blind"). Such speech was understood as a rhetorically powerful warning against some group or behavior, but not as careful historical description.

3. Many of the controversies revolved around *halakhic* differences, over differing understandings of what authentic Jewish behavior should look like. That is, these were "in-house" arguments, not Jesus versus Judaism.

4. In the background of all the conflicts lay Jesus' central proclamation of the gospel. He announced and enacted the dawning rule of Israel's God, the time of Israel's redemption and renewal. And even more controversially, he was himself the eschatological anointed agent of God whose preaching, healing and power over the demonic realm *were the dawning of that rule*. Although some Pharisees were willing to entertain this possibility, most saw it as untrue. Because Jesus was growing dangerously in popularity among the people and thus posed a serious challenge to the Pharisees' desire to lead the people to greater holiness as they understood it, they felt forced to oppose him as a misleader of Israel. If Jesus' message and ministry were from God, then the Pharisees' path to Israel's renewal was no longer the way.

Obviously no teacher can go into all this every time a Pharisee-passage is up for consideration. However, we who carry the responsibility for teaching can consistently take opportunity to bring these points in and to speak of Pharisees in a generous and historically responsible manner. In this way we can all help the church to get this part of our story right and to gain once again an appreciation for these closest cousins of Jesus and the early Jesus movement.

APPENDIX

Interview with a Pharisee

THANKS TO THE MIRACLE of time-transport, we have arranged for Pastor Eduard Smythe of Second Avenue Baptist Church to travel back to the year 40 CE where he was privileged to interview Mordecai Cohen, a fisherman, synagogue elder, and committed Pharisee.

(**Pastor S.**) Thank you, Mordecai, for agreeing to this interview... or should I address you as Rabbi Cohen?

(**M. Cohen**) I'm fine with Mordecai. People sometimes address our more learned members as "rabbi" out of respect, but it's not an official title or anything. Anyway, those of us without scribal training wouldn't expect to be addressed this way.

(**Pastor S.**) Let's begin with a little about yourself... family, profession, and of most interest to my readers, why did you become a Pharisee?

(**M. Cohen**) Well, I've been married for twenty-one years. G-d blessed us with five children, praise his name, and four are still living. Like my father before me, I support my family by fishing in the lake and selling the catch in the thriving town markets. Also like my father, and his father before him, we live according to our inherited family traditions which some refer to with the term "Pharisee."

(**Pastor S.**) You said "some refer" to you as Pharisees. Isn't it clear to everyone that someone belongs to the Pharisees, is a "card-carrying member" so to speak?

(M. Cohen) (chuckles) Well, people do notice that our family holds to certain traditions that other's don't observe, but it's not like we have a "Pharisees club" in Capernaum with a membership list. A few other families here also follow these *halakhic* ways and we do gather occasionally. It certainly makes things easier when there aren't three or four different levels of purity observance. There may be more formally organized meetings in larger cities, but I've only heard talk about them.

(Pastor S.) That's very interesting. I always thought people personally decided or chose to become a Pharisee or not.

(M. Cohen) That does happen, and we who follow this way of greater commitment to Torah do want more of our people to take Moses' words more seriously so as to prepare the way of the Lord. But individual "conversions" are not that common, since it can actually bring difficulties in families and villages. Just imagine, if a son still living at home, or a single family in a village, would begin to observe purity or Sabbath more carefully, differently than the rest. Now there would be tension and disagreements at every meal.

(Pastor S.) Since you mentioned purity, I'd like to probe there a little deeper. Many of the stories in my tradition tell of Pharisees who focused on small, we might even say "picayune," details like washing hands a certain way before meals and forbidding doing helpful things on the Sabbath like pulling an animal out of a pit? How would you respond to our perception that you folks seem to miss the forest for the trees, focusing on trivial details like "how far should one walk on the day of rest" and ignoring loving God and others?

(M. Cohen) I'm not quite sure where to start. First, you might need to explain to me how you decide what is trivial and what is important. In my tradition everything G-d tells us is important, even the small things. So, when he teaches us to rest, to not labor or work, on the seventh day, we take that with utmost seriousness. We Pharisees are known for taking these matters more seriously than most. But we would never ignore his command to love and show mercy to others. I find it insulting that someone would accuse us of this. Now, as to helping an animal or another person on Sabbath, our scribes have wrestled long and hard over such situations. Most in our movement do recognize some emergency situations that require doing something on Sabbath that might normally be frowned upon. The stories of our beginnings tell of the Maccabee brothers making the hard decision to defend themselves, even on the Sabbath day of rest. I'm not sure if this answers your question, but this narrow path between two commandments like "love" and "rest" is something we have thought much about.

(**Pastor S.**) My apologies for causing offense; that was not my intention. Let's move on to your involvement in the local synagogue. You are one of the elders. Were you elected because you are a Pharisee?

(**M. Cohen**) No, my being an elder was not tied to my way of life as a Pharisee and I was not elected. Our synagogue, as you call it, is our community gathering. It can happen anytime there is a community issue needing resolution. Last Tuesday we called a meeting to discuss the way toll-collectors were gouging us and what we could do about it. We always gather on Sabbath, as well, to listen to a Torah reading, discuss, and to pray. My family has been a pillar in this community for some generations, so when my father grew ill, the other community leaders graciously recognized me as his replacement. That's how I became an elder. There was no election, but the other leading families consulted and decided. As to being a Pharisee, they knew our family is righteous and wise and seeks to follow Moses with particular care. But we have been part of this community for decades; these are my friends, even if they do not take all the commands as seriously as we do. We sometimes talk about this, and I know they are thinking about my point of view, but I generally try not to be obnoxious about it.

(**Pastor S.**) You've mentioned Moses and the commandments a number of times. At the risk of offending again, there's something about this I need to get clear for my readers. Why is keeping the commandments, and keeping them in the particular way your movement does, so important? Is that what you believe people, or at least Jews, have to do in order to be saved?

(**M. Cohen**) No offense taken, though I find the question a bit puzzling. "Saved" is not really that common in our religious discussions, but I assume you're referring to enjoying life with our G-d, including the life of the age to come. Or maybe you have more the idea of deliverance in mind, such as at the exodus of our people out of Egypt, or even now our hope for deliverance from foreign oppression. To your question more directly, a Jew doesn't have to do something extra to enjoy true life. That is part of our inheritance as a people. The G-d of Abraham, Isaac and Jacob granted us life with him and hope for a good future out of sheer kindness to our fathers. He loves us because we are his people, blessed be his gracious name. Because we are his people, he has not left us without guidance in this world. He has given us his teaching, his Torah, through Moses. We do not have to obey these commandments in order to get him to love us, but because we are his people we are obligated to walk in his ways, and not in the ways of other gods and peoples.

(**Pastor S.**) One last question, if I may. I lead a group of non-Jews who believe that Jesus of Nazareth was the Jewish messiah. I assume you are aware of him, since he was active in this area before he was killed by the Jewish leaders and the Romans a little over five years ago. Your group, the Pharisees, seems to have opposed him pretty consistently, even hounded him, some would say. Why are you so against him?

(**M. Cohen**) Yes, of course we were aware of Jesus from Nazareth. He made his home here for a while, spoke occasionally in our Sabbath gatherings, caused some disturbance among us, and one of my less-observant fisher-colleagues, Simon, left to follow him. We were initially taken with Jesus. People were talking about him, miracles were reported, he wanted to instruct people about the path of righteousness and he was looking for G-d to rule among our nation. He had all the makings of a prophet of Israel. He was, however, quite abrasive in manner, calling everyone to "repent," even those of us giving every effort to be obedient. And then he taught and did some things that really skated on the edge. He told one disabled man in our community his sins were forgiven, and that without any reformation of ways, or any sacrifice or visit to a priest for mediation. And, although he seemed in some ways serious and knowledgeable about Torah, he was openly careless about holiness, purity, Sabbath and many other matters. He partied with backslidden Jews, healed the children of our oppressors, . . .

(**Pastor S.**) Excuse me for interrupting, but what about him being the Jewish messiah?

(**M. Cohen**) Some of those, like my former colleague, Peter, have been spreading this idea, but this can't be true. Where does it say that G-d's anointed agent of Israel's deliverance will fail!? That our enemies will overcome him and put him to death? That he will promote carelessness toward the commandments, et cetera? No, nothing fits. I never actually heard him make this "messiah" claim myself, though some things he said seemed to head in that direction. He was actually not that clear, talking at times about a "son of man" figure. He tried to gain wide influence among our people by his announcement that deliverance was at hand, that his miracles were the signal of its beginning, and so on. My Pharisee colleagues tried to engage him, but he seemed too sure of himself, often replying "but I say to you." Some in our movement would disagree, but most of us saw him as a dangerous renegade who would ultimately bring harm to our nation.

(**Pastor S.**) Well, that will certainly give my readers something to think about. Thank you, Mordecai, and *shalom*.

Bibliography

Bolded items are of particular interest for further study of the Pharisees.

Amos, Roger. *Hypocrites or Heroes? The Paradoxical Portrayal of the Pharisees in the New Testament*. Eugene, OR: Wipf & Stock, 2015.
Anderson, Paul, et al., eds. *John, Jesus, and History*. Symposium Series (SBL) 44. Atlanta: SBL, 2007.
Attridge, Harold W. *The Interpretation of Biblical History in the Antiquitates Judaicae of Flavius Josephus*. Missoula, MT: Scholars, 1976.
Avery-Peck, Alan J. "Death and Afterlife in the Early Rabbinic Sources: The Mishnah, Tosefta, and Early Midrash Compilations." In *Judaism in Late Antiquity. Pt 4, Death, Life-after-Death, Resurrection and the World-to-Come in the Judaisms of Antiquity*, edited by Alan J. Avery-Peck and Jacob Neusner, 243–66. Leiden: Brill, 2001.
Bäck, Sven-Olav. *Jesus of Nazareth and the Sabbath Commandment*. Åbo: Åbo Akademi, 1995.
Baeck, Leo. *The Pharisees, and other Essays*. SB 122. New York: Schocken, 1947.
Bailey, Kenneth. "Informal Controlled Oral Tradition and the Synoptic Gospels." *AsJT* 5 (1991) 34–54.
Barr, James. "The Hebrew/Aramaic Background of 'Hypocrisy' in the Gospels." In *A Tribute to Geza Vermes: Essays on Jewish and Christian Literature and History*, edited by Philip R. Davies and Richard T. White, 307–26. London: Bloomsbury, 2009.
Bauckham, Richard. "Gamaliel and Paul." In *Earliest Christianity within the Boundaries of Judaism: Essays in Honor of Bruce Chilton*, edited by Alan J. Avery-Peck, 87–106. Boston: Brill, 2016.
Baumgarten, Albert I. *The Flourishing of Jewish Sects in the Maccabean Era: An Interpretation* JSJSup 55. Leiden: Brill, 1997.
———. **"The Name of the Pharisees." *JBL* 102 (1983) 411–28.**
Benovitz, Moshe. *Kol Nidre: Studies in the Development of Rabbinic Votive Institutions*. 2nd ed. Brown Judaic Studies 315. Atlanta: Scholars, 2020.
Berger, Klaus. "Jesus als Pharisäer und frühe Christen als Pharisäer." *NovT* 30 (1988) 231–62.

Beyer, Hermann W. "*Blasphēmia*." In *TDNT*, edited by Gerhard Kittel, 1:622–24. Grand Rapids: Eerdmans, 1964.
Bird, Michael F. *An Anomalous Jew: Paul among Jews, Greeks, and Romans*. Grand Rapids: Eerdmans, 2016.
———. *Are You the One Who Is to Come?: The Historical Jesus and the Messianic Question*. Grand Rapids: Baker Academic, 2009.
———. "Christ." In *Dictionary of Jesus and the Gospels*. 2d ed., edited by Joel B. Green et al., 115–25. Downers Grove, IL: IVP Academic, 2013.
Blomberg, Craig L. *Contagious Holiness: Jesus' Meals with Sinners*. Downers Grove, IL: InterVarsity, 2005.
———. *The Historical Reliability of the Gospels*. 2nd ed. Downers Grove, IL: IVP Academic, 2007.
———. "Midrash, Chiasmus, and the Outline of Luke's Central Section." In *Gospel Perspectives III: Studies in Midrash and Historiography*, edited by R. T. France and David Wenham, 217–61. Sheffield: JSOT, 1983.
Bock, Darrell L. "The Son of Man in Luke 5:24." *BBR* 1 (1991) 109–21.
Bond, Helen. "Herodian Dynasty." In *Dictionary of Jesus and the Gospels*, 2d ed., edited by Joel B. Green et al., 379–82. Downers Grove, IL: IVP Academic, 2013.
Booth, Roger P. *Jesus and the Laws of Purity: Tradition History and Legal History in Mark 7*. JSNTSup 13. Sheffield: JSOT, 1986.
Brandon, S. G. F. *Jesus and the Zealots: A Study of the Political Factor in Primitive Christianity*. New York: Charles Scribner's Sons, 1967.
Brawley, Robert L. *Luke-Acts and the Jews: Conflict, Apology, and Conciliation*. Atlanta: Scholars, 1987.
Broadhead, Edwin Keith. "Mk 1,44: The Witness of the Leper." *ZNW* 83 (1992) 257–65.
Brown, Raymond E. *The Gospel According to John*. 2 vols. AB. Garden City, NY: Doubleday, 1966.
Brownlee, William H. "Messianic Motifs of Qumran and the New Testament." *NTS* 3 (1956–1957) 195–210.
Bryan, Christopher. *Render to Caesar: Jesus, the Early Church, and the Roman Superpower*. New York: Oxford, 2005.
Carroll, John T. "Luke's Portrayal of the Pharisees." *CBQ* 50 (1988) 604–21.
Carson, Donald A., et al., eds. *Justification and Variegated Nomism, Vol. 1, the Complexities of Second Temple Judaism*. Wissenschaftliche Untersuchungen zum Neuen Testament 2/140. Grand Rapids: Baker Academic, 2001.
Childers, Charles L. "The Gospel According to St. Luke." In *Beacon Bible Commentary, Volume 6: Matthew through Luke*. Kansas City: The Foundry, 2010.
Chilton, Bruce. "Gamaliel." In *ABD*, edited by David Noel Freedman, 2:903–6. New York: Doubleday, 1992.
Cohen, Shaye J. D. "The Significance of Yavneh: Pharisees, Rabbis, and the End of Jewish Sectarianism." *HUCA* 55 (1984) 27–53.
Collins, Adela Yarbro. *Mark: A Commentary*. Hermeneia. Edited by Harold W. Attridge. Minneapolis: Fortress, 2007.
Collins, John J., and Adela Yarbro Collins. *King and Messiah as Son of God: Divine, Human, and Angelic Messianic Figures in Biblical and Related Literature*. Grand Rapids: Eerdmans, 2008.
Crossan, John Dominic. *Raid on the Articulate: Comic Eschatology in Jesus and Borges*. New York: Harper & Row, 1976.

Daube, David. "Ἐξουσία in Mark 1 22 and 27." *JTS* 39 (1938) 45–59.
Davies, Philip. "Hasidim in the Maccabean Period." *JJS* 28 (1977) 127–40.
Davies, W. D. *Introduction to Pharisaism*. Philadelphia: Fortress, 1967.
Davies, W. D., and Dale C. Allison. *A Critical and Exegetical Commentary on the Gospel According to Saint Matthew*. 3 vols. ICC. Edinburgh: T. & T. Clark, 1988.
Dawsey, James. "Jesus and the Language of Authority." In *Theology and Authority: Maintaining a Tradition of Tension*, edited by Richard Penaskovic, 14–23. Peabody, MA: Hendrickson, 1987.
De Andrado, Paba Nidhani. "Ḥesed and Sacrifice: The Prophetic Critique in Hosea." *CBQ* 78 (2016) 47–67.
Deines, Roland. *Jüdische Steingefässe und pharisäische Frömmigkeit: Ein archäologisch-historischer Beitrag zum Verständnis von Joh 2,6 und der jüdischen Reinheitshalacha zur Zeit Jesu* Wissenschaftliche Untersuchungen zum Neuen Testament 2.52. Tübingen: Mohr Siebeck, 1993.
———. **"Pharisäer." In *Theologisches Begriffslexikon zum Neuen Testament*, edited by L. Coenen and K. Haacker, 2:1455–68. Neukirchen/Vluyn, 1997–2005.**
———. "The Pharisees: Good Guys with Bad Press." *BAR* 39 (2013) 22, 57–58.
———. **"The Social Profile of the Pharisees." In *The New Testament and Rabbinic Literature*, edited by R. Bieringer, 111–32. Leiden: Brill, 2010.**
Derrett, J. Duncan M. "Receptacles and Tombs (Mt 23:24–30)." *ZNW* 77 (1986) 255–66.
Dewey, Joanna. *Markan Public Debate: Literary Technique, Concentric Structure, and Theology in Mark 2:1–3:6*. Chico, CA: Scholars, 1979.
Dimant, Devorah. "Qumran Sectarian Literature." In *Jewish Writings of the Second Temple Period: Apocrypha, Pseudepigrapha, Qumran, Sectarian Writings, Philo, Josephus*, edited by Michael E. Stone, 483–550. Philadelphia: Fortress, 1984.
Doering, Lutz. "Much Ado about Nothing? Jesus' Sabbath Healings and their Halakhic Implications Revisited." In *Judaistik und neutestamentliche Wissenschaft: Standorte, Grenzen, Beziehungen*, edited by Lutz Doering, Hans-Günther Waubke and Florian Wilk, 217–41. Göttingen: Vandenhoeck & Ruprecht, 2008.
———. **"Sabbath Laws in the New Testament Gospels." In *The New Testament and Rabbinic Literature*, edited by R. Bieringer, 207–53. Leiden: Brill, 2010.**
———. *Schabbat: Sabbathalacha und -praxis im antiken Judentum und Urchristentum* TSAJ 78. Tübingen: Mohr Siebeck, 1999.
Donahue, John R. "Tax Collectors." In *ABD*, edited by David Noel Freedman, 6:337–38. New York: Doubleday, 1992.
Doudna, Gregory L. *4Q Pesher Nahum: A Critical Edition*. Sheffield: Sheffield Academic, 2001.
Dunn, James D. G. "Altering the Default Setting: Re-Envisaging the Early Transmission of the Jesus Tradition." *NTS* 49 (2003) 139–75.
———. "Jesus and Purity: An Ongoing Debate." *NTS* 48 (2002) 449–67.
———. *Jesus, Paul, and the Law: Studies in Mark and Galatians*. Louisville: Westminster/John Knox, 1990.
———. *Jesus Remembered Christianity in the Making, Vol. 1*. Grand Rapids: Eerdmans, 2003.
———. *The Partings of the Ways: Between Christianity and Judaism and their Significance for the Character of Christianity*. Philadelphia: Trinity International, 1991.
———. "Philippians 3.2–14 and the New Perspective on Paul." In *The New Perspective on Paul: Revised Edition*, 469–90. Grand Rapids: Eerdmans, 2008.

Earle, Ralph. "Matthew." In *Beacon Bible Commentary, Volume 6: Matthew through Luke.* Kansas City, MO: Beacon Hill, 2010.

Edersheim, Alfred. *The Life and Times of Jesus the Messiah.* Grand Rapids: Eerdmans, 1971.

Egger, Peter. *Verdienste vor Gott? Der Begriff Zekhut im rabbinischen Genesiskommentar Bereshit Rabba.* NTOA 43. Göttingen: Vandenhoeck & Ruprecht, 2000.

Evans, Craig A. "The Pharisee and the Publican: Luke 18.9–14 and Deuteronomy 26." In *The Gospels and the Scriptures of Israel*, edited by Craig A. Evans and W. Richard Stegner, 342–55. London: Bloomsbury, 1994.

Falk, Harvey. *Jesus the Pharisee.* New York: Paulist, 1985.

Fascher, Erich. "Zur Witwerschaft des Paulus und der Auslegung von I Cor 7." *ZNW* 28 (1929) 62–69.

Ferguson, Everett. *Backgrounds of Early Christianity.* 2nd ed. Grand Rapids: Eerdmans, 1993.

Finkel, Asher. *The Pharisees and the Teacher of Nazareth AGJU IV.* Leiden: Brill, 1974.

Finkelstein, Louis. "The Pharisees: Their Origin and Their Philosophy." *Harvard Theological Review* 22 (1929) 185–261.

Fitzmyer, Joseph A. *The Gospel According to Luke (X–XXIV)* Anchor Bible 28a. New York: Doubleday, 1981.

Fleddermann, Harry T. "A Warning about the Scribes (Mark 12:37b–40)." *CBQ* 44 (1982) 52–67.

Flusser, David, and R. Steven Notley. *The Sage from Galilee: Rediscovering Jesus' Genius* 4th English ed. Grand Rapids: Eerdmans, 2007.

Foerster, Werner. "*Exousia.*" In *TDNT*, edited by G. Kittel et al., 2:562–74. Grand Rapids: Eerdmans, 1964.

France, R. T. *The Gospel of Mark: A Commentary on the Greek Text* NIGTC. Grand Rapids: Eerdmans, 2002.

———. *The Gospel of Matthew.* Grand Rapids: Eerdmans, 2007.

Freyne, Seán. *Galilee, from Alexander the Great to Hadrian, 323 B.C.E. To 135 C.E.: A Study of Second Temple Judaism.* Edinburgh: T. & T. Clark, 1998.

———. *Galilee, Jesus, and the Gospels: Literary Approaches and Historical Investigations.* Philadelphia: Fortress, 1988.

Friedrichsen, Timothy A. "The Temple, a Pharisee, a Tax Collector, and the Kingdom of God: Rereading a Jesus Parable (Luke 18:10–14a)." *JBL* 124 (2005) 89–119.

Furstenberg, Yair. "Defilement Penetrating the Body: A New Understanding of Contamination in Mark 7:15." *NTS* 54 (2008) 176–200.

García Martínez, Florentino. *The Dead Sea Scrolls Translated: The Qumran Texts in English.* Translated by Wilfred G. E. Watson. 2nd ed. Grand Rapids: Eerdmans, 1996.

Garland, David E. *The Intention of Matthew 23* NovTSup 52. Leiden: Brill, 1979.

Garlington, Don B. "'You Fool!': Matthew 5:22." *BBR* 20 (2010) 61–83.

Gerhardsson, Birger. *Memory and Manuscript: Oral Tradition and Written Transmission in Rabbinic Judaism and Early Christianity with, Tradition and Transmission in Early Christianity.* Grand Rapids: Eerdmans, 1998.

Goldingay, John. *Old Testament Theology, Vol. 2: Israel's Faith.* Downers Grove, IL: InterVarsity, 2006.

Goodman, Martin. *Mission and Conversion: Proselytizing in the Religious History of the Roman Empire.* New York: Oxford, 1994.

Gowler, David B. *Host, Guest, Enemy, and Friend: Portraits of the Pharisees in Luke and Acts*. Emory Studies in Early Christianity 2. New York: P. Lang, 1991.
Grabbe, Lester L. *Judaic Religion in the Second Temple Period: Belief and Practice from the Exile to Yavneh*. New York: Routledge, 2000.
———. "Synagogue and Sanhedrin in the First Century." In *Handbook for the Study of the Historical Jesus*, edited by Stanley E. Porter, 1723-45. Leiden: Brill, 2011.
Hagner, Donald A. *Matthew 1-13*. Word Biblical Commentary 33a. Dallas: Word, 1993.
———. *Matthew 14-28*. Word Biblical Commentary 33b. Dallas: Word, 1993.
———. *The New Testament: A Historical and Theological Introduction*. Grand Rapids: Baker Academic, 2012.
Hanson, John S., and Richard A. Horsley. *Bandits, Prophets, and Messiahs: Popular Movements in the Time of Jesus*. Minneapolis: Winston, 1985.
Heard, Warren J., and Kazuhiko Yamazaki-Ransom. "Revolutionary Movements." In *Dictionary of Jesus and the Gospels*, 2d ed., edited by Joel B. Green et al., 789-99. Downers Grove, IL: IVP Academic, 2013.
Heinemann, Joseph. *Prayer in the Talmud: Forms and Patterns*. Studia Judica 9. New York: de Gruyter, 1977.
Hengel, Martin. *Judaism and Hellenism: Studies in their Encounter in Palestine during the Early Hellenistic Period*. 2 vols. Philadelphia: Fortress, 1974.
Hengel, Martin, and Roland Deines. "E. P. Sanders' 'Common Judaism,' Jesus, and the Pharisees: Review Article of 'Jewish Law from Jesus to the Mishnah' and 'Judaism: Practice and Belief' by E. P. Sanders." *JTS* 46 (1995) 1-70.
Herford, R. Travers. *The Pharisees*. New York: Macmillan, 1924.
Holmén, Tom. "The Alternatives of the Kingdom: Encountering the Semantic Restrictions of Luke 17,20-21 (entos ymōn)." *ZNW* 87 (1996) 204-29.
Holmgren, Fredrick C. "The Pharisee and the Tax Collector. Luke 18:9-14 and Deuteronomy 26:1-15." *Int* 48 (1994) 252-61.
Horgan, Maurya. *Pesharim: Qumran Interpretations of Biblical Books*. CBQMS 8. Washington: Catholic Biblical Association, 1979.
Hultgren, Stephen. *From the Damascus Covenant to the Covenant of the Community: Literary, Historical, and Theological Studies in the Dead Sea Scrolls*. Studies on the Texts of the Desert of Judah 66. Leiden: Brill, 2007.
Instone-Brewer, David. *Divorce and Remarriage in the Bible: The Social and Literary Context*. Grand Rapids: Eerdmans, 2002.
———. "Temple and Priesthood." In *The World of the New Testament: Cultural, Social, and Historical Contexts*, edited by Joel B. Green and Lee Martin McDonald, 197-206. Grand Rapids: Baker Academic, 2013.
Jaffee, Martin S. *Torah in the Mouth: Writing and Oral Tradition in Palestinian Judaism, 200 BCE-400 CE*. New York: Oxford, 2001.
Jeremias, Joachim. *Jerusalem in the Time of Jesus: An Investigation into Economic and Social Conditions during the New Testament Period*. Philadelphia: Fortress, 1975.
———. "War Paulus Witwer?" *ZNW* 25 (1926) 310-12.
Johnson, Luke Timothy. *The Gospel of Luke*. Sacra Pagina 3. Collegeville, MN: Liturgical, 1991.
———. "The New Testament's Anti-Jewish Slander and the Conventions of Ancient Polemic." *JBL* 108 (1989) 419-41.
Josephus, Flavius. "Josephus." Edited by H. St J. Thackeray et al. Cambridge, MA: Harvard University Press, 1976-1981.

Kampen, John. *The Hasideans and the Origin of Pharisaism: A Study in 1 and 2 Maccabees*. Atlanta: Scholars, 1988.

Karesh, Sara E., and Mitchell M. Hurvitz. "Pharisees." In *Encyclopedia of World Religions: Encyclopedia of Judaism*, 389–90. New York: Infobase, 2016.

Kazen, Thomas. *Jesus and Purity Halakhah: Was Jesus Indifferent to Impurity?* rev. ed. ConBNT 38. Winona Lake, IN: Eisenbrauns, 2010.

———. *Scripture, Interpretation, or Authority?: Motives and Arguments in Jesus' Halakic Conflicts*. Wissenschaftliche Untersuchungen zum Neuen Testament 320. Tübingen: Mohr Siebeck, 2013.

Keener, Craig S. *Acts: An Exegetical Commentary, Vol. 2, 3:1—14:28*. Grand Rapids: Baker Academic, 2013.

———. *The Gospel of John a Commentary*. Peabody, MA: Hendrickson, 2010.

Keith, Chris. *Jesus against the Scribal Elite: The Origins of the Conflict*. Grand Rapids: Baker Academic, 2014.

Kemeny, Paul Charles, ed. *Church, State, and Public Justice: Five Views*. Downers Grove, IL: IVP Academic, 2007.

Kendall, R. T., and David Rosen. *The Christian and the Pharisee: Two Outspoken Religious Leaders Debate the Road to Heaven*. New York: FaithWords, 2006.

Kilgallen, John J. "Was Jesus Right to Eat with Sinners and Tax Collectors?" *Biblica* 93 (2012) 590–600.

Klawans, Jonathan. *Josephus and the Theologies of Ancient Judaism*. New York: Oxford, 2012.

Krause, Andrew R. *Synagogues in the Works of Flavius Josephus: Rhetoric, Spatiality, and First-Century Jewish Institutions*. Ancient Judaism and Early Christianity. Leiden: Brill, 2017.

Lambrecht, Jan. "Jesus and the Law. An Investigation of Mk 7, 1–23." *ETL* 53 (1977) 24–79.

Lane, William L. *The Gospel According to Mark: The English Text with Introduction, Exposition, and Notes*. New International Commentary on the New Testament. Grand Rapids: Eerdmans, 1974.

Lau, Markus. "Geweißte Grabmäler: Motivkritische Anmerkungen zu Mt 23.27–28." *NTS* 58 (2012) 463–80.

Levenson, Jon Douglas. *The Love of God: Divine Gift, Human Gratitude, and Mutual Faithfulness in Judaism*. Princeton: Princeton, 2016.

Levine, Amy-Jill. "Quit Picking on the Pharisees!" *Sojourners Magazine* 44 (2015) 26–29.

Levine, Lee I. *The Ancient Synagogue: the First Thousand Years*. 2nd ed. New Haven, CT: Yale University Press, 2005.

Liebowitz, Etka. "Hypocrites or Pious Scholars? The Image of the Pharisees in Second Temple Period Texts and Rabbinic Literature." *Melilah Manchester Journal of Jewish Studies* 11 (2014) 53–67.

Ma'oz, Zvi. "The Synagogue of Gamla and the Typology of Second-Temple Synagogues." In *Ancient Synagogues Revealed*, edited by Lee I. Levine, 35–41. Detroit: Wayne State University Press, 1982.

Maccoby, Hyam. *Jesus the Pharisee*. London: SCM, 2003.

———. *Ritual and Morality: The Ritual Purity System and its Place in Judaism*. New York: Cambridge, 1999.

Malbon, Elizabeth Struthers. "The Jewish Leaders in the Gospel of Mark: A Literary Study of Marcan Characterization." *JBL* 108 (1989) 259–81.
Marshall, I. Howard. *The Gospel of Luke: A Commentary on the Greek Text.* The New International Greek Testament Commentary 3. Grand Rapids: Eerdmans, 1978.
———. "Who is a Hypocrite?" *BibSac* 159 (2002) 131–50.
Marshall, Mary. *The Portrayals of the Pharisees in the Gospels and Acts.* FRLANT 254. Göttingen: Vandenhoeck & Ruprecht, 2015.
Mason, Steve. *Flavius Josephus on the Pharisees: A Composition-Critical Study.* Studia Post Biblica 39. Leiden: E.J. Brill, 1991.
———. "Josephus's Pharisees: The Narratives." In *In Quest of the Historical Pharisees*, edited by Jacob Neusner and Bruce Chilton, 3–40. Waco, TX: Baylor University Press, 2007.
———. "Josephus's Pharisees: The Philosophy." In *In Quest of the Historical Pharisees*, edited by Jacob Neusner and Bruce Chilton, 41–66. Waco, TX: Baylor University Press, 2007.
May, David M. "Mark 2:15: The Home of Jesus or Levi?" *NTS* 39 (1993) 147–49.
McCown, Chester. "Luke's Translation of Semitic into Hellenistic Custom." *JBL* 58 (1939) 213–20.
McKnight, Scot. *A Light among the Gentiles: Jewish Missionary Activity in the Second Temple Period.* Minneapolis: Fortress, 1991.
McLaren, James S. *Power and Politics in Palestine: The Jews and the Governing of their Land, 100 BC–AD 70* JSNTSup 63. Sheffield: JSOT, 1991.
Meier, John P. *A Marginal Jew: Rethinking the Historical Jesus: Companions and Competitors.* Vol. 3. New York: Doubleday, 2001.
———. *A Marginal Jew: Rethinking the Historical Jesus: Law and Love.* Vol. 4. New Haven, CT: Yale University Press, 2009.
Metzger, Bruce M. *A Textual Commentary on the Greek New Testament.* 2nd ed. Swindon: United Bible Societies, 1994.
Moore, Clifford H. *Ancient Beliefs in the Immortality of the Soul, with Some Account of their Influence on Later Views.* New York: Cooper Square, 1963.
Moore, George Foot. *Judaism in the First Centuries of the Christian Era, the Age of the Tannaim.* 3 vols. Cambridge, MA: Harvard, 1927.
Morrison, Craig. "What's in a Name? Interpreting the Name 'Pharisee.'" In *The Pharisees*, edited by Joseph Sievers and Amy-Jill Levine. Grand Rapids: Eerdmans, 2021.
Muddiman, John. "Fast, Fasting." In *Anchor Bible Dictionary*, edited by David Noel Freedman, 2:773–76. New York: Doubleday, 1992.
Murphy-O'Connor, Jerome. *Paul: A Critical Life.* New York: Clarendon, 1996.
Neusner, Jacob. "First Cleanse the Inside: The 'Halakhic' Background of a Controversy-Saying." *NTS* 22 (1976) 486–95.
———. *Judaic Law from Jesus to the Mishnah: A Systematic Reply to Professor E.P. Sanders.* Studies in the History of Judaism 84. Atlanta: Scholars, 1993.
———. "Mr Sanders' Pharisees and Mine: A Response to E P Sanders, Jewish Law from Jesus to the Mishnah." *SJT* 44 (1991) 73–95.
———. **The Pharisees: Rabbinic Perspectives. Hoboken, NJ: KTAV, 1985.**
———. "Pharisaic Law in New Testament Times." *USQR* 26 (1971) 331–40.
———. ***From Politics to Piety: The Emergence of Pharisaic Judaism.* Englewood Cliffs, NJ: Prentice-Hall, 1972.**
———. *The Rabbinic Traditions about the Pharisees before 70.* 3 vols. Leiden: Brill, 1971.

———. "The Rabbinic Traditions about the Pharisees before 70 CE: An Overview." In *In Quest of the Historical Pharisees*, edited by Jacob Neusner and Bruce Chilton, 297–311. Waco, TX: Baylor University Press, 2007.

———. *Reading and Believing: Ancient Judaism and Contemporary Gullibility*. Brown Judaic Studies 113. Atlanta: Scholars, 1986.

———. *Torah: From Scroll to Symbol in Formative Judaism*. Philadelphia: Fortress, 1985.

Neusner, Jacob, and Bruce Chilton. *In Quest of the Historical Pharisees*. Waco, TX: Baylor University Press, 2007.

Nickelsburg, George W. E. *Resurrection, Immortality, and Eternal Life in Intertestamental Judaism*. Cambridge, MA: Harvard University Press, 1972.

Oppenheimer, Aharon. *The 'am ha-aretz: A Study in the Social History of the Jewish People in the Hellenistic-Roman Period*. Arbeiten zur Literatur und Geschichte des hellenistischen Judentums 8. Leiden: Brill, 1977.

Owen-Ball, David T. "Rabbinic Rhetoric and the Tribute Passage (Mt. 22:15–22; Mk. 12:13–17; Lk. 20:20–26)." *NovT* 35 (1993) 1–14.

Simpson, J. A., and E. S. C. Weiner, eds. *Oxford English Dictionary*. 2nd ed. Oxford: Oxford University Press, 1989.

Paget, James Carleton. "Jewish Proselytism at the Time of Christian Origins: Chimera or Reality?" *Journal for the Study of the New Testament* 62 (1996) 65–103.

Pickup, Martin. "Matthew's and Mark's Pharisees." In *In Quest of the Historical Pharisees*, edited by Jacob Neusner and Bruce Chilton, 67–112. Waco, TX: Baylor University Press, 2007.

Poplutz, Uta. "The Pharisees: A House Divided." In *Character Studies in the Fourth Gospel: Narrative Approaches to Seventy Figures in John*, edited by Steven A. Hunt et al., 116–26. Grand Rapids: Eerdmans, 2016.

Porter, Stanley. "Levi (Person)." In *The Anchor Bible Dictionary*, edited by David Noel Freedman, 4:294–95. New York: Doubleday, 1992.

Pratheron, James. *Reclaiming the Reputation of the Pharisees*. https://thinkhebrew.wordpress.com/2014/05/21/reclaiming-the-reputation-of-the-pharisees/.

Przybylski, Benno. *Righteousness in Matthew and his World of Thought*. Society for New Testament Studies Monograph Series Book 41. Cambridge: Cambridge University Press, 1980.

Reardon, Timothy W. "Cleansing through Almsgiving in Luke-Acts: Purity, Cornelius, and the Translation of Acts 15:9." *CBQ* 78 (2016) 463–82.

Regev, Eyal. "Pure Individualism: The Idea of Non-Priestly Purity in Ancient Judaism." *JSJ* 31 (2000) 176–202.

Rice, George E. "Luke 5:33–6:1: Release from Cultic Tradition." *AUSS* 20 (1982) 127–32.

Rivkin, Ellis. *A Hidden Revolution*. Nashville: Abingdon, 1978.

———. "Scribes, Pharisees, Lawyers, Hypocrites: A Study in Synonymity." *HUCA* 49 (1978) 135–42.

Robertson, A. T. *The Pharisees and Jesus*. New York: Scribner, 1920.

Rowley, H. H. "The Herodians in the Gospels." *JTS* 41 (1940) 14–27.

Rudolph, David J. "Jesus and the Food Laws: A Reassessment of Mark 7:19b." *EQ* 74 (2002) 291–311.

Runesson, Anders, et al., eds. *The Ancient Synagogue from Its Origins to 200 C. E: A Source Book*. Boston: Brill, 2007.

Saldarini, Anthony J. "Delegitimation of Leaders in Matthew 23." *CBQ* 54 (1992) 659–80.

———. "Pharisees." In *Anchor Bible Dictionary*, edited by David Noel Freedman, 5:289–303. New York: Doubleday, 1992.

———. **Pharisees, Scribes, and Sadducees in Palestinian Society: A Sociological Approach. Grand Rapids: Eerdmans, 2001.**

———. "Scribes." In *Anchor Bible Dictionary*, edited by David Noel Freedman, 5:1012–16. New York: Doubleday, 1992.

Sanders, E. P. *Jesus and Judaism*. Philadelphia: Fortress, 1985.

———. *Jewish Law from Jesus to the Mishnah: Five Studies*. Philadelphia: Trinity International, 1990.

———. ***Judaism: Practice and Belief, 63 BCE–66 CE*. Philadelphia: Trinity International, 1992.**

———. *Paul and Palestinian Judaism: A Comparison of Patterns of Religion*. Philadelphia: Fortress, 1977.

Sanders, Jack T. *The Jews in Luke-Acts*. Philadelphia: Fortress, 1987.

Schams, Christine. *Jewish Scribes in the Second-Temple Period*. Journal for the Study of the Old Testament Supplement 291. London: Bloomsbury, 1998.

Schaper, Joachim. "The Pharisees." In *Cambridge History of Judaism: The Early Roman Period. Vol. 3*, edited by Louis Finkelstein et al., 402–27. Cambridge: Cambridge University Press, 1999.

Schechter, Solomon. *Aspects of Rabbinic Theology: Major Concepts of the Talmud*. New York: Schocken, 1961.

Schiffman, Lawrence H. *The Halakhah at Qumran*. Studies in Judaism in Late Antiquity 16. Leiden: Brill, 1975.

———. *Qumran and Jerusalem: Studies in the Dead Sea Scrolls and the History of Judaism*. Grand Rapids: Eerdmans, 2010.

Schürer, Emil. *A History of the Jewish People in the Time of Jesus Christ*. 5 vols. 2nd and rev. ed. Edinburgh: T. & T. Clark, 1897.

Schürer, Emil, et al. *The History of the Jewish People in the Age of Jesus Christ*. 3 vols. New York: Bloomsbury T. & T. Clark, 2014.

Schwartz, Daniel R. "Josephus and Nicolaus on the Pharisees." *JSJ* 14 (1983) 157–71.

Schwarzfuchs, Simon. *A Concise History of the Rabbinate*. Cambridge, MA: Blackwell, 1993.

Sievers, Joseph, and Amy-Jill Levine, eds. *The Pharisees*. Grand Rapids: Eerdmans, 2021.

Sigal, Phillip. *The Halakhah of Jesus of Nazareth according to the Gospel of Matthew* StBibLit 18. Atlanta: SBL, 2007.

Sim, David C. "Polemical Strategies in the Gospel of Matthew." In *Polemik in der frühchristlichen Literatur: Texte und Kontexte*, edited by Oda Wischmeyer and Scornaienchi Lorenzo, 491–515. Berlin: De Gruyter, 2011.

Smith, Morton. *Jesus the Magician*. San Francisco: Harper & Row, 1981.

Snodgrass, Klyne. *Stories with Intent: A Comprehensive Guide to the Parables of Jesus*. Grand Rapids: Eerdmans, 2008.

Stein, Robert H. *Mark*. Grand Rapids: Baker Academic, 2008.

———. "Synoptic Problem." In *Dictionary of Jesus and the Gospels*, edited by Joel B. Green and Scot McKnight, 784–92. Downers Grove, IL: IVP Academic, 1992.

Stemberger, Günter. *Jewish Contemporaries of Jesus: Pharisees, Sadducees, Essenes.* Translated by Allan W. Mahnke. Minneapolis: Fortress, 1995.

———. "Was There a 'Mainstream Judaism' in the Late Second Temple Period?" *The Review of Rabbinic Judaism* 4 (2001) 189–208.

Stendahl, Krister. "The Apostle Paul and the Introspective Conscience of the West." In *Paul among Jews and Gentiles,* 78–96. Philadelphia: Fortress, 1976.

Stettler, Hanna. *Heiligung bei Paulus: Ein Beitrag aus biblisch-theologischer Sicht.* Wissenschaftliche Untersuchungen zum Neuen Testament 2.368. Tübingen: Mohr Siebeck, 2014.

Sumney, Jerry L. *'Servants of Satan', 'False Brothers' and Other Opponents of Paul.* Sheffield: Sheffield Academic, 1999.

Tasker, R. V. G. *The Biblical Doctrine of the Wrath of God.* 2nd ed. London: Tyndale, 1957.

Thiessen, Matthew. *Jesus and the Forces of Death: The Gospels' Portrayal of Ritual Impurity within First-Century Judaism.* Grand Rapids: Baker Academic, 2020.

Turner, C. H. "Note on 'Succession' Language in Non-Christian Sources." In *Essays on the Early History of the Church and the Ministry,* edited by Henry Barclay Swete, 197–99. London: Macmillan, 1918.

Twelftree, Graham H. "Sanhedrin." In *Dictionary of Jesus and the Gospels,* 2d ed., edited by Joel B. Green et al., 836–40. Downers Grove, IL: IVP Academic, 2013.

———. "Scribes." In *Dictionary of Jesus and the Gospels,* ed. Joel B. Green and Scot McKnight, 732–35. Downers Grove, IL: IVP Academic, 1992.

Udoh, Fabian E. *To Caesar What Is Caesar's: Tribute, Taxes and Imperial Administration in Early Roman Palestine (63 B.C.E.–70 C.E.).* Brown Judaic Studies 343. Providence, RI: Brown Judaic Studies, 2005.

VanderKam, James C. *The Dead Sea Scrolls Today.* 2nd ed. Grand Rapids: Eerdmans, 2010.

———. "The Pharisees and the Dead Sea Scrolls." In *In Quest of the Historical Pharisees,* edited by Jacob Neusner and Bruce Chilton, 225–36. Waco, TX: Baylor University Press, 2007.

Vermès, Geza. *The Dead Sea Scrolls in English.* 4th rev. ed. Baltimore: Penguin, 1995.

Viljoen, Francois P. "Hosea 6:6 and Identity Formation in Matthew." *Acta Theologica* 34 (2014) 214–37.

Von Wahlde, Urban C. "The Johannine 'Jews': A Critical Survey." *NTS* 28 (1982) 33–60.

Waubke, Hans-Günther. "Die talmudische Haberim-Halacha und die Pharisäer." In *Judaistik und neutestamentliche Wissenschaft: Standorte, Grenzen, Beziehungen,* edited by Lutz Doering et al., 108–32. Göttingen: Vandenhoeck & Ruprecht, 2008.

Westerholm, Stephen. *Jesus and Scribal Authority.* Lund: CWK Gleerup, 1978.

Wilckens, Ulrich. "*Hypokrinomai,* etc." In *TDNT,* edited by Gerhard Kittel, 8:559–70. Grand Rapids: Eerdmans, 1964.

———. "*Stolē.*" In *TDNT,* edited by Gerhard Kittel, 7:687–91. Grand Rapids: Eerdmans, 1964.

Wilk, Florian. "Die synoptischen Evangelien des Neuen Testaments als Quellen für die Geschichte der Pharisäer." In *Judaistik und neutestamentliche Wissenschaft: Standorte, Grenzen, Beziehungen,* edited by Lutz Doering et al., 85–107. Göttingen: Vandenhoeck & Ruprecht, 2008.

———. "(Selbst-)Erhöhung und (Selbst-)Erniedrigung in Lk 18,9–14." *BN* 155 (2012) 113–29.

Wilkins, Michael J. "Christian." In *Anchor Bible Dictionary*, edited by David Noel Freedman, 1:925–26. New York: Doubleday, 1992.

Wright, David P. "Unclean and Clean (OT)." In *Anchor Bible Dictionary*, edited by David Noel Freedman, 6:729–41. New York: Doubleday, 1992.

Wright, David P., and Richard N. Jones. "Leprosy." In *Anchor Bible Dictionary*, edited by David Noel Freedman, 4:277–82. New York: Doubleday, 1992.

Wright, N. T. *The Challenge of Jesus: Rediscovering who Jesus was and is*. Downers Grove, IL: InterVarsity, 1999.

———. *Jesus and the Victory of God*. Minneapolis: Fortress, 1996.

Wright, Robert B. "Psalms of Solomon, a New Translation and Introduction." In *The Old Testament Pseudepigrapha*, edited by James H. Charlesworth, 2:639–70. Garden City, NY: Doubleday, 1983.

Yinger, Kent L. *God and Human Wholeness: Perfection in Biblical and Theological Tradition*. Eugene, OR: Cascade, 2019.

———. *The New Perspective on Paul: An Introduction*. Eugene, OR: Cascade, 2011.

Young, Brad. *Meet the Rabbis: Rabbinic Thought and the Teachings of Jesus*. Grand Rapids: Baker Academic, 2015.

Author Index

Allison, Dale C., 146n9, 157n15, 171nn38–39
Amos, Roger, 86n36
Anderson, Paul, 133n20
Attridge, Harold W., 38n19

Bäck, Sven-Olav, 90n1
Bailey, Kenneth, 88n43
Barr, James, 160, 161n8
Bauckham, Richard, 178n2 and n7
Baumgarten, Albert I., 14n20, 47n43
Berger, Klaus, 119n20
Bird, Michael F., 94n14, 132n19, 181n11
Blomberg, Craig L., 88n39, 104n11, 119n20
Bock, Darrell L., 129n14
Bond, Helen, 136n4
Booth, Roger P., 113n2, 114n7, 118n17
Brandon, S. G. F., 136n6
Brawley, Robert L., 83
Brownlee, William H., 143n3
Bryan, Christopher, 136n7
Bultmann, Rudolf, 139

Carroll, John T., 83n26
Childers, Charles L., 151–52
Chilton, Bruce, xviiin11, 178n3
Collins, Adela Yarbro, 103, 132n18
Collins, John J., 132n18
Crossan, John Dominic, 152

Daube, David, 130n15

Davies, Philip, 12n13
Davies, W. D., 146n9, 157n15, 171nn38–39
Dawsey, James, 130n15
De Andrado, Paba Nidhani, 108–9
Deines, Roland, 15n21
Dewey, Joanna, 91n3
Dimant, Devorah, 53n7
Doering, Lutz, 90n2, 95n17, 96
Doudna, Gregory L., 53n7
Dunn, James D. G., 80n13, 88n43, 106n21, 114n7, 120, 182n14

Earle, Ralph, 161n10
Edersheim, Alfred, 48n45
Egger, Peter, 107n24
Evans, Craig A., 154n9

Fitzmyer, Joseph A., 126n4
France, R. T., 93n9, 125n1
Freyne, Seán, 48, 139–40
Friedrichsen, Timothy A., 153n6
Furstenberg, Yair, 114n17

Garland, David E., 164
Garlington, Don B., 166n23
Gerhardsson, Birger, 36n13
Goldingay, John, 70
Goodman, Martin, 165n18 and n10
Gowler, David B., 106n22
Grabbe, Lester L., 5n4, 140n20

Hagner, Donald A., 119n22, 145n7, 167n27, 170n36
Hengel, Martin, 36n13
Herford, R. Travers, 6n6
Holmén, Tom, 126n4
Holmgren, Frederick C., 152n4
Horgan, Maurya, 53n7

Jaffee, Martin S., 36n14
Jeremias, Joachim, 47n43, 48n45
Johnson, Luke Timothy, 96n25, 103, 110, 162

Kampen, John, 12n13
Kazen, Thomas, 59n22, 107n23, 114n7, 118n18, 119n21, 122n28
Keener, Craig S., 178n2 and n4
Keith, Chris, 130
Kemeny, Paul Charles, 138n11
Krause, Andrew R., 45n38

Lambrecht, Jan, 86n35
Lane, William L., 92n7
Lau, Markus, 169
Levenson, Jon Douglas, 71n22
Levine, Amy-Jill, 86n34
Levine, Lee I., 45n38, 138n12, 139
Liebowitz, Etka, 46n40, 146

Maccoby, Hyam, 86n36, 114n4, 159n2
Malbon, Elizabeth Struthers, 87
Marshall, I. Howard, 163, 168
Mason, Steve, 3n1, 5n4, 6n5, 18, 34, 36n11, 37, 38n18, 39n20
May, David M., 100n2
McKnight, Scot, 165n18
McLaren, James S., 140n19
Meier, John P., 45n36, 77, 88, 97n28, 113n2, 115, 118n16
Morrison, Craig, 14n20
Murphy-O'Connor, Jerome, 48n46

Neusner, Jacob, xviiin11, 36n14, 42–43, 58, 59n21, 105, 168, 178n5

Owen-Ball, David T., 137–38

Paget, James Carleton, 165n19
Pickup, Martin, 82n21, 165n17
Przybylski, Benno, 157n13

Rice, George E., 144n4
Rivkin, Ellis, 6n6, 36n13, 41n28
Robertson, A. T., 152n1
Rosen, David, 185n1
Rudolph, David J., 118n15
Runesson, Anders, 138

Saldarini, Anthony J., 5n4, 13n17, 14n19, 25n13, 39n21, 47, 48, 84n29, 139, 161n9
Sanders, E. P., 36n14, 43, 45n36, 59n22, 60–61, 64, 66, 101n5, 105–6, 105–6n21, 152n3, 167
Schams, Christine, 82n19
Schaper, Joachim, 6n6, 22
Schiffman, Lawrence H., 54
Schürer, Emil, 48n45, 102, 152n2
Schwartz, Daniel R., 6n5
Schwarzfuchs, Simon, 173n43
Sievers, Joseph, 86n34
Sim, David C., 161n9
Smith, Morton, 48n46, 139
Snodgrass, Klyne, 153n6, 156
Stein, Robert H., 144
Stendahl, Krister, 181n11
Stettler, Hanna, 107
Sumney, Jerry L., 180n10

Thiessen, Matthew, 119n20
Twelftree, Graham H., 140

VanderKam, James C., 51n2, 53n7

Westerholm, Stephen, 77n8
Wilckens, Ulrich, 172n41
Wilk, Florian, xviiin11, 88, 155n10
Wright, N. T., 94n14, 108n25, 119n19, 125n3, 127n7

Yinger, Kent L., 64n10, 182n15

Subject Index

Akiba, Rabbi, 39
Alexander Jannaeus, King, 19, 53
am ha'aretz, 43–44, 101–3
anti-semitism, xvi–xvii
arrest and trial of Jesus, 81
authority, 78–79, 94, 108, 127–30, 165

beliefs, 24, 37–41, 60–71, 184

character (of Pharisees), 7
    affectionate, 24
    akribeia, 18, 22, 24, 26, 31–33, 76, 119, 152, 184
    haughty, 22, 46, 145–46, 161n10, 162, 170–76
    lenience, 44, 52, 55
    love (for God), 62, 63, 71n22, 98, 107
    ostentatious (*see* haughty)
    pious, 18–19, 21, 32, 45–46, 155–58, 184
    righteous (*see* pious)
    troublemakers, 20
Christianity (first century), 75–76
    Pharisees as followers, 179–80
christology, 93–94 and n14, 129, 186. *See also* messiah.
circumcision, 15, 69, 179–80
corban, 115, 166–7
crucifixion, 83, 84, 131, 134, 140–41

dokein, 19n3

Eighteen Benedictions, 67–68
eschatology, 77–78, 125–27, 135, 143, 186
Essenes, 22, 23, 38–39, 50, 54–56, 78, 85
exousia. See authority.

fate, 37–39

Gamaliel, 42, 84, 177–78

ḥaber (*-im, -oth*), 102, 104–6, 140
hairesis, 5–6, 10, 23n9
halakhah, 53–56, 77, 81, 85, 86, 92–93, 95–97, 168, 184, 186
hasidim, 12–14, 41, 183
healing, 94–98
Herod, King, 17, 20
    relationship with Pharisees, 20–22, 27, 183
Herodians, 78n10, 95, 100n1, 135–36
Hillel, Rabbi, 42, 57, 71, 77n5, 105n16, 166, 167, 168, 178
historicity,
    Gospels, xvii, 87–89, 90, 113n2, 139–40
    inerrancy, 89n44
    Josephus, 3n1, 21n4, 25–26, 39n20, 41
hypocrites, xvi–xvii, 33, 45–46, 86, 97n26, 114–17, 145–47, 159–61, 167, 173, 176
Hyrcanus, John, 6–7, 37

impurity. *See* purity.
invective, 46, 146, 161–64, 173, 175, 186

Jamnia, 56
"the Jews," 85, 133
John, of Gischala, 26
John, the Baptist, 124–25
Josephus,
    biographical information, 3, 8n8
    follower of Bannus, 4–5
    Pharisee himself, 4–5
    writings, 3–4
Judaism,
    common, 60–71, 75
Judas, the Galilean, 23

kashrut, 11, 15, 42, 69, 118
kingdom of God. *See* eschatology.

legalism, ix, xvi, 33, 57, 63–64, 86, 92, 98, 107, 151–52, 156, 185
lepers and leprosy, 107, 113, 121–22
Levites, 65
little tradition. *See* rural attitudes.
location, 48, 85, 139–40, 184
loopholes, 51–52, 116, 117
love, 70–71

marriage, 47, 58
messiah, 76, 94 and n14, 97n27, 98, 126, 130–32
mezuzah, 62n5

name, 14–15, 183
Nicodemus, 131
nomism, covenantal, 61, 63–64

organization, 47
origin, 15
    earliest hint, 5–6
    mid-second century BCE, 6, 183
    related to Hellenization, 8–12, 41, 185

Paul (apostle), a Pharisee, xvii, xviii, 180–82
Philo, 67, 69n18
phylacteries, 62n5, 171

Pollion, 20, 21
popularity, 26–27, 44
prayer, 67–68, 152–54
priests, 9–12, 13, 45, 56, 65–66, 85
    high priest, 6, 7, 9–11, 19, 25, 41, 42, 140, 177
prophecy, 22
providence. *See* fate.
Psalms of Solomon, xvii
purity, ritual, 11, 14, 42, 44, 54, 67, 69–70, 104–7, 112–15, 118, 119 and n20
    contagious, 104n11, 107, 113, 119
    corpse, 107, 112, 122–23
    inside vs outside, 114, 117, 121, 168, 169
    miqvaoth, 70
    relaxation of, 107, 113n2, 118–19, 122, 123

Rabbis
    spiritual descendants of Pharisees, xv–xvi, 56–59
revolutionaries. *See* Zealots.
rural attitudes, 97, 119 and n21, 123

Sabbath, 15, 55–56, 90–99
Sadducees, 6–7, 10, 23, 24, 37, 39–40, 45, 56, 66, 85, 125, 177, 185
Salome Alexander, Queen, 17–20, 22, 37, 183
Samaias, 20, 21, 46
Sanhedrin, 21, 42, 140, 177, 184
schools of thought. *See hairesis*.
scribes, 13–14, 47, 81–82, 83, 84, 91, 94n15, 101, 109, 113–14, 126n6, 183
seat of Moses, 7, 24
Second Temple period, 13
seekers after smooth things, 51–53
Shammai, Rabbi, 57, 77n5, 105n16, 166, 167
Shema, 61–62, 67
sinners, 12, 14–15, 64, 70, 77, 98, 101, 106 and n21,
size, 22, 184
standard of living, 46–48

status and power, 6–7, 24–27, 47n43, 139. *See also* Sanhedrin.
  political, 18, 20, 21, 22, 41–43, 134, 183
    pragmatists, 24, 26, 184
    religious, 20, 24, 42, 45, 84–85 (*see also* seat of Moses; synagogues)
    social, 19, 22, 44, 178, 184
synagogues, 45, 138–39
synoptic gospels, 79–80

tassels, 118, 171–72
taxes,
  temple, 66, 67
  toll-collectors, 106n20, 152–54
  Roman, 66, 137–38
tefillin. –phylacteries.
temple, Jerusalem, 64–65
tithes, 66–67, 166–67
tombs, whitewashed, 161, 169
Torah, 62–63, 67
  burden, 67
  definition, xv, 62n8
  Jesus as observant, 118, 122
  letter vs spirit, 108
  Oral, 36–37, 56, 58
  ritual vs moral laws, 90, 96n25, 107, 109
  "traditions of the fathers," 7, 17, 20, 33–37, 81
  succession chain, 35

views, of Pharisees toward Jesus,
  divided, 84, 98, 131, 133, 186
  favorable, xix, 131, 177–78
  opposed, xviii, 81, 84, 85, 94, 100, 134–35
views, regarding Pharisees,
  modern, xv–xvi, 57–58, 86–89
  Talmud, 56–59
  traditional (Christian), xvii, 63–64, 146, 151, 155, 161, 175, 185

Yavneh. *See* Jamnia.

Zealots, 23, 24, 25, 28, 85, 136

Ancient Documents Index

Hebrew Bible

Genesis

17:9–14	180
17:12–14	69

Exodus

15:24	108n26
16	92
16:2	108n26
17:3	108n26
20:8–11	91
20:12	115
31:15	95n16
34:6–7	71
34:21	91
35:2–3	92

Leviticus

11	69
11:33	168
12	122
12:1–8	70
13–14	54, 121
14	122
15	70, 122
15:12	168
15:19–23	112
21:14	6n7
22	54
24:8	93n11
24:10–11	128
24:14–16	128
24:23	128
27	66

Numbers

5:1–4	122
14:2	108n26
14:29	108n26
15:38–39	118, 171–72
16:41	108n26
18	66
19:11–22	122
19:11–13	112
19:13	123
19:20	123
31:19–24	122
35:2–5	55

Deuteronomy

5:12–16	91
5:16	115
6:1–3	63
6:4	61
6:5–6	63
6:7–9	62
6:9	62n5
7:7–8	62
8:17–19	137

Deuteronomy (continued)

11:18	62n5, 171
14	69
18	66
22:12	172
23:21–23	116
26:12–15	154
29:18	97n27

1 Samuel

7:6	142
21	93n11

1 Kings

21:27	145

Nehemiah

9:1	145

Esther

4:3	145

Job

8:13	160
17:8	160

Psalms

1	103n10
1:1–2	153
12:1	12n14
17:1–6	153
23:5	145n9
26	153
32:6	12n14
35:13	142
51:1	154
81:13	97n27
104:15	145n9
119:30–32	154

Proverbs

1	103n10
14:32	155

Ecclesiastes

8:2	137

Lamentations

3:31–33	71

Isaiah

1:17	167n28
5:7	126n5
5:8–22	164
6:10	97n27
29:13	115
30:10–11	51
40:3	125
54:5–8	143n3
56:7	152
58:5	145
60:21	121
61	127
61:3	121
62:5	143n3

Jeremiah

2:2	143n3
3:17	97n27
7:24	97n27
9:13	97n27
11:18	97n27
13:10	97n27
16:12	97n27
22:3	167n28
25:6	65
29:1–9	137
29:7	9
36:6	142

Ezekiel

16	143n3

40:46	10n11	*2 Maccabees*	
43:19	10n11	5:25	160
44:15	10n11	6:25	160
45:22	101n6	14:6	13n15, 13n16
48:11	10n11		

Daniel

7:13	94
7:14	94

4 Maccabees

6:15	160

Judith

4:13	142

Hosea

2:18	143n3
2:21	143n3
6:4	108
6:6	108, 118, 167n28
7	129

Sirach

45:17	65

Tobit

6:18	153
12:8	142

Micah

3:11–12	65
7:2	12n14

Pseudepigrapha

1 Enoch

10:16	121
84:6	121

Habakkuk

2:4	167n28
2:6–20	164

Jubilees

1:16	121
7:34	121
50:12	92

Zechariah

7:9–10	167n28

Letter of Aristeas

305	114n6

Apocrypha

1 Maccabees

1	41, 106
1:11–15	10–11
1:41–50	11
2:27	11
2:29–41	95
2:41	12, 93
2:42–48	12
7:9	13
7:12–16	13

Psalms of Solomon

4:7	173
4:19	173

Sib. Or.

4:25	65n11

T. Job

9:7–8   175

New Testament

Matthew

1:1	132
3:2	124
3:3	125
3:5–6	124
3:7–17	83
3:7–12	125
3:7–10	124
3:7	82n23, 108n27
3:10	125
4:17	124, 164
5	109
5–7	139
5:16	171
5:17–20	76n4, 83, 86, 157
5:20	82n23, 108n27, 145n7, 156–58
5:21–48	157–58
5:21–22	157
5:22	87, 161, 166n23
5:23–24	109n30
5:27–28	157
5:33–37	166n24
5:39	161
6:1–18	174–76
6:1–6	145
6:5	153
6:16–18	145
7:5	175n49
7:28	130n15
8:1–4	122
8:19	83
9:1–17	91n3
9:1–8	78
9:6	127
9:8	129n12
9:9	106n20
9:10–13	108
9:11	82n22, 83, 101n3
9:13	118
9:14–17	144
9:14	142, 143
9:15	78n9
9:20	172
9:34–35	134
9:34	82n22, 127, 128
10:4	136n8
10:34	136
11:19	142
12:1–14	91n3
12:1–8	91
12:5–6	93n11
12:6	87
12:7	108, 109, 118
12:9–14	88, 97
12:10	97
12:12	97
12:22–32	134
12:24	82n22, 127, 128
12:27	128
12:28	127, 128
12:38	82n22
12:42	87
14:36	172
15:1–20	113, 118, 119–21
15:1–3	83
15:1–9	36
15:1	113n3
15:2	115n9
15:3	33
15:7–9	170
15:7	174n49
15:8	160
16:1–12	125 and n1
16:1	82n22
16:6	82n22
16:12	83
16:19	164
17:24	83
19:3–12	77n5
19:16	83
19:20–22	122
21:15	141
21:33–46	134
21:45	83, 126n6
22:15–22	62n7, 137
22:15–16	141
22:16	135
22:18	161n8, 174n49

ANCIENT DOCUMENTS INDEX

22:34–40	135	1:21	91
22:34	82n23	1:22	78, 128
23	145n7, 159	1:23–28	127
23:1–26	82n23	1:27	128, 130n15
23:2–3	24, 78	1:29–34	127
23:2	83, 171	1:40–45	122
23:4	44, 157	1:44	70, 107, 113, 122
23:5–12	171–74	2:1—3:6	80, 91, 100
23:5	118, 145n7	2:1–12	81n17, 88n41, 91
23:12	172	2:5–17	80n15
23:13	135, 164–65	2:5	128
23:14	164n14	2:6	80n16, 81
23:15	101, 165	2:10–11	127, 128
23:16	165–66	2:10	78
23:17	166 and n23	2:13–17	100–108
23:21–22	166	2:15–17	81n17, 91
23:21	64	2:16	80n16, 81, 82
23:23	166–67		and n22
23:24	33	2:18–22	80n15, 91, 143
23:25	168	2:18	142
23:26	168	2:19–20	143
23:27–28	169	2:21–22	143
23:29	169–70	2:23–28	55, 80n15, 91, 96
23:30	169	2:25–26	93
23:31	169	2:27	87, 93
23:33	170	2:28	87, 93
23:34	170	3:1–6	80, 88, 91, 113, 167
23:37	170	3:1	91
24:51	161 and n8, 175n49	3:2	94
26:6	122	3:4	96
26:25	173n45	3:5	97
26:28	129n13	3:6	83, 95, 100, 135
26:49	173n45	3:15	78, 128
26:63	132	3:18	136n8
26:64	132	3:20–27	81n17
27:62	83, 141	3:22–27	134
28:18	128	3:22	81, 82n22, 113n3, 128 and n10
Mark		5:21–24	123
1:1	132	5:21–23	45n39
1:14–15	125, 127, 130n15	5:25–34	122
1:15	77, 87, 101n5, 164	5:27	122
1:16–20	127	5:35–43	45n39, 123
1:21–22	129	6:2	91
		6:7	128
		6:30–44	113

Mark (continued)

6:53–56	113
6:56	118
7:1–6	83
7:1–8	80n15, 81n17
7:1–23	87, 113–19
7:9–13	167
7:10–12	88
7:1	81
7:2–4	120
7:3–4	81
7:3–5	20, 81
7:5	81
7:16	117n12
8:11–13	80n15
8:11	82n22
8:14–21	80n15
8:15	82n22, 135n1
8:30	132
8:31	81, 82n20, 132
9:5	173n45
9:11	81
9:14–29	81n17
9:14	81
10:2–9	80n15
10:2–12	77n5
10:33	81
11:1–10	132
11:15–19	81n17
11:18	81
11:21	173n45
11:27–33	81n17, 128
11:27	81
11:28	78
12:1–12	126
12:13–17	80n15, 137
12:13	81, 126n6, 135, 141
12:18	40
12:28–34	71, 81n17, 135
12:28	81
12:37–39	171n37
12:38	81
13	126
13:3–4	135
14:1–2	81n17
14:1	81
14:2	140
14:3	122
14:43–50	81n17
14:43–46	163
14:43	81
14:45	173n45
14:53–65	81n17
14:53	81
14:55–64	94
14:62	132n17, 172n42
15:1–5	81n17
15:1	81
15:21–32	81n17
15:31	81

Luke

1:1–4	83
1:32	132
1:59	69n18
2:11	132
2:21	69n18
3:7–9	125n1
4:16	91
4:18–19	78, 127
4:21	127
4:31	91
5:12–16	122
5:17 – 6:11	91n3
5:17–26	88n41
5:17	84n28
5:21–26	127
5:21	94n15
5:24	128–29 and n8
5:27–32	108
5:29–32	144
5:29	100n2
5:30	82, 94n15, 101n3, 101n4, 142
5:33–39	144
5:33	142
6:1–5	91
6:1	92
6:2	83
6:6–11	88, 97
6:6–7	139n15

ANCIENT DOCUMENTS INDEX

6:6	96n24	18:12	145, 167
6:11	83	19:1–10	108n26
6:15	136	19:20	141
7:11–17	123	19:28–40	135
7:24–30	134	19:39	83, 141
7:29–35	84n28	20:19–20	84n27
7:29–30	125	20:19	126n6
7:30	84	20:20–26	137
7:34	142, 144	20:23	161n8
7:36–50	83, 84n28	20:45–46	171n37
7:36	131	21:6	65
7:47–48	129n13	22:36–38	136
8:43–48	122	22:67	132n17
10:13–17	45n39		
10:19	128	*John*	
10:25–28	135		
11:15–19	128	1:19–28	125
11:20	127	1:24	85
11:37–41	113, 121	1:38	173n45
11:37–39	83	1:49	173n45
11:37	131	3:1–15	131
11:39–45	84n28	3:1–2	146
11:39–41	168	3:2	173n45
11:40	168n32	3:26	173n45
11:42–52	164n14	4:1–3	85
11:42	66, 166, 167n28	4:3	85n31
11:43	139n15, 174	4:26	133
11:44	169 and n34	4:31	173n45
11:46	82	5:18	91
11:47	169	6:25	173n45
11:52	164–65	7	132
11:53	82, 94n15	7:1	85
12:1	159	7:32	84, 85, 102
12:54–56	163	7:40–44	102
13:10–16	96n23, 97n26	7:45–52	131
13:10	91	7:45	84
13:31	83, 131	7:46	130n15
14:1–6	83, 84n28	7:47–49	102
14:1	131	7:48	130
14:7–11	172	7:49	70n19, 101, 102
15:1–32	109–110	8:3	84n30
15:2	94n15	8:59	97
16:14	46, 84n28	9	85
17	126	9:1–12	97
17:14	70	9:2	173n45
17:20–21	84n28, 125, 135	9:6–7	97
17:22–37	135n1	9:7	97
18:9–14	84n28, 151–56		

John (continued)

9:15–16	96n23
9:16	90, 98, 131
9:22	85
9:27	98n30
9:28	98
9:30–34	98n30
10:19	131
10:22	12
11:8	173n45
11:47	84, 140
11:48	140
11:57	84, 141
12:19	141
12:42	85
17:1–3	133
18:3	84, 85, 141
19:38–42	131

Acts

1:13	136
2:46	76
3:1—4:4	76
5	178
5:12–20	177
5:17–26	76
5:33	177
5:34–39	84
5:34	42, 140
5:39	178
5:42	76
9:1–2	101
10	118
11:26	76
15	118, 179, 180
15:5	84, 131, 179
15:7–21	180
21:21	69n18
21:26–36	76
22:1	173n44
22:17	76
23:6–10	179n8
23:6	42, 84, 140, 181
23:8	40
24:18	76
25:9	76
26:5	23n9, 33, 84
26:28	76

Romans

2:25	69n18
3:1–2	69n18
11:7	97n27
11:25	97n27
14	120

1 Corinthians

7:8	58
12:31	182
14:12	182

2 Corinthians

3:14	97n27
7:7	182
9:2	182
11:24	76

Galatians

1:7	180
1:13–14	180
1:14	32
1:15–16	180
1:23	180
2:3–4	180
6:12	180

Philippians

3:2–3	181
3:5–6	181
3:5	xviii, 69n18
3:7–11	181
3:8–9	182
3:15	182

Colossians

1:28	182
4:12	182
4:13	182

Titus

2:14	182

1 Peter

4:16	76

Dead Sea Scrolls

CD

1.18–21	51
10.20–23	55
10.22–23	92
11.11–17	95

1QS

3:15–17	39n21
4:9–11	162
8:5	121
11:8	121
11:10–11	39n21

1QH

10.14–15	52
10.31–32	52

1QH^a

15.26–32	68
15.34	154

4QMMT

B 55–58	55
B 71–72	54

4QpIsa^c (4Q163) frag. 23

2.9–10	52

4Qcatena (4Q177) frag. 9

2.12–13	52

4QpNah (4Q169) frgs. 3+4

1.6–8	52
2.2, 4	53
3.3, 7	53

4Q268

frag. 3	95n21

Rabbinic Writings

m.'Abot

1:1	36
3:15	39
4:22	40

m. Ber.

7:1	103

m. Demai

2:2–3	104–5
2:3	102
2:16–17	103

m. Giṭ.

4:2–3	178n6

m. Ḥag.

2:7	102

m. Ned.

9:1	116

m. Neg.

14:3	55

m. Pesaḥ

4:8	55

m. Šabb.

7:2	92n5
14:3	96n22
14:4	96n22
18:3	95n19
19:2	95n19
22:6c	96n22

m. Soṭah

5:3	55
9:15	178n6

m. Ṭehar.

8:9	55

m. Yad.

4:7	55

m. Yoma

6:4–5	55
8:6	95

b. B. Bat.

9b	175

b. Ber.

28b	154
33a	39

b. ʿErub.

54b	36n12

b. Menaḥ.

95b	93n11

b. Nid.

16b	39

b. Pesaḥ.

88b	178n6

b. Šabb.

31a	71

b. Soṭah

22b	175

b. Taʿan

24b	145n6

b. Yoma

19b	45n36
85b	93n12

y. Šabb.

7:9b	92n5

t. ʿAbod. Zar.

3:10	103

t. Ned.

1.6.4	116

t. Šabb.

12[13]:8–13	96n22
14[15]:3	95n20

Avot de Rabbi Nathan

5	46n41

Mek. Exod.

31:13–14	93n12

Uktzin

3:6	167

Sipre on Num

15:37–41	172n40

ANCIENT DOCUMENTS INDEX

Greco-Roman Writings

Josephus

Life

1–6	7n8,
8	19n3
9	32n3
10–12	4
12	38, 41, 44, 46n41
20–23	43
21	26n14
189–98	26, 41, 43
189–94	140, 178
190–92	47
191	27, 32, 33
197	47

Antiquities

13.163	38
13.171–73	5–8, 12
13.172	37–39
13.173	39
13.288–98	20
13.288	44
13.289	6, 7
13.290	7, 46
13.294	44, 55
13.296	7, 26, 44
13.297	7, 34, 35, 37
13.298	7, 44
13.299	7
13.310	7
13.376	53
13.400–432	19–20
13.401–2	44
13.408–9	140
13.408	33, 35, 37
14.172–76	21, 42
14.172	27, 46
14.176	46
15.3–4	20, 42
15.3	21n4, 43
15.370	20, 22, 42, 43
17.41–45	21, 43
17.41	22, 27, 31, 33, 34, 46, 146
17.42–43	22
17.43–45	43
17.149–67	43
18.3	24n10
18.4	43
18:9–10	24n10
18.9	23
18.11–25	28
18.12	35n11, 46
18.13	38, 39
18.14	40
18.15	25, 44, 45
18.16	36n11, 40
18.17	24, 44, 45
18.18	39
18.20	22n7
19.332	32n1
19.347	38
20.43	32n1, 32n3
20.201	32n1
20.268	92n8

War

1.85–98	53
1.85–106	19
1.85	19
1.107–9	17
1.108	19, 32n3
1.110–14	17–19
1.110	31, 32, 46, 76n3
1.111	134
1.208–11	21n4
1.568	18n2
1.571	21, 22, 43
1.648–55	43
1.648	32n1, 32n3
2.117–18	24n10
2.117	43
2.118	23, 137
2.119–66	23–25
2.162	31
2.163	38, 39, 40, 46
2.166	39, 40, 44
2.411–18	25–26
2.411	43, 140
2.563	43
2.264	162
3.374–75	40
4.159	43

War (continued)
4.385	162
5.377–405	35n9
5.443–44	162
6.109	38

Apion
1.29	32n3
1.32	32n3
1.36	32n3
1.54	32n3
1.225–26	162
2.149	32n3
2.171	63
2.186–87	65–66
2.218	40

Philo

Flacc.
5:29	162

Hypoth.
7.3, 5	166n22

Prob
	75

Legat.
19.131	162

Migr.
89–93	69n18

Spec. Laws
1.299–300	67

Seutonius

Aug.
76	142n2

Early Christian Writings

Ignatius

Magn.
10:2–3	75n1

Didache
8:1	145n6

Gos. Thomas
39	165n16

www.ingramcontent.com/pod-product-compliance
Lightning Source LLC
Chambersburg PA
CBHW020407230426
43664CB00009B/1211